Language Change

and

Linguistic

Reconstruction

Language Change

and

Linguistic

Reconstruction

HENRY M. HOENIGSWALD

THE UNIVERSITY OF CHICAGO PRESS

Library of Congress Catalog Number: 59-12287

THE UNIVERSITY OF CHICAGO PRESS, CHICAGO 37
The University of Toronto Press, Toronto 5, Canada

© *1960 by The University of Chicago. Published 1960. Second
Impression 1961. Composed and printed by* THE UNIVERSITY OF
CHICAGO PRESS, *Chicago, Illinois, U.S.A.*

PREFACE

IN THESE pages an effort has been made to analyze certain formal properties of language change and to make explicit some of the procedures which lead to the reconstruction of change and thus to the recovery of lost language structures. This is done by developing from the fundamental notions of synchronic linguistics the framework in which the recognized processes of change take their place—not as entities different in kind but as special instances of the wider process of replacement and merger (with its corollaries) as it affects utterance constituents of different length and complexity. The extent to which detail has been gone into varies, in part by necessity, since some types of change are less naturally codified than others.

One particular limitation is important, although it, too, is a limitation in extent rather than in principle. Semantic, grammatical, and phonemic systems (and their replacement through time) are here thought of as analyzable into individual contrasts between two elements each (and their replacement through time). The present study is very largely concerned with such individual contrasts and their changing status. While it is of course true that individual contrasts are defined, synchronically at each stage, by the system as a whole, there can be no ambiguity in their separate treatment from stage to stage so long as it is possible to identify elements of the two successive systems as homologous. Just what are considered "two elements" in contrast remains dependent on the particular segmentation (phonemicization, etc.) which is employed as a starting point. It is always desirable to investigate two successive entire systems in more than one way: by selecting longer or smaller elements (e.g., clusters or distinctive features rather than phonemes) or by considering more than one binary contrast at a time. When the latter is done, and a comparison is made between the formulation obtained and a first formulation involving fewer or differently selected data, the result is sometimes hailed as an explanation rather than a description; if the second formulation comprises events which are later or earlier than others, these events are likely to be referred to as goals or as causes. As it is our chief concern to find a consistent notation to carry out and justify operations of reconstruction, we have generally adopted a given phonemic or morphemic analysis and tried to state replacements, mergers, and other changes singly for the elements represented.

Emphasis, then, is not on the outward setting under which replacements develop or on the small-scale processes which in the aggregate produce the effects that can be observed, analyzed, and used for purposes of reconstruction. No attempt is made, for instance, to go beyond recent advances in the study of language contact or to deal in detail with the presumable machinery of the analogical process. It is not that knowledge on these points is not desirable—very much to the contrary—but the history of historical linguistics has shown that formal reasoning based on a comparison of contrasts is fruitful even in the absence of uninterrupted documentation. The present effort merely aims to make that reasoning more explicit and to provide a unified formal language for its various phases.

I wish to thank the colleagues and students who have given me invaluable help by discussing and criticizing my ideas and by reading the manuscript, wholly or in part. Very special thanks are due to Isidore Dyen, Gordon H. Fairbanks, Eric P. Hamp, Zellig S. Harris, and George L. Trager. Furthermore, grateful acknowledgment is made to the Committee on the Advancement of Research of the University of Pennsylvania for recommending, and the University's Board of Graduate Education and Research for awarding, two grants for the purpose of preparing printer's copy.

H. M. H.

TABLE OF CONTENTS

1. INTRODUCTION   1
   Time within the Discourse. Time within the Corpus. Change in Time.
   Formulation of Change. Earlier and Later Stages.

2. INTERPRETATION OF WRITTEN RECORDS: GRAPHEMICS   4
   Fundamental Notions. Phonemic Interpretation: Synchrony; Diachrony. Phonetic Interpretation.

3. MORPHOLOGICAL CHANGE: PRELIMINARIES   13
   Correspondence. Synchronic Foundations: Morphemic Distribution;
   Allomorphic Distribution; Synonyms; Multiple Meaning and Homon-
   ymy. Amorphous Pseudo-Change: Obsolescence without Replace-
   ment; Emergence in New Discourses. New Constructions. Phonemic
   Substitution and Homonymy in Borrowing.

4. MORPHOLOGICAL CHANGE: REPLACEMENT PATTERNS   27
   Replacement without Split or Merger: Morphemic Pattern; No Change;
   Borrowing and Invention; Semantic Change; Analogic Change.
   Merger: Morphemic Pattern; Borrowing; Merger with Nil; Syncretism.
   Split: Morphemic Pattern; Borrowing and Semantic Change; Differ-
   entiation of Allomorphs; Shortening and Increment. Disappearance
   and Emergence of Morph Boundaries. Excursus. Discussion: "Change,"
   Semantic and Analogic; Grammatical Change.

5. MORPH AFFINITY IN REPLACEMENT   48
   Affinity Based on Morphophonemic Alternation; on Dialect Borrow-
   ing. Doublets. Total Replacement in Dialect Borrowing: Sound
   Change. Effects of Sound Change: Alternation and Homonymy.
   Review.

6. DETAIL   59
   Productivity: Analogic Creation. Disturbances in the Productive Pattern. Productivity of Allomorphs. Reinterpretation of Dialect Borrowings and Morphological Change. Taboo. Hyperforms, Phonemic and
   Other.

7. RECONSTRUCTION OF GRAMMATICAL AND SEMANTIC FEATURES . . .   68
   Internal Reconstruction. Sets of Correspondences: Comparative
   Method.

8. SOUND CHANGE: PRELIMINARIES   72
   Phonetic Properties: Alleged Gradual Character; Types of Condition-
   ing and Ease of Articulation; Phonetic Plausibility and Hyperforms.
   Replacement Pattern in Sound Change: Regularity; Reduction (and
   Redistribution) of Contrast; Effects Other than Reduction of Contrast.
   Replacement Pattern and Predictability. Convergence Areas and
   (Sound) Change.

9. PATTERNS OF SOUND CHANGE 86
Types of Sound Change in Constant Environments: Absence of
Phonemic Change; Reassignment; Unconditional Merger and Loss; Primary Split. Secondary Split; Split through Merger, without Residue.
Appendix: Interlocking Changes; Borrowed Phonemes.

10. ALTERNATIONS 99
Split and Alternation; Internal Reconstruction: From Primary Split;
from Secondary Split; Summary. Effects of Subsequent Change on
Alternation: Further Sound Change; Further Analogic Change;
Borrowing.

11. RELATIVE CHRONOLOGY 112
Widened Conditioning. Split without Residue. Split of a Merged
Phoneme: "Rectangular Pattern". Irreversibility of Merger. System
Stability and Relative Chronology.

12. COMPARATIVE METHOD 119
Sets of Correspondences: In Phonemically Unchanged Daughter Languages; Sets Resulting from Sound Change in One Daughter Language;
from Sound Change in Each Daughter Language (Duplicate Merger,
Composite Sets; Intersecting Conditioning, Duplicate Split, Split
Based on Duplicate Merger). Reality of Reconstructions. Sample Reconstructions.

13. CLASSIFICATION 144
Reconstruction from More than Two Related Languages. Three-Language Phonology: Descent, Subrelationships; Examples; Generalization for More than Three Languages. Three-Language Morphemics.
Subgrouping and Internal Reconstruction: Overlapping Innovations;
Duplication; Amorphous Change and Subgrouping. Glottochronology
and Subgrouping.

BIBLIOGRAPHY 161

INDEX 167

1. INTRODUCTION

1.1. Time within the Discourse

Since descriptive linguistics deals with the arrangement as well as with the inventory of speech segments, it deals with TIME. In English ("E"), /l/ follows, but does not precede, /s/ after pause; endings follow stems; certain pronouns follow their antecedents; answers follow questions; the sentences and paragraphs of a text occur in a unique order.[1] The incidence of segments is in part determined by that of other segments in the corpus.

1.2. Time within the Corpus

In a corpus sufficiently long, however, there will be breaks (sometimes characterized physically as stretches of silence) such that no segment determines any segment across a break. The utterance *Look at the tall fellow over there!* may follow a conversation about the weather; but presumably none of its elements is in any way either restricted or called for by any part of that conversation. The two stretches are, or are parts of, two different DISCOURSES. Some discourses are extremely long (narratives, expositions, literary works); others may have only the length of one sentence, including sentences of minimal length.[2] The relative place in time of any two or more discourses within the corpus is linguistically irrelevant. It is as though it were assumed that the speaker would have reversed the order of his discourses if the life-situation leading to his uttering each of them had been reversed; or, in more common parlance, that, even if he did not say such-

---

[1] More precisely, while segments occur in arrangements (i.e., in some order), segment CLASSES (phonemes, morphemes) occur in CONSTRUCTIONS. Generally, material quoted in italics is either in conventional script (or transliteration) or in phonemic transcription; slants (//) are used for the latter when necessary.

[2] Harris, *Lg.* 28. A discourse is thus the true minimum free form. "Sentence" in many languages is a convenient name for a stretch such that its intonation occurs over discourses as well and also such that it cannot be cut without residue into smaller stretches of which the same is true. In other words, sentences are the segments marked by minimum free intonations. In many languages, also, any discourse may, in theory, have one (monster) compound sentence for a transform, while two different discourses do not necessarily enjoy that possibility: the sentence *My friend is going to move and water freezes at 32°.* is not likely to turn up in any corpus. In this sense our "total environment" as we shall use it below might indeed be thought of as the list of all sentence environments for a given form; but it will be better to think of it as the sum of all of its discourse environments. See Hoenigswald, *Sixth Congress* 160; Harris, *Lg.* 33.

1

and-such at a given time, he could have done so. So long as that is true, the investigator looks upon an idiolect (i.e., the corpus of utterances by one speaker) as something static; ignoring seconds, minutes, and hours, he defines his study of it as SYNCHRONIC.[3]

1.3. Change in Time

Disregard of time, however, becomes once more untenable as the idiolect corpus grows to a length of many discourses and begins to cover long periods (say, years), or as several idiolects, sufficiently similar to one another, are added together to form a dialect corpus which may then extend beyond the individual life-span. It is not only that old discourses cease to be repeated, or previously unreported discourses emerge; such AMORPHOUS change may, after all, be thought of as a mere reflection of the disappearance and emergence of new life-situations outside the language and, consequently, as an indication of constancy rather than mutability in language. It is rather that disappearing discourses may be REPLACED, in what must be called the "same" life-situation, by new discourses. The study of the effects of loss, emergence, and, more properly, replacement of discourses, that is, the study of linguistic CHANGE, is the subject matter of HISTORICAL (DIACHRONIC) linguistics. Some of the knowledge gathered in historical linguistics may be utilized for purposes of linguistic RECONSTRUCTION, be it INTERNAL reconstruction or the process of triangulation known misleadingly as the COMPARATIVE method.

1.4. Formulation of Change

In synchronic linguistics the flow of speech and silence in the corpus is mastered by segmenting it and by stating how the segments thus formed occur. Similarly, both amorphous fluctuation and replacement are best formulated not for individual discourses but for classes made up of all the discourses containing a certain element. Thus in English all the discourses with *whelm* (other than after *over-*) have (nearly) disappeared; those with *eme* have been replaced, by and large, with discourses that are similar except that *uncle* replaces *eme;* discourses containing /⧺kn . ./ have been replaced by similar ones with /⧺n . ./ instead. This is conveniently abridged by saying that *whelm, eme,* and /⧺kn . ./ themselves have disappeared; that *eme* has been replaced by *uncle;* and, finally, that /⧺kn . ./ has been replaced by, or "become", /⧺n . ./, or, alternatively, that initial /k/ before /n/ has been lost.

---

[3] Or "descriptive". But Martinet, *Économie* 15, refers to mere descriptiveness in diachronic work, which he contrasts with "explicatory" diachronic work, in which questions of causation are raised and answered. (See Preface and 8.3.)

As the last example indicates, there are at least two styles of expression, both used conventionally although not equally favored in all areas of language structure. Either the length and complexity of the segment for which the statement is made are chosen so as to make the statement UNCONDITIONAL (*"over-whelm* [two morphological segments] is NEVER lost"; "/#kn/ [three phonemic segments] ALWAYS becomes /#n/") or else CONDITIONAL statements are made for segments of uniform, preferably minimum, complexity (*whelm* disappears from the language—i.e., discourses containing *whelm* disappear—UNLESS *over-* precedes; *eme* is replaced by *uncle;*[4] *k*, IF after pause and before *n*, is replaced by absence of any segment, symbolized "Ø" or "ø"). The former style is more immediate and concrete; the latter, more suited to rigorous manipulation—it is, incidentally, the familiar method for the tabulation of sound changes.

1.5. Earlier and Later Stages

Replacement change cannot be formulated unless the EARLIER STAGE and the LATER STAGE have each been subjected to synchronic phonemic and grammatical analysis (3.1).[5] Apart from instances in which scientific description is directly available, this requires the solution of one of two preliminary tasks: either WRITTEN RECORDS must be interpreted paleographically, epigraphically, and, of course, linguistically, or one or both stages must be RECONSTRUCTED, internally or comparatively, from later evidence. The particular analysis used in any of our examples, and the phonemic and morphological notation representing it, will not as a rule be explicitly justified. It is taken for granted that different purposes may call for different notations and that there is no one true phonemicization or morphemicization of a a nguage, as long as the systems offered are convertible into one another. Specifically, the validity[6] of a procedure in historical linguistics must never be dependent on one particular notation, although one particular notation may well facilitate one particular argument.

---

[4] Here the two styles happen to coincide.

[5] Distinguished diachronic work can be done, and was of course done from 1800 on, on the basis of conventional or implicit synchronic formulations. But much time and effort could have been saved if historical theory had been built on more explicit synchronic foundations. At any rate, the champions of a "synthesis" of historical and descriptive work underemphasize an important point: the two are not independent, and any historical statement contains, avowedly or otherwise, at least two synchronic statements—one for each of two or more stages—already. (See Von Wartburg 125; Hoenigswald, *Lingua nostra* 13.49.)

[6] As distinct from the form in which it is stated.

2. INTERPRETATION OF WRITTEN
RECORDS: GRAPHEMICS

Insofar as our source of information for the stages of linguistic change is reconstruction (1.5), its interpretation will be studied later (chaps. 10 and 12). Here we are concerned with the interpretation of written records. In dealing with such records, the investigator faces a number of tasks. Among other things, he may have to discover the nature of the script; its internal consistency regardless of the acoustic shape which it renders; and its relation to physical sound.

2.1. Fundamental Notions

All writing may be considered as being subject to segmentation into graphs.[1] Graphs such that their mutual occurrence is either entirely predictable from or else not at all correlated with other graphs in the sequence are allographs of each other[2] and form a GRAPHEME each; the various "connected" and "unconnected" shapes of letters in the Arabic script (which are entirely determined) or the accidental unevenness in the production of the "same" letter in longhand writing (entirely undetermined—at least so considered for the sake of the argument) are examples. Very special cases aside, graphemes "normally symbolize phonemes, morphophonemic alternations, or morphemes".

In PHONEMIC representation one grapheme may correspond to two or more different phonemes ("th", a "compound grapheme", insofar as its graph nature is concerned, represents both /θ/ and /ð/ in English writing); conversely, a grapheme may spell a sequence of two phonemes ("x" in English script). Syllabic writing is a systematic use of graphemes to represent phonemes combined in "syllables". In MORPHOPHONEMIC representation graphemes indicate morphophonemes; in the clearest case, automatic morphophonemes (10.1.1) are written, in an otherwise phonemic script, by the grapheme expressing the basic alternant ("Wald" for /vált/ in German script; /d/ before pause does not occur in the language, but the morpheme has an allomorph /váld/ occurring before vowel). MORPHEMIC representation is achieved in one of two typical ways: by the use of single graphemes, one each for a morpheme (as partly in Chinese characters), or for the spe-

---

[1] Much of the following is based on Hall, *Acta linguistica* 7. See also Bloomfield, *Language* chap. 17; Hockett, *Course* chap. 62.

[2] I.e., either complementary or freely alternating.

cial purpose of writing homonymous morphemes (3.5) by making use of existing (or especially devised) inconsistencies in a phonemic or morphophonemic writing system (e.g., "eight / ate", "amiss / a miss" in English writing). The three types of representation listed here may be mingled in various ways (as in Japanese usage, where morphemic representation through Chinese characters, and syllabic, i.e., phonemic, *kana* writing are employed together; or in our use of numerals in an alphabetic context; also see above on morphophonemic script).[3]

The nature of a script needs rarely to be discovered from purely internal evidence;[4] in fact, it is doubtful whether graphs could always be identified, be organized into graphemes, and otherwise be interpreted without the aid of information concerning the use of the same or a similar writing in texts already analyzed (e.g., texts using the same writing for another language or for a later stage of the same language). Still, the number of different graphemes in the inventory creates a presumption, at least for the purpose of deciding between three frequent types: logographic (single grapheme— single morpheme), syllabic, and alphabetic. Generally, languages have more different morphemes than "syllables" and more syllables than phonemes.

Pure logographic scripts are difficult to test for internal consistency. Nor can they be expected to provide evidence for changes which leave the morpheme structure intact, such as the replacement of one morph by another with the same meaning (4.1), although they will bring out, if used consistently, changes in morpheme order. More interesting historical indications are obtained when the morphemic character of logographic writing breaks down, and graphemes are used to represent phoneme sequences (often syllables) which are homonymous with morphs, under the "rebus" principle.

2.2 Phonemic Interpretation: Synchrony

Phonemic writing systems, especially alphabetic ones, are more tractable.[5] An ideally consistent alphabetic script will employ one grapheme per phoneme; there should be no overlapping between graphs belonging to different graphemes (including component graphs of compound graphs). If a contrast is not represented (θ and δ, or the degrees of stress, in English writing), this cannot as a rule be discovered through graphic evidence alone.

---

[3] Junctures which are sometimes one-phoneme morphemes can be represented by such devices as spaces, punctuation marks (e.g., on Latin alphabetic inscriptions), hyphens, etc.

[4] Friedrich, *Extinct Languages;* Bennett, *Lg.* 34.

[5] On this and much of the following see Penzl, *Studies Presented to J. Whatmough;* Sturtevant, *Pronunciation.*

On the other hand, if more than one grapheme does service for one phoneme, the situation is different. It may simply be that variant spellings exist side by side (i.e., in what are obviously spellings of the same forms, as in "grey / gray" or the like); more commonly in alphabet history, one of the competing spellings is used in some morphs and another in other morphs, with the result of providing a measure of morphemic representation within the framework of alphabetic writing. In this case great importance must be attached to occasional (but still, in order to exclude mere accident, recurrent) deviations or misspellings (/f/ is spelled "ff" in *stuff* but "gh" in *rough;* "ruff" will occur as a symptomatic misspelling). Such deviations are to be expected more confidently in cases where the variant spellings in the usual orthography are irregularly distributed (i.e., where the forms spelled in a given way require listing) and less so in cases where there is a good deal of predictability from the graphemic surroundings (e.g., English /k/ mostly spelled "k" before "e, i", mostly "c" before "o, u, r").

Sometimes an important check on the graphemic data is provided by metrical and other artistic conventions based upon phonemic structure: rhyme, alliteration, stress or other accent pattern, and quantity. Distinctions which would otherwise be lost may appear in this way. Thus a study of Latin texts yields, say, a grapheme "E". "Morphs" spelled with it show little variation, either fully established or even only deviant. It may be provisionally concluded that "E" represents one phonemic entity. It is then discovered that certain positions (henceforth identified as "heavy" positions) in a Latin line of verse may be filled (1) by all syllables in which "E" is followed by two or more consonant letters or (2) by syllables in which "E" is followed by one consonant letter—but only in some morphs, never in others.[6] There are certain other positions in verse ("light") which may be filled (3) only by syllables with "E" followed by one consonant letter—again with the proviso that many morphs are excluded. There is a small number of morphs written with "E" plus one consonant letter which occur both in heavy and in light position; but these are all homonymous, with one meaning used one way, the other meaning the other way:

"Heavy" Position	"Light" Position
(1) LECTVS 'gathered; bed'	
MENSA 'table'	
ESTIS 'ye are'	

---

[6] Assuming that the concepts "vowel" and "consonant" letters have already been justified from an interpretation of the written corpus. Certain groups of consonant letters, like "TR", function like single consonant letters to a certain extent.

(2) CREVIT 'grew'   (3) REVOCAT 'calls back'
    VERVS 'true'   MERVS 'pure'
    INVENIT 'found'   INVENIT 'finds'
    LEVIS 'slippery'   LEVIS 'light in weight'

This state of affairs (and a similar one for other "vowel letters") suggests that, at least before one consonant plus vowel, "E" spells two different entities one of which (in CREVIT, VERVS) is metrically equivalent to a sequence consisting of the other (as in REVOCAT, MERVS) plus another consonant. The phonemic entity in REVOCAT, MERVS is tentatively labeled /e/; that in CREVIT, VERVS, /e:/. The forms meaning 'found', 'slippery' have /e:/; those meaning 'finds', 'light' have /e/. LECTVS, MENSA, and ESTIS remain undetermined. Comparative evidence will further show both that /e/ and /e:/ develop differently in the daughter languages of Latin (e.g., /e/ > Italian ["Ital."] /ɛ/, /iɛ/; /e:/ > Ital. /e/) and that they have different pre-Latin antecedents; it will further show the MENSA and LECTVS in the meaning 'gathered' have /e:/, while ESTIS and LECTVS 'bed' have /e/.[7] These conclusions are, finally, in some cases confirmed by explicit description on the part of Latin grammarians. In addition, we see that a feature of stress which independent reasoning will indicate differentiated íNVENIT 'finds' from INVÉNIT 'found' becomes (nearly) predictable once the latter form is interpreted as having /e:/ rather than /e/.[8] It is a favorable circumstance that the rules of Latin metrics are simple and squarely based on phonemic structure. English rhyme, for instance, would make a much less safe guide, as the so-called eye rhymes of the type "move / love" (e.g., in nineteenth-century poetry) show.

2.3. Phonemic Interpretation: Diachrony

The preceding example shows how a variety of indications may be used in order to ascertain the extent to which phonemic representation is consistent in an alphabetic script. Quite commonly, the very result of such an examination carries, in addition, a diachronic implication. This is because inconsistency points to one or both of two typical sources: (1) the nature of the writing system at the time when it is first adapted (or the prevailing preconceptions about writing when it was first devised *de novo*—a far rarer event) and (2) the conservatism of an uninterrupted scribal tradition in a typical literate or partly literate society which brings it about that language change is ignored and that the language continues to be represented as

---

[7] The data on this particular example are somewhat uncertain, but see Leumann, *Lateinische Grammatik* 105.

[8] The rule is that a Latin word of three or more syllables is stressed on the penult, if heavy (including through /:/), or else on the antepenult.

though it had not changed. The deviant spellings mentioned above as an indication of such inconsistency are then in fact attempts at readapting the script to the changed state of the language.

When an alphabet is applied to a new language, it may already carry inconsistencies developed in its older history; to these, new ones may be added in the process of adaptation.[9] The two layers are not different in nature and will therefore not be distinguished in the brief exposition which follows. The alphabet may provide more graphemes than are needed. The final consequence is frequently that the superfluous ones are dropped from use (although not necessarily from ornamental or other secondary uses of the alphabet);[10] but the disappearance may be incomplete and, in any event, slow. The graphs may, for instance, develop a complementary distribution which would make them into mere allographs within one grapheme. In English spelling, "k" and "q" are somewhat in that position;[11] the Phoenician source alphabet had two graphemes representing two phonemes, /k/ and /ḳ/, respectively; the successive Greek, Etruscan, Roman, and medieval European adapters of the alphabet devised several ways of regulating the use of each graph in a mutually exclusive fashion.[12] It would be absurd to believe that the Greeks (in certain areas, in archaic times), in writing /ka/ as "ka" but /ku/ as "qu", practiced "allophonic" writing when they were simply bringing order into the use of graphs along lines suggested by the names of the letters (borrowed from *kāph* and *ḳōph*, respectively) and by the practice of teaching spelling through syllables consisting of consonant-vowel sequences. Another possible use for phonemically unneeded graphs lies in the irregular morphemic representation which was mentioned earlier (2.1): the Roman alphabet available for German contained such graphs as "v" and "f" (graphemes representing phonemes in Latin and in the Romance languages in which the Latin writing tradition was kept alive). The later German use is in part one of morphemic differentiation, witness such modern examples as "viel" 'much' and "fiel" 'fell' (both representing /ffyl/). Assamese has one voiceless apical stop /t/, but As-

---

[9] On the scripts of the world and on the history of writing—more an anthropological and archeological problem than a linguistic one—see Diringer, *Alphabet;* Gelb, *Study of Writing;* Kroeber, *Anthropology* chap xi.

[10] E.g., use as numerals.

[11] These letters are probably altogether complementary positional allographs: "q" always before "u" followed by another "vowel letter" (including "conquer," "quay", in addition to "conquest", "quail"); "k" never thus (this includes "awkward"). Note that this complementation has no phonemic meaning insofar as these small marginal points are concerned. Only cases like "Iraq" spoil the picture.

[12] Hoenigswald, *Lg.* 29.185.

samese writing (in an Indic alphabet) represents it with two graphemes, "t" and "ṭ", so identified after the phonemic representation which they carry when used for two phonemes with retroflex and dental allophones in other Indic languages.[13] From the Assamese point of view, the distribution is by morphemes. It is of course part of the linguistic background that the morphemes arbitrarily spelled with "ṭ" are, by and large, cognates of the morphemes spelled with a phonemically distinctive "ṭ" in the sister languages.

The last example indicates that the effect of sound change may be largely the same as that of the introduction of a foreign script. The linguistic correspondence of Assamese morphs with /t/ to morphs in other Indic languages with either /t/ or /ṭ/ is the result of a phonemic merger; it will be shown that most sound changes are essentially mergers (chap. 9). If Assamese had been written down before the /t/-morphs and the /ṭ/-morphs had lost their mutual distinction, and if no subsequent spelling reform had taken place, the outcome would have been the same: an oversupply of graphs; a period in which there is morphemic representation; and possibly a script reform in which one of the two graphs is abolished and replaced by the other. Instead of, or mixed in with, morphemic representation (and depending on cultural attitudes toward orthography), there may simply exist free variation or confusion between the graphs. Such free variation may, at any rate, be expected in occasional deviant writings. These writings are a good indication of merger having taken place.

In merger, two phonemically different entities (a, b) are replaced by one phoneme (m [cf. 8.2.2]). The replacing phone is often physically more similar to one of the two phones which it replaces than it is to the other; it may, in fact, even be possible to say that the replacing phoneme occupies a place in the new phonemic system which is structurally the same as that which one of the replaced phonemes used to occupy in the old, but comparable, system (cf. 8.4). If, in this sense, m equals a but not b, and if the alphabetic script has available two graphs, "a" (the earlier representation of a) and "b" (for earlier b), to write the new m, both occasional misspelling and generally accepted script reform will take the form of altering the spelling of given morphs either by replacing "a" with "b" or by replacing "b" with "a". The replacement of "b" by "a" is known as "inverse spelling". In Latin around 150 B.C. the spelling "EI" comes to be used not only for morphs which had been spelled thus before but also as a replacement of "I" (when "long," i.e., /i:/; see above for the parallel /e:/). The innovation indicates that the old contrast existing between /ej/ and /i:/ was merged;

---

[13] Emeneau, *Lg.* 18.248.

from other evidence it is quite clear that the resulting phone was [i:], phonemically /i:/. Of the two available spellings " EI " and " I ", the inverse " EI " had the advantage of avoiding the ambiguity of letting " I " represent /i/ as well as /i:/ (see above, 2.2).

Thus, but for inverse spelling, morphemic representation (2.1) in an alphabetic or syllabic framework frequently carries a diachronic meaning; it is then in fact ETYMOLOGICAL REPRESENTATION.[14] If the phonemic merger in the language has been conditional rather than unconditioned (involving at the same time a phonemic split which separates the merged from the unaffected residual phones), and if morphophonemic alternation results (chap. 10), the representation is, in particular, morphophonemic (i.e., it has synchronic meaning as well; cf. 2.1), although the reverse is not true: morphophonemic spellings may be devised long after a split has separated the erstwhile co-allophones.

By contrast with a surplus of graphs, a script when adapted to a new language may offer too few graphs either because of discrepancies between the two sound systems or because of traditional disregard for the rendering of certain contrasts in writing. No alphabet in actual use seems to reflect all phonemic distinctions; from various historical accidents in the development of the script entire types of phonemes have remained unrepresented —stresses, quantities, vowels (in the Semitic alphabetic script). Phonemic change may also create more contrasts than are conveniently rendered by means of the available graphs. So long as this remains true, the contrasts are recognizable only by other than graphic means (e.g., metrical or orthoepic testimony [see 2.2]); phonemic split as such leaves no alphabetic trace. However, under favorable conditions new graphemes may be devised to remedy the shortage; this is done by inventing or modifying graphs or by employing new compound graphemes. Thus, after a period of using "c" both for /c/ [k] and for /g/ [g] (owing to adaptation from a source in which one grapheme was sufficient), the Latin alphabet adds a modified "c", viz., "G", to the list for the purpose of rendering /g/. If it can be shown, for instance by means of comparative reconstruction, that the contrast thus being written for the first time had existed, morph by morph, at an earlier period, it is also certain that it was merely the script which, before the addition of the new sign, failed to bring out an existing distinction, since

---

[14] Inverse spellings are etymologically deceptive. Sometimes the very merger which makes the extra graph available leads to an association which favors an inverse spelling; witness the famous instance of E "delight", which in the normal course of events might have been expected to keep the French spelling with ". . lit . ." (< Lat. *dēlectāre*) if it had not been for its association with "light".

phonemic merger is irreversible (cf. 11.4). Latin *c* and *g* correspond (cf. 12.1), by and large, to two different phonemes each in the sister languages (e.g., Greek *k, g;* Germanic *h, k;* Slavic *s, z*) and therefore reconstruct as two different phonemes at the pre-Latin stage (chap. 12); consequently, they must have been different also during the period when both were rendered by "c".

2.4. Phonetic Interpretation

Up to this point we have considered how written records may be made to yield elements of the language structure as it was when the records were committed to writing; moreover, we have seen under what conditions earlier and different structural features, and hence linguistic change, may be reconstructed from the analysis of a conservative writing tradition or of metrical conventions. Strictly speaking, only consistency in the rendering of phonemic contrast has been studied. It remains to show how the physical nature of the phones of a language might be determined from written records.

Internal evidence alone is probably never quite sufficient to establish phonetic values. Certain properties are so common to writing systems in general that simple conclusions from them are nearly self-evident; for example, the use of space as an indication of pause, terminal intonation, or morphological division, but not, say, as the representation of a vowel phoneme. It has also been ordinary practice to utilize simple typological preconceptions about the language (thought of, perhaps, as representing so-called universals in human speech), as when a given graph is read as vowel sign in order to avoid having to recognize unusually long consonant clusters. Indications of that sort are, however, so crude that they are not much in evidence outside the first stage in decipherment from scratch. The more detailed results are achieved with the help of connected data already known. There are the phonetic values which the same writing system has for other languages (including that from which it was adapted or those for which it was adapted from the language represented in the records under discussion). There is the evidence of borrowings (oral) from or into a language with known phonetic values which must be interpreted in terms of sound substitution, that is, with the proviso that rendering a phone of one language by a given phone in another implies no simple physical "identity" but merely the fact that no other phone of the borrowing language (and in the particular environment in the phone sequence as said and as heard) was in some sense of the word "more similar" than the one used in the rendering.[15] Thus the fact that in some types of German /oŋ/ [ɔŋ] will render a

---

[15] See 3.9; Haugen, *Lg.* 30. 382; Weinreich, *Word* 13.

French /ɜ/ [ʒ] means no more than that other available segment sequences of German (such as /o:/ [o:] or /on/ [ɔn] or /o:n/ [o:n]) were less close.[16] It also happens that phoneticians (as in India), orthoepists, or language teachers provide explicit testimony. Finally, the comparative method sheds light of a sort on the phonetics of reconstructed proto-languages or of sister languages (chap. 12, end). Among the indications which make it possible to narrow down the allophonic range for the Latin phoneme written with "c" there are these: In the Etruscan alphabet (from which the Latin alphabet was, in part, adapted) the corresponding grapheme stands roughly for [k]. Loanwords from Greek render a Greek [k] with "c". In Greek and elsewhere, Latin words and names are transcribed with [k]-graphs.[17] Roman grammarians say in effect that "c" is [k]. Latin morphs spelled with "c" correspond to phonemes with [k]-allophones in a number of sister languages (e.g., Oscan, Greek, Hittite); further study of all sister languages indicates that [k] is a plausible value for the ancestor language. The same Latin morphs (insofar as they have survived) appear later (in the descendant languages) either throughout with /k/ [k] (in modern Sardinian) or else in more variable forms which nevertheless plausibly reconstruct into a [k]-like phone.

---

[16] A minor source is the representation of animal cries and other sounds of nature by orthographic means (Sturtevant, *Pronunciation* 26).

[17] For elaborate use of "secondary transmission" see Schwyzer, *Griechische Grammatik* 1.150–65.

3. MORPHOLOGICAL CHANGE: PRELIMINARIES

3.1. Correspondence

Two idiolect corpora (languages) may have properties which make it possible to match segments and segment classes of one with segments and segment classes of the other as CORRESPONDING. Under certain further conditions (more fully discussed in chap. 13) the two corpora are recognized as two STAGES, EARLIER and LATER, respectively, of one language (or, what amounts to the same thing, as ancestor and descendant languages). A correspondence between two stages is a REPLACEMENT.

A comparison may serve to illustrate the notion of correspondence and replacement. Let there be two archives, one containing straight documents; the other, documents written in a substitution cipher. Some documents exist in both forms (A, A') and hence in both archives; others exist in straight form only (B), while still others exist in cipher only (C'). The order in which each archive keeps its papers is irrelevant. The cryptanalyst studies the recurrence of the letters, spaces, etc., and thus finds (1) the A' documents, (2) their A originals, and (3) the cipher linking the two.[1] In some important ways the discourses of the two stages of a language behave like the documents in the two archives. Some discourses ("A", "A' ") of the two stages are matched or nearly matched—the more probably so the shorter the discourses are; to the extent that this is true, correspondences can be formulated, segment by segment, or segment class by segment class. Other discourses have no counterpart at the other stage; they are either "lost" ("B") from the language or newly made up ("C' ") at the later stage.

The letters of the two alphabets represented in the two archives may be thought of as paralleled by the segment classes (e.g., the morphemes or the phonemes) of the two stages. If a letter happens to be represented only in the B portion of the first archive, the cipher will have no equivalent for it. This may happen relatively rarely. But the same observation holds for letter sequences: the particular sequences which occur in B but not in A will have no equivalent sequences in the cipher. On the other hand, the cipher may contain (in the C' texts but not in the A' texts) letters and letter sequences which do not correspond to any letters and letter sequences in the straight

---

[1] To the ordinary cryptanalyst deciphering messages, the discourses in A and B certainly have no order, since they all exist in his mind as "possible". His problem is simply to identify the A' messages (Hoenigswald, *Lg*. 35).

alphabet. By the same token, the disappearance and new emergence of discourses from one language stage to the next may involve—by default, as it were—the disappearance of old, and the fresh appearance of new, segment classes. According to the length of sequence affected, these are instances of conditioned or unconditional (see 1.4) disappearance and emergence. In either case, since no replacement is present, the "change" is AMORPHOUS.

Amorphous change will alter the gross phonemic structure only by accident. It is unlikely that those discourses which drop from the language through lack of opportunity for their use share any phonemic peculiarities. If a phoneme combination (a cluster, syllable, etc.), a phoneme, or a distinctive feature were exceptionally rare, this might of course accidentally occur. The converse is more relevant; in cases where new discourses carry with them new morphs, specifically, borrowed morphs, new phonemic entities may in fact make their appearance.

The parallel of the two archives carries further. Physical resemblance has no part in defining correspondence. Actually, a passage in cipher is bound to look unlike the corresponding original; if there is a resemblance, it is an accident. Just so, phonetic similarity between the phones that make up corresponding phonemes, phonemic identity of the morphs in corresponding morphemes, and identical morph order in corresponding constructions are certainly not essential. Historical linguistics is full of cases in which a replacement (or generally a correspondence) relation exists between physically very dissimilar elements. French ("F") *le cheval* 'the horse' is one of the replacements for Latin ("Lat.") *equus;* the Indo-European phoneme sequence *$\#dw$- is replaced by Armenian $\#erk$-; and so on. Nevertheless, some kind of affinity or resemblance often prevails, and, once the separate nature of the question is clearly understood, it is a matter of interest to investigate those affinities. The two chief criteria for the treatment of linguistic change are, then, (1) the REPLACEMENT PATTERN (e.g., no replacement—as in amorphous change; one-to-one replacement; two-to-one replacement or merger; one-to-two replacement or split)[2] and (2) the AFFINITY which exists between the phones and morphs figuring in the replacement process (e.g., phonetic similarity in phones, phonemic identity in morphs, increase or decrease in the number of segments). This latter investigation leads frequently (3) to a consideration of the SOURCE for the replacement (e.g., borrowing versus redistribution of available morphs or "semantic change"). Finally, (4) there are those larger traits characteristic of changing languages and of speech communities affected by change which

---

[2] Merger and split do not have ready prototypes in ordinary substitution ciphers.

seem to have a bearing upon the PREDICTABILITY of change. All these factors also enter into the procedures used for reconstruction. Owing to the incompleteness of our knowledge of the small-scale processes involved, these various criteria tend to stand out against one another all too sharply; the replacement pattern and the affinities obtaining between replaced and replacing segments then appear as properties of the "gross results" of change, seemingly amenable to formal statement, while the remainder may be open only to extrapolation from such observation as has been reported—not to mention the countless extralinguistic factors which are part of the picture.

3.2. Synchronic Foundations: Morphemic Distribution

Synchronically, the sums of all discourse-long environments for two segments,[3] A and B, may differ as shown in Figure 1. This is the most general

	I	II	III	IV
A	x	x	-	-
B	x	-	x	-

FIG. 1

instance. There are pairs of discourses (I, with A or B filling the blank) the members of which differ only in that one has A, the other B; that is, A and B substitute for each other or contrast (minimally) with each other in that particular class of environment frames. There are other discourses (II) in which, of the two segments considered, only A occurs. There are others still (III) in which only B occurs. And there must be a fourth class of environment frames (IV) in which neither A nor B occurs. Note that these four classes are defined entirely by the distribution of the segments A and B— they may or may not have other distinguishing characteristics. Class II will be referred to as the class of CHARACTERISTIC environments for A, III as the class of characteristic environments for B, and I as the CONTRASTIVE environment class for both A and B.[4]

The stretches considered (A, B) may be mere phone sequences (taken, e.g., from a phonetically written record); they may also be morph se-

---

[3] Haugen, *Lg.* 29. Since segments are unique, "tentatively defined segment classes" would be more precise than our "segments". As more forms are studied, the number of environment classes needed (see immediately below in the text) increases rapidly: n contrasting (morphemic, phonemic) elements define 2^n environment classes. Applied to morphemes in particular, this is one of the more elementary indications of how complex semantic relations are.

[4] It is called "contrastive" inasmuch as it PROVIDES contrast. A contrasts with B in any environment so classed (see Bloch, *Lg.* 24; *Lg.* 29; Haugen, *Lg.* 27). H. Spang-Hanssen (*Eighth Congress* 184) quite independently uses a similar graphic representation, though his purposes are quite different.

quences (conveniently thought of as already phonemicized). Since in some ways an understanding of morphologic change makes it easier to judge sound change, we shall for the time being concentrate our attention on morphs and their combinations.

Morphs and morph sequences which are distributed among all the other morphs of the language in the manner illustrated in Figure 1—which are, in other words, in contrast with each other—are said to differ in MEANING, the difference in meaning being related to their respective characteristic environments.[5] If *A* and *B* are single morphs, they must be assigned to different MORPHEMES. If they are morph sequences, they must contain at least one morph each to be assigned to two different morphemes.

Most English "words" when paired are such *A*'s and *B*'s. Take *robbers* and *grow;* these share a few environments such as, for example, the very simple minimal frame ╫———╫ (with an appropriate intonation morpheme such as *!*) (I). Neither occurs in the sentence-long discourse frame *He is highly* ———. (IV). The characteristic environments of *robbers* (II: *The* ——— *came and took everything.*) and those of *grow* (III: *They showed tremendous* ———*th.*) are many.[6] To be pointed, however, these comparisons should be

---

[5] Sledd, *Lg.* 33.264: "The native speaker interprets the forms in a single sentence partly by their known distribution in all the other sentences he has heard since childhood". Single sentences, i.e., single-sentence discourses, are often too short to be characteristic, and it may be difficult to frame "definitions", i.e., to devise characteristic one-sentence environments for definienda. It must not be forgotten that the environment classes here referred to are formed, ideally, from all discourse-long environments of the corpus. The property in question is called "meaning" because what is here pictured as a measurable corresponds rather well to the common-sense understanding of meaning, both "lexical" and "grammatical". It is worth pointing out that, if synonymy (3.4) equals total interchangeability, there can be no forms, and not even a "few" forms, which "possess" different meanings but have no characteristic environments. This has been claimed for such items as *red* and *green*. A comparison with *economics* /e/ and *economics* /iy/, which are more nearly synonyms (3.4), shows the difference: it is possible to say *This ribbon is neither red nor green*, but the utterance *This is neither economical* (/e/) *nor economical* (/iy/) is no more possible (without restressing the first syllable) than *This ribbon is neither red nor red*. Thus, as between *red* and *green*, the environment *This ribbon is neither* ——— *nor green* is a characteristic environment for *red*—not to mention the fact that the wider environments for the two phrases *red as blood* ("normal") and *green as blood* ("paradoxical") in the corpus ought to be very different. It is quite true, however, that the need for going to these arguments makes of words like *red* and *green* a special semantic subclass, not too far removed from such forms as numerals or proper names (see Hoenigswald, *AJPh* 79.293).

[6] If the environment classes are delimited after the morphs are identified but before they are organized into morphemes, the fact that *Grow!* contains

made after all discourses have been reduced, sentence by sentence, to their kernel form. This eliminates the myriad differences between environments that are transformationally linked. Rather than *robbers* and *grow*, it is pairs like *rob* and *grow*, *grow* and *grow up*, *five* (——) and (——) *in steadily diminishing numbers* that interest us. For *rob* and *grow*, class I is exemplified by the one-sentence discourse frame ——*ers have an easy time these days;* class II by *They are* ——*ed of their best chance;* class III by *This tree has been* ——*ing nicely;* class IV by *Let's* —— *to the movies*—or, rather, by the chains of kernel sentences from which each of these four short discourses is a transform.[7]

3.3. Synchronic Foundations: Allomorphic Distribution

Sometimes two morphs (morph sequences) occur in the fashion shown in Figure 2. That is, there are no discourses in which they contrast. This is

	II	III	IV
A	x	-	-
B	-	x	-

FIG. 2.—In the tabulations that follow, the mutually exclusive environment classes identified by Roman numerals are thought of as exhaustive, that is, as adding up to the sum of all discourse-long environments in the language.

	II	III	VIII	IX	VII	IV
A	x	-	x	-	-	-
B	-	x	-	x	-	-
(*C*	x	x	-	-	x	-)

FIG. 3

particularly true of positional allomorphs, where the larger picture is somewhat as given in Figure 3. *A* and *B* complement each other in II,VIII as against III,IX respectively; neither occurs in IV,VII.[8] In addition, there is a class of morphs, here exemplified by one *C*—with one environment class (VII) which is characteristic with regard to both *A* and *B*, one in which there is contrast with *A*, and one in which there is contrast with *B*. {*A; B*}, on the one hand, and *C*, on the other, assume morphemic distribution:

---

a zero allomorph of *you* (Harris, *Lg.* 33.335) has not yet been discovered. Intonations are here in part disregarded, i.e., assumed for simplicity's sake to be held constant. Of course, intonation morphemes are subject to the same analysis as other forms. They have been neglected in comparative work.

[7] Harris, *Lg.* 33.

[8] Column II, column III, and column IV of Figure 2 are simply renamed II,VIII, III,IX, and IV,VII, because they have to be subdivided once each when *C* is brought in.

II,III is the contrastive environment class; VIII,IX, the characteristic environment class for {A; B}; VII, the characteristic environment class for C; IV, the class of environments in which neither {A; B} nor C occur. If A = *sleep*, B = *slep*, C = *hope*, an example of II would be *You cannot ——— forever.*; of III: *He had always ———t.*; of VIII: *You look ———y.*; of IX *Sorry, I over———t.*; of VII: *I ——— you're all right.*; of IV: *Don't ——— from it!.*[9]

3.4. Synchronic Foundations: Synonyms

If two morphs or morph sequences occur as in Figure 4, they are in free variation with each other and deserve to be called SYNONYMS. The nearest phenomena to real synonyms are perhaps "stylistic" doublets like E

	I	IV
A	x	-
B	x	-

FIG. 4

/e/*conomics* and /iy/*conomics*.[10] If they were truly interchangeable, they might be said to be (or contain) allomorphs in free variation. The assertion —probably valid—that there are no synonyms proper in natural languages means that one can devise (i.e., find in a sufficiently large corpus) characteristic environments for any morph. The number and complexity of these characteristic environments, and the number and status of those contrastive environments (under I) which the two forms in question share to the exclusion of other forms, are presumably the formal equivalent of their semantic similarity.

3.5. Synchronic Foundations: Multiple Meaning and Homonymy

By a cursory charting, let a number of morphs (A to G) be distributed as given in Figure 5. Various common characteristic environments are labeled (1) to (8). B, C, and E appear as semantically related, and so do, in their turn, D, F, and G: they share environment classes formed from (1, 2, 3, 6, 8) and from (4, 5, 7), respectively, without overlap beyond the trivial kind represented by class I. This picture is marred only by A, which occurs in environments belonging to both characteristic environment classes. To the

---

[9] Complementation carries with it this possible complication: -(e)n and -ed are, on the whole, in complementary distribution—*lived, waxed*, but *given*. However, they "contrast" in *hewed:hewn*, and zero and -ed "contrast" in *hanged:hung*. One solution is of course to split *hang* (and perhaps also *hew*) into two entities (Bloch, *Lg.* 23.406 [= *Readings in Linguistics* 247]). The phonological parallel lies in phones which are said to be partly in complementation and partly in free variation, like the [t^c] (*tin, hat*) and [t^1] (unreleased) (*hatpin, hat*) of English.

[10] Harris, *Methods* 198.

extent that forms in natural languages approximate the solitary status of A, they are said to have different meanings as they occur in environments belonging to one or the other class. If $A = $ E $bank$, B to G might be equated with such items as *shore, slope, business, side, post office*, and *vault*, respectively; and (1) to (8), with all kinds of specific discourse frames. On the other hand, a discourse frame such as *Can you see the other——?* might represent class I. In particularly clear-cut cases one speaks of two homonymous morphs (and morphemes) A; or, with a slight departure from conventional usage, of one HOMONYMOUS (that is, polysemous) A.[11]

	I	(1)	(2)	(3)	(4)	(5)	(6)	(7)	(8)	... IV
A	x	x	x	x	x	-	x	x	-	-
B	x	x	-	x	-	-	x	-	x	-
C	x	x	x	x	-	-	-	-	x	-
D	x	-	-	-	x	-	-	x	-	-
E	x	-	x	x	-	-	x	-	x	-
F	x	-	-	-	x	x	-	-	-	-
G	x	-	-	-	-	x	-	-	-	-

FIG. 5

3.6. Amorphous Pseudo-Change: Obsolescence without Replacement

Since there is no linguistic answer to the question why a given discourse occupies its location in the idiolect corpus (1.2), the disappearance of discourses from otherwise similar idiolects or the emergence of new discourses in such idiolects is not linguistic change in the strict sense. Just as the location of a discourse in the idiolect depends on the speaker's "needs" or surroundings, the occurrence or non-occurrence of discourses in an aggregate of idiolects must be looked upon as a matter of the extralinguistic, historical conditions under which the speakers live. When change—for example, physical, technological, social change—overtakes the community, old discourses will disappear and new ones will appear. As this affects the idiolect corpora, this may be said to alter the language in one sense; it will, for in-

---

[11] See n. 9 above. Figure 5, the comments upon it, and the uses made of it later are not meant to be a mere recourse to "areas" of meaning and to other spatial metaphors commonly used in discussions on meaning ("coherence", "gaps between meanings"). Rather they are meant to help justify these metaphors by suggesting what underlies them. Meaning CONTENT (common content, similar content . . .) is not introduced at all into our picture. The classes BCE, DFG, (1–2–3–6–8) and (4–5–7) are defined by one another, not by denotata. Note that the order in which the rows and columns are arranged is without significance; it was deliberately chosen so as not to represent any preconceived relation between denotata. (See also Harris, *Methods* 202; Wells, *Eighth Congress* 662.)

stance, have an obvious influence on morph frequencies and inventories, that is, on the lexicon. On the other hand, it may be viewed merely as an extension of the normal speech activity exercised by the individual speaker in meeting new situations with new discourses, so that, as has often been remarked, it is not the language that has changed but the "things" or "signifiés". If it has also been said that, every time a form is used in a new sentence context (better: discourse context), it takes on a new meaning, this emphasizes the close affinity which nevertheless exists between the case under study and the instances of more properly so-called semantic change.[12]

The obsolescence and the fresh appearance of discourses have formal linguistic interest insofar as these processes are not random but affect all those discourses marked by the presence of a given form; it is this form itself which is then said to become obsolescent or emergent in the lexicon.[13]

Obsolescence may affect all the discourses containing a given form of one-morpheme length. Thus E *jess* (nearly) disappeared with the art of falconry and with the discourses in which "jesses" were referred to. This disappearance also affects the total distribution of every other form which used to occur in the same discourse with *jess* (e.g., the plural morpheme is *jesses*); but in many cases the effect must be infinitesimal.[14]

If the stretch which marks the set of obsolescent discourses is longer than one morph, say, a two-morph sequence AH, representing the two-morpheme construct AH, the matter can be stated in two ways: (*a*) as unconditional disappearance of AH from the lexicon or (*b*) as conditioned disappearance of A (WHEN in construction with a following H) and of H (WHEN following A [see 1.4]). A and H each may be said to have SPLIT into a surviving and an obsolescent portion. In either case, as before, this also affects to a minute degree all the other forms in the obsolete discourses. The choice of statement depends on a variety of factors. For instance, if AH stands out in syntactic analysis as a constituent, or if either A or H or both are "bound"—if AH is a "word"—(*a*) is more customary and perhaps preferable. On the other hand, if in addition to AH such forms as AJ, AK, and AM disappear, while AN, AO, and AP survive, it is often more convenient to register the event as (*b*) partial, or conditioned, obsolescence of A (the corresponding conditioned obsolescence of H may or may not affect

---

[12] Bloomfield, *Language* 435.

[13] The longer the marking form, the more it approximates the entire individual discourse, and the more rarely it recurs in the corpus.

[14] There is a hierarchy of relative weight of forms constituting environments. It is clear, for instance, that the disappearance of an English verb has a far stronger effect on the meaning of the nouns which function as its subject or as its object than it has on adverbs like *always* or *certainly*. Such hierarchies emerge neatly from a table of transformations (Harris, *Lg.* 33).

a substantial portion of the occurrences of H; it is, in any case, not considered further). Typically, A (when considered along with other forms, $B, C, \ldots$) will have had "two meanings" in the sense explained above (3.5); we need only substitute H, J, K, and M, on the one hand, and N, O, and P, on the other, for the numbered sample environments representing non-overlapping classes in Figure 5. A has become obsolete in "one of its meanings". Thus, in older French, *moudre* (as reconstructed) was neatly homonymous ('to milk', 'to grind', the source of the homonymy being sound change, < Lat. *mulgere* 'milk' versus *molere* 'grind').[15] It was lost where it had the first of the two meanings, but it was kept where it had the second.

Trivial examples of (nearly) unconditional as well as of conditioned obsolescence without replacement exist in the guise of the many nounlike and verblike expressions denoting objects or operations which vanish from the speakers' experience, like the *jesses* cited above. One variety of conditioned obsolescence is perhaps of general importance: the survival of metaphor without its underlying literal counterpart. Like other vocabulary having to do with horses, E *reins* is no doubt being lost from many people's speech, except in phrases such as *reins of government*. Where *reins* (A) patterns with *cord*, *thongs*, etc. (as B, C, and E), it is being dropped; where it patterns with *hold*, *authority*, etc., it continues.

Processes viewed here as individual instances occur in great strength at the same time (i.e, between the same earlier and later stage) and then produce a specific cumulative effect; in fact, contemporary changes often give the impression of working toward a different language structure. Part of the machinery of typological revolution consists precisely in disappearance not of individual morphemes but of morpheme classes without replacement or with a replacement pattern so complex as to render the transformation altogether profound. This is particularly true where morphemes with grammatical rather than lexical distributions are eliminated or where entire form classes, and hence constructions as such, are destroyed.[16]

---

[15] Gilliéron; see Von Wartburg 131. In this instance, to be sure, there was replacement (by *traire* < Lat. *trahere* 'draw'). E *reins*, on which below, was lost in one meaning without clear replacement (granting the facts as described for the average modern speaker). It is considered, however, that the mechanism of obsolescence is fundamentally the same, whether or not replacement ensues. The "gross effect" (3.1) is different. (See also Menner, *Lg.* 12.)

[16] By contrast, other possible cumulative effects of disappearance without replacement have a more accidental character. Thus split into a preserved and an obsolescent portion may happen to eliminate a particular allomorph from a morpheme. Accidental elimination of a phoneme (or cluster, or phonemic component) through obsolescence of all the morphemes the members of which contain it is less probable.

3.7. Amorphous Pseudo-Change: Emergence in New Discourses

Just as old forms are lost along with the discourses that contain them, so new discourses will bring in new forms.[17] The counterpart of obsolescence (without replacement) is new creation (not constituting replacement). The occasions for such new creation, insofar as they are understood, are much of the same nature as those for obsolescence: new conditions, physical or social, in the speakers' life-situation bring about new discourses; new discourses mean a gain in the total distribution of the forms of the language, whether these be minimal or complex. Closely linked with positive cultural innovation (rather than with mere falling into disuse of cultural traits) as these processes are, they have attracted great interest in the history of language study. On the whole, more attention has been paid to the external circumstances under which they typically take place than to the change in the structural balance which they may or may not bring about in the language.

Forms one morph long may make a first appearance. If we ignore for the moment the kind of back formation which may introduce such morphemes by subtraction (below, chap. 5), there are two conceivable SOURCES: deliberate invention (rare) and borrowing from an outside source. *Gas*, introduced (into Dutch) in 1644, is the classical case of invention;[18] a word like E *tea* (ultimately from South Chinese) is a simple instance of borrowing. There is no difference in the manner in which both types spread within the language community once an individual has invented the morpheme and once the first member of the speech community has introduced the loanform into a native context. Linguistic literature is full of loanword histories that illustrate the very process here being considered: the importation from outside of new "names" for new "things"; in other words, innovation without item-by-item replacement.[19] When new one-morpheme forms emerge, this

---

[17] The term "form" is used in contexts where the distinction between segments, sequences of segments, segment classes, constructs, etc., does not matter.

[18] Actually, there was only some superficial tampering with an older usage (Kluge, *Et. Wb. s.v.*). Modern examples of synthetic brand names or the like would fit better, Eastman's *Kodak*, for instance.

[19] Loanshifts, i.e., "loans" which do not import the phonemic shape of the foreign word (Haugen, *Norwegian Language* 2.391), are essentially amorphous extensions of a special kind, namely, such that, instead of conforming to the native analogic pattern (6.1), they fill an environmental slot corresponding to one existing in the influencing language. In American Portuguese *correr* 'run' comes to include the meaning 'run for office'. In New Guinea Pidgin English, *barata* (<*brother*) and *sista, susa* (<*sister*) have come to mean 'relative of same generation and same sex' and 'relative

necessarily adds new environments to the environment ranges of all the forms in the newly created discourses—to what extent will depend on the previous width of those ranges. In this sense it is true that the introduction of the morpheme *tea*, and its occurrence in such a close-knit construction as *plenty of tea leaves*, has also somewhat altered the distribution of *leaves*, and to a far lesser extent that of *plenty of*, in the corpus.

Thus new discourses differ from old ones not only by containing new morphs but by having existing morphs enter into new combinations. By contrast with borrowed or made-up morphs, their occurrence goes up, not from zero to a positive value (of discourse-long environments), but from some positive value to a higher value. The usual attitude toward this process is somewhat uncertain. It is not regarded as the classical variety of semantic change (on which more below, chap. 4). Like partial obsolescence, and for the same reason, it seems to call for little special attention; it reflects not so much change in language as it reflects change in life (see 1.3). After the steamship was invented, the morph (i.e., as in all these cases, the morpheme) *ship* moved into such frames as the one-sentence discourse, *The ——needs a new boiler*, or *This is a steam ——*. Few would label these new uses "change" or even "extension" of meaning, except those whose business it is to treat meanings systematically rather than anecdotally, namely, lexicographers. In the eyes of some lexicographers, at least, such innovations necessitate a new "definition". In the main it is only when such an extended distribution becomes a homonymous one (see 3.5) through disappearance of "intermediate" occurrences (see 7.1), or if the newly acquired occurrences survive at a later time while some of the original occurrences disappear (in either case with or without replacement), that the history of the form takes on, in retrospect, the proportions of a semantic change. German ("G") *Feder* 'feather' was at first amorphously extended into environments such as *mit der Feder schreiben* 'write with a quill'; that is, it was extended into the meaning 'quill'. Only after the disappearance of utterances like *mit einer frisch ausgerupften Feder schreiben* 'write with a freshly plucked goose quill'—that is, as the extralinguistic historian says, only after the disappearance of goose quills—does the "change of meaning" from 'feather', 'quill', to 'pen' become clear cut.[20] Thus, also, G *Wand* means 'wall'

---

of same generation but of opposite sex', respectively (see Murphy, *Book of Pidgin English* 60, 94, a reference I owe to Ward H. Goodenough), presumably under the influence of "foreign" (i.e., indigenous, non-English) speech. (See Hall, *Ricerche Linguistiche* 1; Weinreich, *Word* 14.374.)

[20] In the common-sense view the disappearance of the quill "causes" the change of meaning (meaning taken as an inherent quality of words), and the change of meaning "causes" the disappearance of the sentence.

long after houses have ceased to be built with wattled walls; in addition, the word does not occur any longer in the meaning 'something twisted' (from *winden* 'twist') which it had before the extension.[21]

The extension of morphemes from very limited (and often closely "bound") positions into wider (and often more "free") positions takes on a rather special complexion and is known by a separate name, BACK FORMATION.[22] The verb *chauffe* was the result of such a drastic extension. The first occurrence of the morph was of course in *chauffeur* /šówfer/; it cannot be older than the borrowing of that French word and the coming into being of the morpheme boundary before /er/ -*e(u)r* upon borrowing (below, chap. 5; owing to analogy with *driver* and *drive*, etc.). From its limited occurrence before -*er* it was extended to all kinds of other positions, such as *He ——s* or *They don't know how to ——*.

3.8. New Constructions

In considering an individual case of borrowing, it is irrelevant whether the borrowed form is complex or minimal in the language from which the borrowing is made (the SOURCE LANGUAGE).[23] But, if enough complex forms make their appearance, the recurrence of their constituent forms in the borrowing language will make them analyzable. If so, the construction binding the constituent forms together may in itself be native, that is, part of the older stage, while only the morphs themselves are new—thus the relation between *audac(ious)* and -*ity* (borrowed) duplicates that between *bold* and -*ness* (native); it may, of course, also be an entirely new construction in itself. The further status of such borrowed constructions depends on the degree in which the morphs, and not only the relation between them, fill existing slots. In the last-named example they nearly do. Not only did Old English ("OE") have adjectives and suffixes making nouns out of adjec-

---

[21] Bloomfield, *Language* 428, 435.

[22] The term is badly misleading; it reflects the usual undue preoccupation with "words" as privileged units in language. It suggests that a longer form (typically bound) like *chauffeur* exists first and that the new occurrences of one of its constituents (as in *chauffe-s*) are often free or are independent lexemes (*chauffe* is a "word"). But implicitly, i.e., from the choice of their examples, writers on the subject agree that the starting distribution of the form need not be bound (Leumann, *Lat. Gr.* 195 ff.). Reinterpreted ("misunderstood") loanwords like *chauffeur* have the virtue of proving that one particular occurrence (before -*er*) came first. After all, # —— # ("between pauses") is only one of the many environments for a form! (See also below, 4.4.)

[23] The emergence of new constructions is the counterpart to the loss of constructions when it is a cumulative effect of the disappearance of discourses.

tives, thus providing room for a borrowing like *audacity;* the specific items, *audac(ious)* and *-ity,* come rather close to being equivalents of existing items (*bold* and *-ness*) except for the matter of "style".[24]

3.9. Phonemic Substitution and Homonymy in Borrowing

When forms are borrowed, they are adapted to their new surroundings.[25] The degree of adaptation, or (from the viewpoint of the source language) distortion, probably differs with the circumstances of the transfer. More widespread full bilingualism will hold back distortion, at least in its less systematic form, which is represented by the extreme lexical transformation of borrowed items which goes under the name of FOLK ETYMOLOGY as in E *goose-berry* from **groze-berry* (cf. F *groseille*). At any rate, borrowing entails phonemic substitution or the rendering of the foreign form by what is vaguely called the nearest phonemic shape in the borrowing language. Here we shall merely hint at two ambiguities hidden in that plausible-sounding statement. First, at the present stage of typological knowledge, it is simply not predictable just what the native phoneme sequence nearest to a foreign sequence is, even if full particulars of both phonemic systems are given. German loanwords from English words beginning with *sw-* are often taken over, in true word-of-mouth borrowings, as /tsf/ (as though spelled *zw-;* "Zwetter" *sweater* is an example); why this is closer to the English model, as heard through the intermediaryship of the German phonemic system than /šf/ ("Schwetter"), would be difficult to deduce without the help of ad hoc assumptions. On the contrary, it is precisely loanword phonology that may provide the clues for what is "nearest" phonemically in any relevant sense. The other difficulty is a familiar one to theorists and practitioners of phonemics: where (if anywhere) is the dividing line between a sequence of recognized phonemes which merely fails to occur in the borrowing language and one which is phonemically excluded? Possibly, the degree of facility with which a new sequence of existing phonemes can be uttered is determinable from a true sample of all phoneme sequences existing in the language, but it would be wrong to suppose that serious attempts can be made as long as phonemic statement stops arbi-

---

[24] As determined by the occurrence of other forms in wider environments, *perish* is likely to occur with *return, receive; die* with *come back, get* elsewhere in the discourse. The difference between *audacity* and *boldness* is more denotative or lexical (i.e., more determined by nearer environments and co-occurrence classes of a simpler type) than these examples. (See also Joos, *SinL.* 13.68.)

[25] Haugen, *Norwegian Language* 2.392 ff.; *Lg.* 30; Weinreich, *Word* 13, with reference to his earlier work.

trarily at consonant clustering or monosyllabic utterance.[26] In a strict (and useless) sense only such borrowings as are rendered homonymously with existing stretches of speech could be guaranteed against phonemic resistance. Some borrowings are indeed homonyms to existing forms (e.g., G *kosten* 'cost' < Lat. *cō(n)stare:* G *kosten* 'taste') in the sense that, barring accidental circumstances, their distribution with regard to other verbs is likely to show the familiar two-meaning pattern (Fig. 5). This has some bearing on the chances for the reconstruction of meanings (chap. 7).

---

[26] It is reasonable to suppose that new combinations of existing distinctive features, and new clusters of existing phonemes, with certain provisos satisfying "pattern congruity" and taking into account the asymmetrical nature of the articulators (which excludes some combinations of distinctive features and furthers others), come relatively easy (see Martinet, *Économie* 95).

4. MORPHOLOGICAL CHANGE: REPLACE-MENT PATTERNS

The preceding discussion has been preliminary only. Linguistic change proper begins where it is possible to distinguish what happens to the language from what happens to the speakers' surroundings. As indicated before (1.3), that state is approached as the obsolescence of segments is compensated by the distributional growth of other segments—that is, according as there is replacement.

The present chapter is concerned with the behavior of morphemes in the replacement process (replacement pattern) and with the behavior of morphs within both unchanging and changing morpheme structures.

4.1. Replacement without Split or Merger

4.1.1. Morphemic Pattern

The simplest replacement pattern provides a one-to-one correspondence between one morpheme of the earlier stage and one morpheme of the later stage (Fig. 6). A represents a morpheme (i.e., all the morphs comprised in

		I	II	III	IV
EARLIER STAGE:	A	x	x	-	-
	$(B$	x	-	x	-)
LATER STAGE:	M	x	x	-	-
	$(..)$				

FIG. 6

a morpheme) at the earlier stage; as a morpheme, it contrasts with other morphemes like B. At the later stage, a morpheme M occurs in the same (more precisely, in the corresponding) environments. The choice of different symbols, "A" and "M", recalls the fact that a morpheme is defined synchronically, that is, by all the other morphemes of the same stage, and that their correspondence relationship from stage to stage is discovered by a separate step.[1] Strictly, different Roman numerals should have been chosen to label the environment classes merely as corresponding.

The replacement of A by M may also be represented as shown in Figure 7. On the horizontal axis we may imagine an array of the morphs or morphemes of the earlier stage, with their environment frames; the vertical axis

---

[1] See 3.1. This somewhat Saussurian conception should meet some of Allen's criticism, *TPL* 1953; see also Holt, *Sixth Congress* 98.

contains the same information for the later stage.[2] At the appropriate intersection on the grid inside the entry in Roman numerals ("I II") indicates
the environment class ("I,II") in which the replacement is valid. When
convenient, we may also express the inside entry in this fashion: "$A > M$"
(read: "A is replaced by M").[3]

4.1.2. No Change (beyond Possible Sound Change)

This replacement pattern may be satisfied in a number of morphically
different ways.

The morphs making up the morphemes A and M may correspond
phonemically. The notion of phonemic correspondence will be elaborated
later (chap. 8); it involves the presence or (as a limiting case) absence of
sound change.

If the two stages are close together in time, most of their morphemes will
appear "replaced" in this minimal fashion. The *here* in *Come here* as uttered

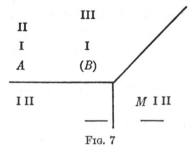

Fig. 7

today replaces *here* in *Come here* as uttered a generation ago. The morphs
correspond phoneme by phoneme; as it happens, the phonemes, in turn,
are represented by physically similar phones. But this is not essential: the
knock /knók/ of several centuries ago is replaced by /nók/ with a phonemic
correspondence between k and $\emptyset$ (4.2.3). In Armenian *erku* 'two' the stretch
erk- is the phonemic replacement of an Indo-European ("IE") *dw- (3.1).

4.1.3. One-to-One Replacement by Borrowing or Invention

Just as an amorphously emergent morph, so a replacing morph may be
a borrowing. OE (and later) *ēam* was replaced by (French) *uncle;* Middle
English ("ME") *ey* was replaced by *egg* (from Scandinavian); *inwit* by a

---

[2] For use of the same graph in connection with sound change see chaps.
9, 10, and 12, with fuller explanation. The alignment of the index numbers
(I II III) shows the contrastive-characteristic pattern for A and B at the
older stage. The upper portion of the diagram equals in effect Fig. 1,
turned around 90°, with column "IV" omitted.

[3] The corresponding statement for phonemes, $a > m$, is customarily read
"a BECOMES m"; the two are, however, entirely parallel. (See chap. 9, beginning.)

more recent *conscience* (from French). A striking instance of a somewhat different nature may be found in Greek ("Gk.") *ke(n)* in those dialects in which it is the equivalent of *án*. Since *án* may be inherited and since *ke(n)* has no plausible etymology, the latter may well be a borrowing.[4] In any case, it is an impressive fact that the very specialized "use" or "meaning" of the two is practically the same. The two words are "particles", that is, the kind of item which in conventional grammar occupies a border-line position between grammar and lexicon. Here, perhaps, it is particularly clear how definitions or translations (as found in the dictionary), and rules about occurrence in construction (e.g., "secondary tense in the protasis, secondary tense with *án* [*ke(n)*] in the apodosis"), are merely two ways of dealing with the same subject: the environment in which *án* or *ke(n)* occurs.

It is also quite conceivable, again in parallelism to amorphous creation (3.7), that new morphs are brought about by an act of artificial invention and then spread.

4.1.4. One-to-One Replacement by Existing
Morphs (Semantic Change)[5]

The morph or the allomorphs representing M may have phonemically corresponding counterparts at the earlier stage; but these counterparts do not at that stage fill the corresponding morphemes. OE *cēace* as a morph is (phoneme by phoneme) replaced by present-day *cheek;* but the morpheme made up of the morph *cheek* does not replace the morpheme made up of the morph *cēace;* instead it replaces, by and large, the OE *wonge* (Figs. 8 and 9).

		I	II	III	IV
OLD ENGLISH:	*wonge*	x	x	-	-
	cēace	x	-	x	-
MODERN ENGLISH:	*cheek*	x	x	-	-
	jaw	x	-	x	-

FIG. 8

As it happens, the morph *wonge* disappears from the language (i.e., it does not turn up in any morpheme).[6] The morph *jaw* is probably a borrow-

---

[4] Ionic-Attic: *án;* Doric: *ka;* others: *ke(n)*; Schwyzer, *Gr.Gr.* 2.568 (uncertain etymologies for *ke(n)*). Some environments may have been original with *ke(n)*.

[5] On this term, and on the term "analogic change", see 4.6.

[6] There is the compound *wangtooth*. It is true that *wonge* had 'jaw' as an occasional meaning. This process, and even more a fuller picture like that given under 4.5, furnishes the morphological equivalent for the "push-chain" and drag-chain changes in phonology (Martinet, *Économie* 78). See also Kuryłowicz, *Voprosy yazykoznaniya* 1935.3.73.

ing from French; it comes to fill the morpheme in question under the provision of the preceding section. The morphemes in their relative permanence are evidently represented by their environment ranges (I,II and I,III)— that is, by their meanings. We may say that the environment range I,II defines the meaning 'cheek' and the environment range I,III the meaning

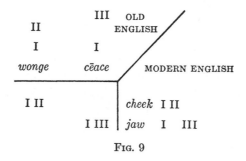

FIG. 9

'jaw' or, at least, that the difference between them defines the difference in meaning. The morphs (*wonge, cēace-cheek, jaw*) give the appearance of moving in and out of a fixed framework of meanings. Since all replacements are not one to one, this stability is by no means absolute. But it seems true that the fundamental morphemic structure of languages changes far more slowly than the surface movements of the morphs suggest.

4.1.5. *Replacement between Two Co-allomorphs* (*Analogic Change*)

Morphemic one-to-one replacement may be complicated by submorphemic replacement processes among co-allomorphs. In the trivial case the allomorphs themselves are replaced one to one. This occurs typically if the later stage has a morph with corresponding phonemes (i.e., at most, "sound change" [see chap. 8]). The *-en* of *oxen* and the *-es* of *boxes* are in no significant way different from the *here* of *Come here* as these forms recur in successive corpora. Consider, however, the instance illustrated in Figure 10.

		II	V	III	IV
EARLIER STAGE:	A	x	x	-	-
	B	-	-	x	-
LATER STAGE:	M	x	-	-	-
	N	-	x	x	-

FIG. 10

A and *B* are complementary; they are in reality only allomorphs forming a morpheme {*A*; *B*}. The upper half of the diagram describes the same state of affairs as does Figure 2, except that the environment class labeled "II" is here subdivided, for reasons which have nothing to do with the earlier stage as such, into "II" and "V". From the synchronic point of view there is only one environment class, "II,V".

At the later stage, M and N are allomorphs of $\{M;N\}$. M replaces A in the environment class II ("A-in-II"). N replaces (1) A-in-V and (2) B-in-III. This is represented in another way in Figure 11. For example, in the

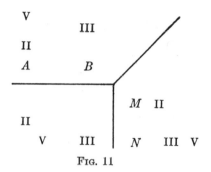

Fɪɢ. 11

following diagram,

	give—	wax—	live—	IV
-en	x	x	-	-
-ed	-	-	x	-

has in modern English become

-en	x	-	-	-
-ed	-	x	x	-

Fɪɢ. 12

or:

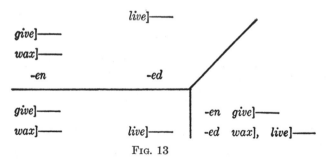

Fɪɢ. 13

Figures 12 and 13 depict the transfer of *wax* from the "strong" to the "weak" conjugation, that is, the substitution of *waxed* for *waxen*. In this example the morphs M and N are sequences of phonemes corresponding to those of A and B. Sometimes such allomorphs are created ex novo: in Middle English, *weared* (past tense; past participle) was replaced by *ware; worn*. Later the past tense *ware* was replaced by *wore*. Insofar as the allomorphs of the stem alone (i.e., disregarding the accompanying alternation in the suffix) are concerned, we have, first, Figure 14*a* and, then, Figure 14*b*.

EARLIER STAGE:	*wear*	x	x	x	-
LATER STAGE:	*wear*	x	-	-	-
	ware	-	x	-	-
	wore	-	-	x	-

Fig. 14*a*

SECOND LATER STAGE:	*wear*	x	-	-	-
	wor(e)	-	x	x	-

Fig. 14*b*

A more extreme case, in which the need for the new subenvironment V is eliminated, is given in Figures 15 and 16. *M* replaces {*A*; *B*} throughout

		II	III	IV
EARLIER STAGE:	*A*	x	-	-
	B	-	x	-
LATER STAGE:	*M*	x	x	-

Fig. 15

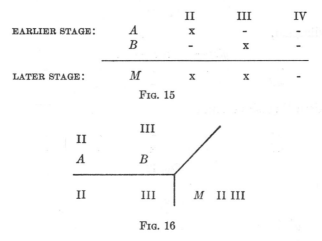

Fig. 16

by replacing *A* as well as *B*: the alternation is eliminated. In dialects of English in which the plural of *roof* is no longer *rooves* but *roofs*, the allomorphs have been rearranged as shown in Figures 17 and 18. Here *M* corresponds phonemically to one of the erstwhile allomorphs ("*A*"; in other words, *roof* of the later stage equals *roof* at the earlier stage). Again, there

		II = —— 'plural suffix'	III	IV
EARLIER STAGE:	*roov*	x	-	-
	roof	-	x	-
LATER STAGE:	*roov*	-	-	-
	roof	x	x	-

Fig. 17

is no necessity that this need be so. An alternating morpheme, like any other, may be filled by a new morph. Simple one-to-one replacement of non-alternating (one-allomorph) morphemes, as treated earlier (4.1.3–4.1.4), may be regarded as a limiting case of co-allomorph redistribution. It would be correct to say, for example, that, when *uncle* is substituted for OE *ēam*, one allomorph (*ēam*) has gone from exclusive to zero occurrence, while another (*uncle*) has moved in the opposite direction.

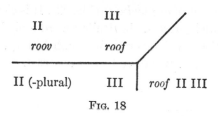

FIG. 18

4.2. Merger

4.2.1. Morphemic Pattern

The total distribution of one morpheme at the later stage may come close to equaling the sum of the distributions of two morphemes at the earlier stage (Figs. 19 and 20). The slots originally filled and defined by *A*

		I	II	III	IV
EARLIER STAGE:	*A*	x	x	-	-
	B	x	-	x	-
LATER STAGE:	*M*	x	x	x	-

FIG. 19

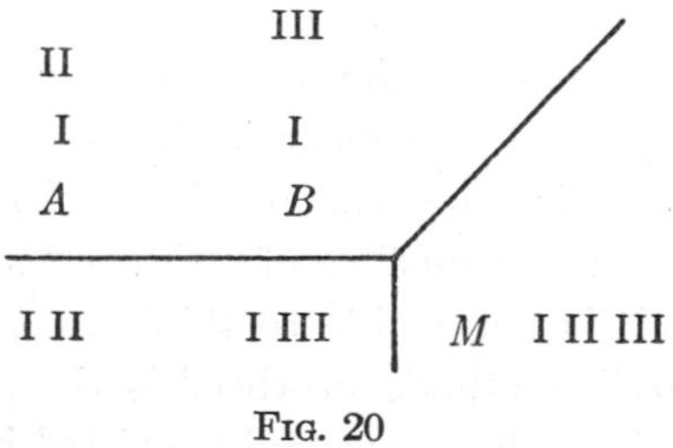

III
II
I   I
A   *B*

| I II | I III | *M* I II III |

FIG. 20

exclusively (II), by *B* exclusively (III), and by *A* and *B* interchangeably (I) are later filled by *M* only. From the point of view of the later stage (and always assuming a background of other existing forms, *C*, *D*, . . . , whose distribution is not directly relevant), I, II, and III can no longer be distinguished. The semantic difference between *A* and *B* has disappeared; a more or less obligatory "concept" has ceased to be part of the language.

4.2.2. *Merger and Borrowing; Merger and Semantic Change*

The morph representing *M* may have various types of origin (see 4.1.3–4.1.4). It may, for instance, be a borrowing: thus Lat. *patruus* 'paternal uncle' and *avunculus* 'maternal uncle' have been replaced in Italian by a loanword (from Greek) (Fig. 21). In other cases *M* corresponds in phonemic shape to either *A* or *B;* from the same earlier stage as in the preceding example (Latin) another later stage (French) has *oncle*, as the phoneme-by-phoneme equivalent of *avunculu(s)* (Fig. 22). It is clear that, with regard to Lat. *avunculus* and *patruus*, the Italian word and the French word are morphemic equivalents whatever their morph history. In each later stage there has been merger of what used to be contrast.

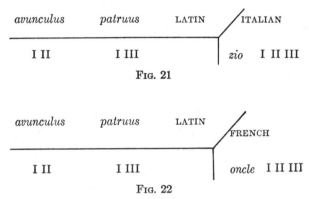

FIG. 21

FIG. 22

In actual history merger is perhaps never carried out thus neatly. For one thing, there must always be some admixture of amorphous occurrence of *M* when new discourses come into being and of loss of *A* when old ones fall into disuse, and this will keep the border line unsharp. Furthermore, certain restrictions may prevent the replacement from being simple. While *avunculus* may be supposed to appear for both *avunculus* and *patruus* in most frames, this is certainly not the case in the Latin equivalents of "He has two *avunculī* and one *patruus*" or of "His *avunculī* and his other maternal relatives". Here it is reasonable to think that such a phrase as the explicit *"mātris frātrēs"* 'mother's brothers' is the proper replacement for *avunculī*. Since this phrase has presumably existed in the corpus before, it has widened its distribution, while *patruus* and *avunculus* have not been replaced invariably by one and the same, but sometimes by one, sometimes by another, form in a pattern which, then, involves splitting of distributional slots as well as merger. In this sense our models suffer from the distortion which is inevitable if anything less than the system of all forms and all distributional frames in the language is considered.

Thus, while the change whereby the morph (sequence) *avunculus* comes to denote a paternal as well as a maternal uncle may reflect a "widening" in the relational logic of the denotata, it is not altogether a widening in linguistic distribution. This is so because the older-stage *avunculus*, with its logically narrower meaning, is just for that reason appropriate in the discourse environments calling for such a meaning. In spite of their quantitative associations, semantic labels like "widening", "narrowing", and "metonymy" do not directly characterize the changing occurrence of forms. They are content classifications, not really different from "metaphor", "litotes", "hyperbole", "pejoration", and the like. Their formal linguistic analysis, while not inconceivable in principle, would presuppose a rigorous charting of semantic "fields" somewhat along the lines indicated earlier.[7]

4.2.3. Unconditioned Merger into Nil

In certain circumstances, especially when the replacing form contains either more or fewer morphemes (in construction with one another) than the replaced form, any morpheme-by-morpheme statement requires the notion of $\emptyset$ or "nil". Synchronically, $\emptyset$ denotes the absence of morphemes, with the following proviso: it is said to occur (in fact, any number of $\emptyset$'s are said to occur) as a part of any occurring construct.[8] It is possible, for instance, to say that *good friend* includes not only the obvious segmental and suprasegmental morphemes, the construction morpheme of the kernel, and the transformation (here considered as a morpheme, too) but also any number of $\emptyset$'s. On the other hand, $\emptyset$ is said not to occur with **very friend* (a construct not in the language).

Clearly, a morpheme may either be replaced by $\emptyset$ and thereby create a new occurrence of $\emptyset$[9] or merge with an occurring $\emptyset$.[10] In either case, of

---

[7] See 3.5 and Ullmann's discussion, *Principles* 154, of the formal aspects of the theory of semantic fields evolved by Trier and others.

[8] Hoenigswald, *Lg.* 35. When $\emptyset$ is recognized as an allomorph, it is called "zero"; in the opposite case, where a positive morph (a phoneme sequence) is entirely predictable, we have an empty morph:

	POSITIVE MORPH	NO MORPH
MORPHEME	regular	zero
NO MORPHEME	empty morph	total $\emptyset$

We are here concerned with total $\emptyset$ and, in principle, empty morphs, i.e., with morphemic $\emptyset$.

[9] This parallels phonemic reassignment (9.1.2).

[10] Normally, of course, there is one-to-one replacement of earlier-stage $\emptyset$ by later-stage $\emptyset$. Note that, in spite of their phonemic identity, the two $\emptyset$'s are not the "same" morphemically; for one thing, $\emptyset$ has different morphemes to contrast with at each stage.

course, this means that the morpheme disappears from the sequence, thus shortening or simplifying it (Fig. 23). Some very sweeping cases of this sort may be seen in the history of the several European languages which have "lost their inflections", although this process is difficult to separate from the effects of sound change (see 5.5).

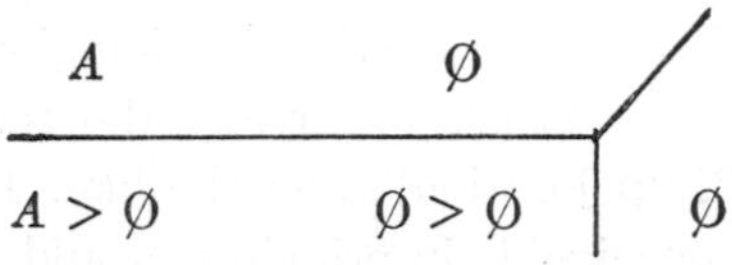

FIG. 23

4.2.4. Morphemic Merger through Developing Complementation: Syncretism

A particularly interesting form of merger exists when morphs which originally contrast recur, at the later stage, in phonemically corresponding shape but in complementary distribution and therefore as co-allomorphs (Fig. 24). At the earlier stage A and B contrast; their contrastive environ-

		I	IX	II	VII	III	VIII	IV
EARLIER STAGE:	A	x	x	x	x	-	-	-
	B	x	x	-	-	x	x	-
LATER STAGE:	N	-	x	x	-	-	x	-
	O	x	-	-	x	x	-	-

FIG. 24

ment is labeled "I,IX"; the two characteristic environment classes, "II,VII" and "III,VIII", respectively. At the later stage there is in effect one replacement, M, or $\{N; O\}$, occurring in the combined environment classes except IV. Its allomorphs N and O correspond phonemically to A and B, respectively; they are complementarily distributed. But the terms of their complementation are not (or at least not necessarily) related to their former contrasting distribution. E go and *wend* (*one's way*) did at one time contrast; now their distribution is practically complementary, with *wend* preceding the appropriate allomorph of the past-tense suffix, and go otherwise.[11] At the older stage the meaning distinction between *wend* 'turn (tr.)' and *go* was such that *go* did not occur in III,VIII, while both occurred in I,IX. This had nothing to do with the presence or absence of a following past-tense ending. Subclasses II, VIII, and IX are those in which the past-

---

[11] Jespersen, *Grammar* 6.75. The continued existence, at the later stage, of *wend one's way* is disregarded.

tense ending does follow; as it happened, that was the basis for the re-arrangement.

Another typical example is given in Figure 25. The morphs in question are case suffixes (Indo-European dative singular and locative singular, respectively). At the older stage (Indo-European), I,IX is the environment class in which both occur; II,VII represents the specific constructions in which the dative appears (e.g., with 'to give' present in the clause); III, VIII, those in which the locative appears (e.g., with 'remain' or 'be seated').

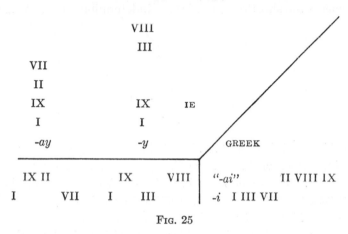

FIG. 25

Different types of noun stems precede either suffix. At the later stage (Greek) -ai remains after certain stems (e.g., the o-stems, where the word-end appears then contracted into -ōi) and also replaces -y after those same stems. Conversely, -i remains after certain other stems (e.g., consonant stems) where, in addition, it replaces -ay. The result, usually called SYN-CRETISM, is that "-ai" and -i in Greek are at the later stage mere allomorphic alternants of the same suffix, the meaning of which combines the meanings (uses, distribution) of the original morphemes, much in the same way in which F oncle and Ital. zio combine the meanings of Lat. avunculus and patruus.

4.3. Split

4.3.1. Morphemic Pattern

In an earlier connection it was pointed out that, if we wish to make state-ments about stretches and segment classes of standard (say, minimum) size and complexity only, we shall have to recognize conditioning, or split (see 1.4). Thus, as we have seen, a morpheme may split into a replaced and an amorphously lost portion. Likewise, of course, it may split into two differ-ently replaced portions. We then have the situation given in Figure 26.

Here the original environment class defined by the occurrence of A ("I,II, III") is broken up into three parts: one in which M and N contrast (I), and one each (II and III) characteristic of M and of N. This split may be viewed as at least partially conditioned, in that A in one meaning has gone to M; in another, to N. In a sense A-in-I has no true replacement; the ambiguous discourses in which both M and N contrast later on are recognizable as corresponding to the former A-in-I discourses only from a study of the extralinguistic situation. In the formal sense they may be compared with documents too short or otherwise too indeterminate to serve as a basis

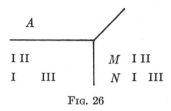

FIG. 26

for establishing a cipher (see 3.1). Thus older E *flesh* (as a morpheme) has been split into two morphemes, one filled by the morph *meat*, the other by the morph *flesh*. The two contrast in *their* —— *is tender* but not in *he eats more* —— *than bread* (*flesh* no longer occurs) or *a deep* —— *-wound* (*meat* does not occur). The last two discourse stretches may more properly be called replacements of (possible) older ones, with *flesh* filling the blanks each time, whereas of the first this is less strictly true. This means perhaps that neither *this is meat; its meat is tender* nor *this is flesh; its flesh is tender* are replacements of the original *this is flesh; its flesh is tender*, even from the extralinguistic point of view: the concept "animal matter regardless as to whether it is used as food or not, and equally regardless of any of the infinite other possible conceptual subdivisions" is no longer in the language structure.[12]

4.3.2. *Split and Borrowing; Split and Semantic Change*

It remains to discuss some of the morphic varieties of morphemic split. In the example just cited, one of the later contrasting morphs is the phonemically corresponding equivalent to the one original morph. The other (*meat*) comes from a different morpheme (see below). In other typical forms of split, one of the morphs is a borrowing; this is essentially the well-known history of some of the English words for domestic animals and their meats:

---

[12] One could thus maintain that contrast in I has been created amorphously. The process of secondary phonemic split is in some respects parallel (9.2). (See below, chap. 8.) For the example see Bloomfield, *Language* 430.

(*calf—veal; sheep—mutton; swine* [*pig*, etc.]—*pork*; etc.) (see Fig. 27). The morphs *veal, mutton,* and *pork* are French loanwords.[13]

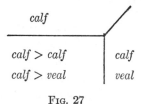

FIG. 27

4.3.3. Contrast Developing from Allomorphs: Differentiation

There is, furthermore, syncretism (4.2.4) in reverse. If the earlier *A* is allomorphically complex and is in fact equal to {*B; C*}, with *B* and *C* in complementary distribution, the allomorphs may simply develop, at the later stage, full contrast (Fig. 28). Allomorphs have become DIFFERENTIAT-

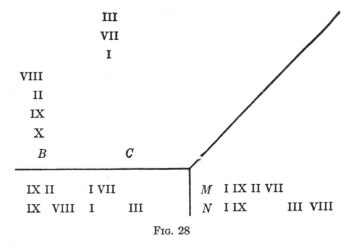

FIG. 28

ED into DOUBLETS. The Latin noun stem for 'god, divine' once had, owing to an earlier conditioned sound change (4.1.1), two alternants, *de-* and *deiv-* (nominative singular *deus;* genitive singular *deivī*). Each was extended into the former domain of the other so that later there are two paradigms: **deos* (later *deus*), genitive *deī;* and *deivos* (later *dīvus*), genitive *deivī* (*dīvī*). The new contrast serves to some degree the distinction between noun and adjective—*deus* 'god', *dīvus* 'divine, god'—as well as a difference in style. IE **lewkʷ-* appears in pre-Sanskrit and Sanskrit at first in the form of an alternating *loc-/lok-* 'look, perceive', here too, the alternation has a background of conditioned phonemic split: *loc-* had its place before certain suf-

---

[13] Haugen, *Norwegian Language,* 2.378, with discussion.

fixes; *lok*, before certain others. After rearrangement, both erstwhile alternants form full-fledged paradigms; they are near-synonyms, but certain differences in meaning have developed.[14]

4.3.4. *Role of Nil in Split Processes: Shortening and Increment*

A morpheme may split up in such a way that its replacement in some environments is Ø. The result, known as SHORTENING or (in some cases) ellipsis, is familiar: *private* has replaced *private soldier; Calico* seems to have replaced *Calico cloth; the Coast* is possibly gaining at the expense of *the West* (*Pacific*) *Coast;* and so on. The pattern is somewhat as shown in Figure 29.

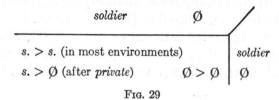

	soldier	Ø	
s. > *s.* (in most environments)			soldier
s. > Ø (after *private*)	Ø > Ø		Ø

FIG. 29

The counterpart of shortening is INCREMENT or conditioned split of Ø. A construct like F *un homme* 'a man, one man' replaces, by and large, both Lat. *hominem* (in certain environments; namely, those calling for the "indefinite article") and Lat. *ūnum hominem* 'one man' (Fig. 30). Consider

	Ø	*ūnum*	
Ø > Ø (in most environments)			Ø
Ø > *un* (in some other environments)	*ūnum* > *un*		*un*

FIG. 30

also such a process as the replacement of many Latin nouns by their diminutives in Vulgar Latin as attested by the Romance languages (e.g., F *oreille* 'ear', phonemically not from *aurem* 'ear' but from *auriculam* '(dear) little ear').

4.4. Disappearance of Morph Boundaries without Shortening and Emergence of New Morph Boundaries without Increment

A form may continue without replacement of any of its parts and without having its phonemic shape altered and yet change its status from complex to simple, due to losses involving its constituent morphs elsewhere in the corpus. It is the morpheme boundary that disappears by default, as it were. Lat. *vidua* 'widow' and (*dī-*)*vido* 'I divide' come from an old compound meaning 'set asunder': *wy-* 'asunder' + *dhē* 'put, set'. But, since *wy-* has dis-

---

[14] See 10.2.2.1 and Wackernagel, *Ai. Gr.* 1.148.

appeared elsewhere in Latin and *dhē* has been obscured also through losses in its occurrence and through sound change, the forms become unanalyzable. It is usually impossible to decide, though, how much of this is due to losses elsewhere and how much to semantic change of the complex form AS A WHOLE: it may be argued—and the argument would hold for many parallel instances—that, even if *vi-* existed in other constructions as a recognizable morpheme, the occurrence of *vidua* is such that it is not predictable from the occurrence of its one-time component parts. The problem is to determine the chronology of events: the specialization in the meaning of the reanalyzed form might have preceded (as it did in the case of *vidua* insofar as our reconstructions tell us) or followed the loss of the other instances of the former component morphs.[15]

On the other hand, a morph may have to be reanalyzed into a complex form. In a simple instance there may be a morph /a . . b . ./ = *A* at the older stage; a new (perhaps borrowed) morph /a . ./ = *B* appears in the

		sheep——	peas——	day——
EARLIER STAGE:	-s*	-	-	x
	-zero	x	x	-

* To include /z/ and /s/ (*day-s*, *hat-s*).

FIG. 31

morph sequences *BC*, *BD*, *BE*. If some of these belong to the same substitution class as /a . . b . ./ does, the latter is now *BF*, with a newly created morph boundary.[16]

A somewhat special and more complicated case is the following. In older English the singular of *peas(e)* was *peas(e)* (parallel to *sheep / sheep*), with a zero allormorph of the plural morpheme (Fig. 31). When *peas(e)* (plural) was reinterpreted as *pea-s* rather than *peas* + zero, this set up a new morph *pea*, which occurred at first only before *-s* 'plural'. When this morph widened its distribution to occur in other ("singular") environments, it became a back formation, like *chauffeur* cited above (3.7). It is different from *chauffeur* in that this particular back formation competed with the earlier singular, *peas(e)*, and finally replaced it, while "*chauffe*" was a new item in the semantic inventory. On the other hand, the singular *pea* differs from *Calico* (which might also be called a back formation in the wider sense) in that the latter does not crowd out, but rather continues to compete morphemically (with characteristic environments for each) with, *Calico*

---

[15] If only one of two component morphs becomes thus isolated, it nevertheless continues as a unique morph (*huckle-* in *huckleberry*; *kith* in *kith and kin*), with the morph boundary intact.

[16] The stretches "a . ." and "b . ." stand for identical phoneme sequences. The example would have to be adjusted to cover "portmanteau" and other types of morphs.

cloth (see 4.3.4). We may summarize this by charting the behavior of the forms *peas(e)* and *pea* before ("II") the plural morpheme (whichever allomorph— /z/ or zero—represents it) and ("III") elsewhere (Fig. 32). It is probable (see below, chap. 6) that speakers going through stage 2 and through the creation (though not the replacement) phase of stage 3 did not have the singular occur, or at least did not have it occur as often as the plural, and that the replacement phase was only carried out in a dialect or style in which the old singular had survived and into which the new singular was then borrowed. It is of course a peculiar feature of this example that the newly created boundary between *pea-* and *-s* constitutes a change from simple (one-morph) to complex only so long as the zero allomorph in *peas(e)*,

		II ——'-pl.'	III otherwise	
STAGE 1:	*peas(e)*	x	x	
	pea	-	-	then by reinterpretation:
STAGE 2:	*peas(e)*	-	x	
	pea	x	-	then by back formation:
STAGE 3:	*peas(e)*	-	-	
	pea	x	x	

Fig. 32

		sheep——	*peas*——	*days*——
EARLIER STAGE:	Minus zero	x	x	-
	Minus *s*	-	-	x

Fig. 33

sheep, etc. (plural), is not recognized. Morphemically speaking (i.e., once the zero allomorph is substituted for mere absence of a morph), the boundary is not an addition to the list of existing boundaries, but it is an existing boundary shifted: *peas(e)* + zero has become *pea-s*.[17] This is a special case of the process which is also observable in an example like *a napron, my napron* producing *apron* by way of *an apron, mine apron*. In these forms both *peas(e)* and *pea*, both *napron* and *apron*, were available as unique morphs playing the role of *huckle-* in present-day *huckleberry*: "*huckleberry* minus *berry* = *huckle*" parallels not only "*peas(e)* minus zero = *peas(e)*", "*anapron* minus *a = napron*", but also "*peas(e)* minus *-s = pea*", "*anapron* minus *an = apron*". The outcome depended on whatever advantage *-s* had over zero, or *an, mine*, over *a, my* (see below, chap. 6). Using subtractive singular morphs in the environment of the plurals from which the singulars are derived, we may rewrite the last diagram as Figure 33. Such rewriting is needed to bring the emergence of the new singular *pea*, which is clearly an-

---

[17] See below, n. 23.

other example of analogic change, into line with the more ordinary type of Figure 12 (Fig. 34).

		sheep——	peas——	days——
LATER STAGE:	Minus zero	x	-	-
	Minus *s*	-	x	x

FIG. 34

4.5. Excursus

In this section we return briefly to a previous example, in order to comment on some typical aspects of the interlocking of the processes whereby morphs are made to move across the morphemic system of a language. When *flesh* went, in part, to *meat* (4.3.1), there was a true morphemic split (Fig. 35). As a morph, *meat* used to fill a different morpheme, filled at the later stage, more or less clearly, by *food* (whose provenience is here not further investigated) (Fig. 36). But in a few isolated phrases like *sweetmeats* or *meat and drink*, *meat* is replaced by itself (i.e., by its phonemic correspondent at the later stage) so that the morpheme represented in the right-hand column in Figure 37 has, to a minute extent, split up. However, this second split fails to create a serious merger, in spite of the twofold entry on the second horizontal line: only for those speakers to whom *meat and drink*

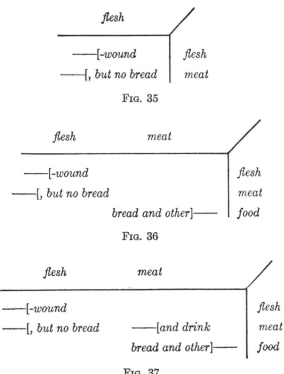

FIG. 35

FIG. 36

FIG. 37

may conceivably mean both (1) 'something to eat and something to drink' and (2) 'a roast and something to drink' (the latter with *meat* in its "non-idiomatic", ordinary meaning) has a real merger taken place. Even so, the merger is not on a par with *avunculus* and *patruus* above: presumably, F *oncle* shows no detectable homonymy in the sense of Figure 5, while *meat* (granting the usage just described) falls into two homonymous parts, as any dictionary will confirm (Fig. 38). Thus the complete picture, with all the relevant environment classes represented, is given in Figure 39.[18]

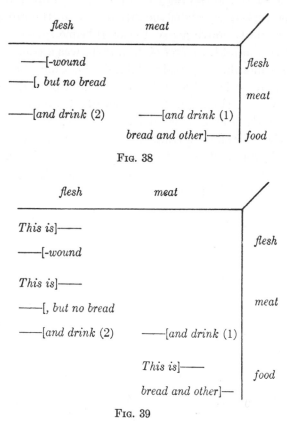

Fig. 38

Fig. 39

4.6. Discussion

It appears from the preceding that certain simple, well-tested notions like the notion of (synchronic) contrast (with the concomitant distinction between morphs and morphemes) and the notion of correspondence between elements of different corpora will produce a framework which defines the known varieties of morphologic change with regard to each other—and also incidentally, as will be shown later, in parallelism to the various types of sound change.

---

[18] See also the examples in chap. 6.

4.6.1. "Semantic Change"

This is perhaps particularly apparent in connection with so-called semantic and analogic change. The phrase "semantic change" or "change of meaning" is properly applied to morphs; if a morph at a later stage appears otherwise than as part of a corresponding morpheme—if, in other words, it has changed its morphemic environment—it is quite rightly said to have changed its meaning. Thus *avunculus, cēace-cheek, flesh, meat*, taken as morphs (i.e., identified phonemically), have all undergone semantic change. With amorphous extension, the usage is, for good reasons, somewhat uncertain (3.7). On the other hand, even foreign loan morphs are sometimes credited with semantic change; to the extent that languages in contact exhibit correspondences (of the kind utilized in more or less literal translation), morphs may indeed be declared to have changed an identifiable morphemic status in the process of passing from one language to another.

As has been explained earlier, a great deal of semantic change takes place within remarkably stable morpheme systems (4.1.3). This has led many students of language to view the world of denotata as absolute, with each denotatum correlated to (but constituted independently of) the "words"—namely, the morphs—of the language. Furthermore, the "fields" of meaning which it is possible, in theory at least, to identify and describe—somewhat along the lines indicated above (3.5)—as morphemic subsystems have a way of resembling each other from language to language. Some may, in fact, be universal. As a result, semantic change lends itself to classification by meaning content.[19] "Widening" and "narrowing" have been mentioned (4.2.2). In areas of the morpheme table where "good" and "bad" connotations are operative (in the sense that Fig. 5 would reveal these elements of meaning as suitable tags for observable common characteristic environments), morphs moving in and out of the resultant morphemic locations will "improve" or "deteriorate" in meaning. In other areas where a study of homonymy sets off elements of meaning such as "literal" and "transferred," there will be the types of semantic change known as "metaphor" (as when the ancestor of E *bitter*, originally 'biting', comes to assume its present meaning). At present these processes can be studied profitably only by relating their instances directly to their non-linguistic historical setting; insofar as this setting is itself in some way systematic, the semantic change, too, acquires the appearance of system. Thus, spectacular growth of metaphor at certain times has been explained by reference to such movements as the Christianization of Germanic Europe or the popularization of eighteenth- and nineteenth-century philosophy. Yet the true nature of

---

[19] See Ullmann, *Principles* 199, and n. 7 above.

semantic change is revealed by the way in which unique historical events, like the circumstances of Judge Lynch's life, are reflected in the vocabulary.

4.6.2. Semantic Change and Grammar

The illusion of a closed inventory of types of semantic change becomes even more difficult to maintain once attention is directed away from the nouns (in Latin, English, and other similarly built languages), with their spurious property of being "names for things in the real world". Other parts of speech, including those characterized by "grammatical" rather than "lexical" meanings, are equally subject to morphological (including semantic) change;[20] the same is true of relatively "bound" morphs like roots and affixes (as some of our example illustrate), of suprasegmentals (e.g., intonations), and also of constructions—that is, morphemes the morphs of which are arrangements of morph classes. "Syntactic change" may be of this latter sort; the general changeover from the "synthetic" build of some of the older Indo-European languages (like Sanskrit or Latin) to the "analytic" syntax of their descendants (like Hindi or French) often manifests itself in rather neat one-to-one replacements (of the type Lat. *amā-t-ur* 'love-he-passive* = he is loved' > F *il est aimé* 'he-is-loved') in which change in morph order is at least one factor.

Another matter which is here in principle accounted for but which is difficult to illustrate in a general way is that of parallel semantic change affecting morphs from entire subclasses of morphemes. Metaphor, in particular, is often seen to operate on more than one morpheme within a semantic field. In order to arrive at a satisfactory formulation, one would need more effective synchronic methods for the extracting of semantic long components.[21]

4.6.3. Analogic "Change" and Semantic "Change"

If the word "change" in the phrase "analogic change" were used, in customary parlance, consistently with the function it has in the phrase "semantic change", it ought to refer to the allomorph as it alters its occurrence (4.1.4); in that case the morphs -*ed* and -*en* would each be said to have "changed" (namely, to have moved into new, or out of old environment slots, just as *meat* and *flesh* are said to have undergone change by a similar movement). But this is not the practice; rather, it is said that the "past participle of *wax*" (or: "the past participle ending after *wax*" or the like) has been analogically changed from (*wax-)en* to (*wax-)ed*. In other words, in the case of co-allomorphs, change is attributed to the morpheme as it is filled by different morphs rather than to the morph as it fills a different morphe-

---

[20] Note the examples in 6.4.
[21] As is possible in paradigms (Harris, *Lg.* 24).

mic slot. The analogous style for describing a semantic change would be to say that "the designation for the concept 'edible animal matter' has been changed from *flesh* to *meat*".[22] Once allowance is made for this shift from one viewpoint to another, it is easy to see that the essential difference between change of meaning and analogic change proper lies only in the status of the morphs: *-ed* and *-en* contrast neither before nor after the change but simply continue to dovetail within the same morpheme; *flesh* and *meat* contrast before as well as after the change, although over different environment classes.

4.6.4. Analogic Change and Analogic Creation

In addition, the very word "analogic" is a source of confusion. "Analogic change", so called, must be kept distinct from "analogic creation" or "analogy", the principle which may be assumed to channel various kinds of linguistic innovation, including both "analogic change" and change of meaning (see chap. 6).

4.6.5. Analogic Change and Grammar

Analogic change, too, may affect very different types of morphemes (see 4.5.2); but, as the complementary distribution of allomorphs is characteristically simple and clear cut (compared with the differences between characteristic portions of morpheme distributions [see 3.2–3.3]) and therefore easily described, it is traditionally a part of grammar (rather than of the lexicon). What is sometimes called "grammatical change" is therefore in part (and in certain language structures more than in others) identical with analogic change. Once again, constructions may be involved, along with segmental and suprasegmental morphemes; as usual in this department, our powers of synchronic analysis are not sufficient to give us much understanding of the subtle analogic changes presumably at work.[23] Here belongs the often-observed development whereby free (that is synonymously alternating [see 3.4]) word order becomes fixed and meaningful; thus the "inversion" which distinguishes a question from a statement in French is not inherited from Latin. This would seem to parallel our instances of differentiation (4.3.3).[24] But these examples are far from clear, if only because the accompanying intonation morphemes are almost unknown.

---

[22] Hoenigswald, *Indian Linguistics* 16.

[23] See, especially, Bloomfield, *Language* 420; Hockett, *Course* 429. So-called contamination (as in Lat. *pr(eh)endere* 'take' × *reddere* 'give back' → Vulgar Latin *rendere* 'give back' is still imperfectly understood, despite its obvious connection with folk etymology (3.9) and the processes described in 4.4.

[24] Thus, to be sure, it is not strictly "analogic change".

5. MORPH AFFINITY IN REPLACEMENT

So far we have recognized only the two extreme degrees of formal affinity between outgoing and incoming partners in replacement processes: (1) phoneme-by-phoneme correspondence (i.e., identity under sound change, as between *avunculus* and *oncle*) and (2) absence of any formal regularity (as between *avunculus* and *zio*, *patruus* and *oncle*, *soldier* and Ø in *private* (*soldier*), etc.). Actually, intermediate degrees of affinity exist, when the phonemic differences between two morphs matched in replacement recur in other such pairs, without, however, constituting general phonemic correspondences.[1] We shall therefore from now on have to consider SETS of replacements rather than individual cases. There are certain typical conditions under which such intermediate affinity is likely to arise; the ability to distinguish between them is crucial for reconstruction, both internal and comparative.

5.1. Phonemic Affinity in Morphophonemically Related Replacement Partners

First, phonemic affinity in replacement may stem from a morphophonemic relationship that existed between the old and the new form. Synchronically, co-allomorphs are of two kinds: SUPPLETIVE or MORPHOPHONEMICALLY RELATED. The phoneme discrepancies between suppletive co-allomorphs (e.g., E *go; wend*) are not significantly repeated in allomorphs making up other morphemes in the language. By contrast, /láyf/ 'life' and /lív/ 'live' are morphophonemically related: l/l recurs trivially in uncounted morphemes, alternating and non-alternating; ay/i (or a/i and y/ϕ; or a/ϕ and y/i; whichever notation is preferred) recurs in {*light; lit*}, {*define; defin(itive)*}, etc.; f/v recurs in {*life; (a)live*}, {*gif(t); give*}, etc. The recurring pairs of alternating phonemes are known as MORPHOPHONEMES. According as morphophonemically related allomorphs contain trivial morphophonemes (e.g., the l/l in {*life; live*}), they are phonemically similar; but similarity is not required to establish morphophonemic relationship. Also the extent of similarity found varies with the underlying phonemic analysis. Thus f/v will fall into a non-trivial and a trivial half if a common distinctive feature, or common distinctive features (labiality, fricativity), have been extracted on that level.[2] The recurrence of a putative morphophoneme outside the

---

[1] That is, the environments in which the replacements recur can be stated only in terms of specific morphs and morphemes.

[2] In this example labiality and fricativity are trivial; voice is non-trivial.

morpheme in which its presence is suspected may be low or nil; since allomorphs are most fruitfully considered as either entirely suppletive or morphophonemically related (see below), the guiding rule must still be that any two co-allomorphs which contain more recurring morphophonemes, trivial and otherwise, than is attributable to random chance are morphophonemically related in their entirety and that the non-recurring or poorly recurring pairs which they also contain are unique morphophonemes. It will be shown later that suppletive and morphophonemically related allomorphs have very different histories: the latter typically arise from sound change (except that syncretism from accidentally similar or even morphologically related sources may produce deceptive instances); the former, as we have seen already, arise from syncretism (4.2.4) (except insofar as they are merely the last remnant of extreme sound change).[3]

Morphophonemically related allomorphs may become partners in "analogic change" (4.1.4). If so, the incoming form may be "similar" phonemically to the replaced form—that will depend on the proportion of trivial to non-trivial morphophonemes. Certainly, however, as co-alternants of other morphemes undergo corresponding analogic changes during the time span inclosed by the same earlier and the later stage, it will appear as though the PHONEMES had been replaced by other phonemes in a parallel fashion. Thus if E *hooves* and *rooves* both are found to have been replaced, respectively, by *hoofs* and by *roofs* at the end of some one time span, one might describe the replacement as one of phonemes (/v/ by /f/) rather than of morphs in the forms cited. Likewise, Lat. *honōs* (gen. *honōr-is*) 'honor' was in the course of documented history replaced by *honor;* on the other hand, a reconstructed older Lat. **poritus* 'placed' (cf. *situs* 'let') gave way to *positus*.[4] This illustrates that analogical phoneme replacements ("*s* to *r*", "*r* to *s*"), while recurrent, do not have the "regularity" of sound change (in the technical sense): if a given phoneme replacement occurs and recurs,

---

[3] In Scottish Gaelic, the plural of *ben* 'wife' is *mrā̆-ăn* ($<$IE $*g^w(e)n\tilde{a}$). The alternation $b \sim m$ seems to have been for a long period restricted to this noun, and the same is substantially true of $n \sim r\tilde{\ }$. Yet both alternations are created by conditioned sound change. Such morphophonemic uniqueness (or absence of recurrent morphophonemics) must not be confused with lack of phonemic similarity. In Plœmel Vannetais (Breton) *kok* 'coq' alternates with *ǿr]-ǿǰ-[ir* 'les coqs', where $k \sim$ zero, $o \sim \phi$, $k \sim ǰ$ all recur. (I am indebted to Éric Hamp for these examples.)

[4] It is likely that **positus* with the rare, non-productive prefix *po-* was in existence before the third-century sound change of intervocalic *s* to *r*. It is possible, however, that the internal open juncture /+/ which must be recognized in some compounds played a role in the conditioning of the sound change $s > r$. That this role was not a simple one is shown by *dirimo* $<$ **dis-emo* 'separate'. See Hill, *Lg.* 30.

the reverse replacement may also be expected (according as one or the other allomorph has widened its domain). Furthermore, not all the allomorphs are affected; only those which happened to give ground to their partners (E *knives*, Lat. *flōs* [gen. *flōr-is*] 'flower' remained). What is characteristic from the viewpoint of the later stage is, then, that the phoneme replacement affects allomorphs, that is, that it is associated with constructions in which morphophonemes play a role (e.g., in English or Latin derivative affixation, inflection, etc., but not the sentence construction in which "isolated" adverbs, etc., find themselves); that it may well go on in either direction; and, perhaps most diagnostic of all, that the very phonemes involved in the replacement still figure at the same time in morphophonemic alternations: *knives* exists alongside *roofs* (in the speech of those who do not say *rooves*), *flōs* alongside *honor*. As is true of other typical effects of analogical change, these diagnostic traits may happen to be missing in a border-line case, with the result that we cannot tell whether a phonemic replacement is essentially a rearrangement of allomorphs or true "sound change". A brief graphic résumé (using the Latin example) is given in Figure 40.

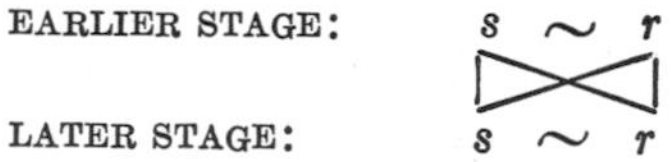

EARLIER STAGE: *s* ~ *r*

LATER STAGE: *s* ~ *r*

FIG. 40

Here, ~ indicates that there is a class of morphemes in which *s* and *r* alternate (*flōs/r, honōs/ōr,*[5] *s/ritus*); the sign is repeated at the later level because the class still exists (*flōs/r-* has remained unaltered, as indicated by the vertical connecting lines—as it happens, there have been no additions to the class of alternating morphemes). The northeast-southwest connecting line represents *positus;* the northwest-southeast line, *honor.*

5.2. Phonemic Affinity in Replacement Partners from Dialect Borrowing

The other, even more important, source of phonemic correspondence in replacement is borrowing from a cognate source, or dialect borrowing. Just as the existence of morphophonemically related allomorphs in the language had been taken for granted in dealing with analogical phoneme change, so we shall for the time being accept as given the presence of cognate languages or dialects, that is, of languages in which some morphs with like meaning (in other words, with corresponding distributions in each language) exhibit phonemic recurrence in the sense defined earlier (5.1). There the recurrence

---

[5] The alternation between *o* and *ō* (automatic, with basic *ō* yielding to *o* before *-r* at the end of a polysyllable) is disregarded from here on.

was one between the earlier and the later stage only; in the present instance there is a three-way phonemic recurrence among source dialect, earlier stage, and later stage.

Thus, in corresponding morphs, Iranian phonemes frequently answer Indic phonemes of such physical similarity that they would be rendered, under borrowing with sound substitution (3.9), precisely by those phonemes which also appear in the indigenous Indic form. In a few respects, however, the discrepancy between the sound systems is sufficient so that a borrowed form can be distinguished from a native one. Indic *a* corresponds to Iranian *a;* Indic *m* to Iranian *m;* but Indic *gh* to Iranian *g.* In a later form of Indic, Urdu, the Iranian ("source language") *garm* 'warm' is borrowed to replace the Indic form with *gh-* (Sanskrit ["Skt."] *gharma*). In a sense, *gh-* in this and other such loanwords may be said to have "become" *g.* Or, also in the Indo-Iranian subfamily of Indo-European, it seems that some Indic dialects (at a reconstructed stage) regularly match an *r* of the other dialects with an *l* of their own.[6] But in historical times we see chiefly the results of considerable borrowing (largely by the *r*-dialects from the *l*-dialects). Where these borrowings have superseded the corresponding original forms, *r* (the reconstructed antecedent for whichever phoneme occurs) has "become" *l.* In cultures where literary borrowing from an artificially preserved older stage is common (India, western Europe), this variety of phonemically regular borrowing is important. Lat. *plēbem* 'populace' is at once the ancestor (by "sound change" [see 5.4]) of Ital. *pięve* 'parish' and, through scholastic and literary channels, a potential source for the replacement of this form.[7] If *pięve* had disappeared completely, it would be true that *plębe* 'populace' has replaced it. Owing to the special circumstances in the historical setting, the phonemic replacements (two non-trivial ones in one and the same morph: *i* by *l* and *v* by *b*) have a special and characteristic phonetic effect: they cancel the result of the earlier sound change in which two entities, *l* and *b*, went to *i* and *v*, respectively. The sense in which the earlier *l* and *b* (of Latin) and the later ones (of Italian) can be looked upon as the "same" remains to be clarified (see 8.4).

If the dialect borrowings, instead of dislodging the phonemically corresponding indigenous forms, rather exist side by side, that is, in contrast, with them, they produce DOUBLETS analogous to the doublets of analogic origin (5.1). Some added detail from the history of the IE *lewk^w-* mentioned earlier (see 4.3.3) provides an illustration. Probably, *lewk^w-* gave Indo-Iranian *rauč-/rauk-* by sound change (*č/k* conditioned by the first segment

---

[6] Burrow, *Sanskrit Language* 82.

[7] Hall, *Leave Your Language* 172.

of the following suffix, if any). The Sanskrit forms *loc-/lok-* are borrowings from an *l*-dialect in accordance with what has been said above. But there was no complete replacement; Sanskrit has a third root morpheme *roc-* (with *c* generalized; no *k*), meaning 'shine'.[8]

Both phonemically corresponding doublets (i.e., doublets with phonemic recurrences) and phonemic replacement in forms may, then, be the result of one of two rather different processes: the rivalry of allomorphs and the rivalry of dialect varients. Allomorphic origin can be inferred if the pair of phonemes involved in the contrasting doublet or in the comparison between old and new also functions as a morphophoneme—Skt. *c* ~ *k* does so function elsewhere in the language. Dialect borrowing (in this context often referred to as dialect mixture) leaves no such parallelism behind—Skt. *r* and *l* are found in doublets as well as in individual continuations of the same reconstructed Indo-Iranian *r* but not in morphophonemic alternation, except in the sense dealt with below (see 6.6).[9] The relationship between

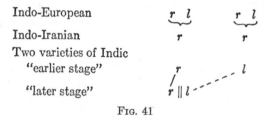

FIG. 41

Skt. *c* and *k* might be diagrammed exactly like that between Lat. *s* and *r* (Fig. 40). By contrast, the history of *r* and *l*, doublets aside, is as given in Figure 41 (the two stages previous to the "earlier stage" in the replacement process illustrate the background of sound change leading up to the dialect difference in the first place). The dotted line represents the borrowing; the sign ‖ stands for "not a morphophoneme". The fact that Indo-European had a contrast between an "r" and an "l" is not immediately relevant. The vertical line represents such items as *rudhira-* 'red', *roc-* 'shine'; the oblique dotted line, *lok-*, etc.

5.3. Phonemic Affinity in Replacement from Subphonemic Dialect Differences

For the effects of dialect borrowing it makes little difference whether the discrepancy between the source language and the borrowing language is on,

---

[8] The history of such doublets in Indo-Iranian suggests that the noun *loka-* (from *$lowk^w$-o-*) 'open space' acted as the pivot for this development. Of the *r-* and the *l-*forms, only the former belong to the oldest language.

[9] These quasi-alternations are neither phonemically regular nor grammatically meaningful. If anything, they carry a stylistic "connotation".

or below, the phonemic level: either degree of discrepancy may lead to sound substitution and hence to recurrent replacements of phonemes in morphs. In other words, two varieties of speech—local, social, generation-bound, or whatever else their nature may be—within the same speech community (i.e., presumably characterized by complete mutual intelligibility and "bilingualism") may be so similar as to exhibit only subphonemic but no phonemic diversity; yet, in the course of interaction, they may undergo or induce phoneme replacement. Let there be a community with two such varieties, (a) and (b), in each of which a voiceless dental stop and a voiced dental stop contrast, with the contrast occurring entirely in corresponding

> (a) /tem/   /del/
> (b) /tem/   /del/
>
> FIG. 42

morphs so that the two dialects are identical from the phonemic level upward (Fig. 42, where /tem/ and /del/ are examples of morphs with /t/ and /d/ in near-identical surroundings).

> (a) [tem]   [del̥]
> (b)   [tem]   [del]
>
> voiceless . . . . voiced
>
> FIG. 43.—Read ₒ = voiceless

Subphonemically, however, the allophonic ranges might be found located on a scale, say, of increasing voicedness from left to right, as shown in Figure 43.[10] Supposing that the suggested calibration does indeed measure

> (a) [etem]   [edel]
> (b)   [etem]   [ed̬el]
>
> voiceless . . . . voiced
>
> FIG. 44

the degree and type of similarity which is operative in sound substitution (3.6), the borrowing of /del/ from (a) into (b) would lead to a /tel/, which would then either continue as a doublet of /del/ or replace /del/. In the latter event, the effect would again be a change of the "same" morph in (b) from /del/ to /tel/, and the same would hold for all other morphs with /d/ and /t/ in comparable position (here, "initial before /e/ . . .").

On the other hand, the allophonic ranges in different (e.g., intervocalic) surroundings may have occupied different relative locations on the physical scale, somewhat perhaps as in Figure 44. Here the speakers of (b) will pick

---

[10] Hoenigswald, *SinL* 10.

up [d] = /d/ of (a) as [d̦] = /d/ (not as [t] = /t/). In short, phonemic replacement is found (1) where the outside form has dislodged the indigenous form and (2) in statable phonemic surroundings, that is, by positional allophones.

5.4. Total Replacement in Dialect Borrowing: Sound Change

It may be asked what the effect would be if dialect loans replace a very large set of forms—perhaps all the morphs in the language. This would not have been a realistic question to ask in the case of allomorphic replacement (5.1), since there it depends on the language structure to what extent replacement is even possible. Dialect borrowing is a different matter, however. Dialect differences of subphonemic and submorphic magnitude must be generally present in speech communities. Borrowing from one to the other, by definition, encounters no structural resistance (chap. 6); nearly all (not only some) borrowed forms have ready-made slots to fall into. Also by definition, it is largely a background phenomenon, below the threshold of observation and therefore immune from manipulation on the part of speakers. Supposing that one of the two dialects in the community, (a), functions as a model (has "prestige"), the other, (b), may then well borrow from it to the overwhelming extent which cannot be expected under conditions of contact between mutually unintelligible languages or even between closely related dialects that nevertheless do show diversity on the level of contrasting segments. One could at best argue whether such complete or near-complete dialect borrowing does not, in effect, amount to learning of (a) rather than borrowing from (a).[11] The answer may well be that this distinction disappears where the two contiguous forms of speech resemble each other in that exceedingly high degree.

In any event, the effect of total or near-total morph replacement from a subphonemically different dialect would be a change of certain positional allophones of certain phonemes into other existing phones in all or nearly all the forms in which those positional allophones occur.[12] That effect is well

---

[11] On learning as distinct from borrowing see Haugen, *Lg.* 33; Weinreich, *Word* 14.

[12] Examples like those quoted from the (Swiss German) Glarus dialect by Bloomfield, *Language* 339 (from Winteler's work), in which the name of a local feature (a minor mountain ridge) shows an aberrant development, fit excellently into this picture, if, as is at any rate probable, the aberrant development is the last remnant of the earlier local speech. Technically, so long as there is a remnant, all the other cases are borrowings; as soon as the remnant, too, vanishes, the borrowing has become a sound change. This raises the question, important for the reconstructing and classifying scholar, of how to deal with languages which have been swamped with borrowings —especially dialect borrowings. From the point of view of the spreading

known; it goes by the name of regular SOUND CHANGE. It is hard to escape the conclusion, speculative though it is, that sound change is generally the result of internal stresses and strains within one speech community and that its mechanics is fundamentally that of borrowing with sound substitution. With the aid of such a view a great obstacle to the acceptance of sound change can be overcome: the inability to conceive a process so contrary to ordinary speech activity as the elimination of existing contrasts. Naïvely, any speaker of a language can imagine that he will at some future time carry out, along with his fellow speakers, lexical borrowing (especially with total, one-to-one replacement) or that he will drop words from his vocabulary. But no speaker of English can easily see himself giving up the contrast between, say, *clip* and *lip*, *click* and *lick*, *clock* and *lock*. Yet that is more or less what happened to *knight* and *night*, *knit* and *nit*, *knot* and *not* a few centuries ago. If it could be shown that that change began with a purely phonetic disparity, and with a subsequent effort (a "misunderstanding" [see 6.4]) on the part of some members of the community to reproduce what is a less prominent (non-released? voiceless-nasal?) phone in the /kn/ of the source dialect of their high-prestige neighbors and substitute for it their own /n/, an important difficulty would disappear, and one would begin to understand why "correction" by the hearer, which allegedly keeps centrifugal tendencies from getting out of hand, sometimes fails to preserve contrasts, be they heavily used in the vocabulary or not.[13] Considering sound change a special case of borrowing does not imply taking a position on its so-called causes; specifically, it is not an indorsement of a modified "substratum theory" to the exclusion of other factors worth investigating. Quite proba-

---

dialect the aberrant form is the "borrowing"—viz., from the "substratum" dialect (see chap. 13, end). It seems that local remnants have a better chance of survival if they do not involve unique phonemic entities (8.3) but fall in with an ordinary phone of the spreading dialect. Since neighboring dialects are often typologically the same or very similar, this condition is frequently easy to fulfil.

[13] Of course, the cluster /kn/ was far less well "integrated" than /kl/ and /kr/ and therefore possibly more exposed to the action of forces here envisaged. So long as it existed, however, it cannot be said to have been closer to extinction in any one speaker's usage than were the other distinctive units in the phonemic system. See also Hall, *AGI* 42.154.

Naert, *AL* 2 (here somewhat modified), has made it probable that Lat. *ct* (/kt/) > Rumanian *pt* is the result of borrowing back and forth, not, to be sure, between close dialects, but between languages having similar systems, yet slight phonetic discrepancies in these systems: Lat. *ct* was rendered as /kt/ [xt] by Illyrian or Thracian neighbors, but [xt] (with lip rounding, [x^wt]?) was "more similar", in the local LATIN system to /pt/ (spirantic allophone?) than to *ct*; on borrowing back, the result was therefore *pt*. See also Rothe, *Einführung* 41. Cf. also below, 6.4 and 8.1.1.

bly, unevenness in the phonemic structure, functional load, and other statistical or physical properties of the language as such have something to do with the incidence of the "internal borrowing" that we seem to see at work in sound change (chap. 8).

5.5. Grammatical Effects of Sound Change:
Alternation and Homonymy

Sound change is likely to alter the phonemic structure of the language.[14] It also reacts on grammatical structure, and that in two ways. First, conditioned sound change (i.e., a process of merger affecting only some, not all, of the allophones of a phoneme in a given way) may create morphophonemically related allomorphs (5.1), which in turn, like all competing morphs and especially like all allomorphs, are subject to mutual extension, narrowing, and displacement. This interplay of sound change and analogical change between allomorphs will be dealt with later (chap. 10); its understanding is a crucial tool of linguistic reconstruction. Second, sound change, like one other replacement process—borrowing—may create homonymy with another existing form: the merger of early Gk. (e.g., Mycenean) k^w with t before e in Attic Greek let *k^w*élos 'end' fall together with télos 'tax levy' into télos, meaning both. The distribution of the new télos in discourse environments presumably shows some of the characteristics of homonymy described earlier (3.5). It may happen that the meanings of two coinciding forms are similar (i.e., their distributions may have been paralleled by those of other forms in the language) to begin with, in which case the merger becomes unrecognizable from the later point of view: OE æhher 'ear (of corn)' and ēare 'ear (animal or human)' became alike through sound change. Whether their present distribution pattern would justify distinguishing two meanings (Fig. 5) is certainly doubtful.[15]

The homonymy created by sound change may be homonymy with "nil" (∅), that is, disappearance of a morph, if the sound change happens to affect all the phonemes making up the morph. This has much the same effect as morphological shortening (4.3.4), but the difference is apparent in the fact that the same phonemic sequence is affected where it has no grammatical standing—provided, of course, that the sequence exists in both roles. Homonymy, and particularly morpheme loss, created by sound

---

[14] This is not so if one change restores to the system what another has taken away (8.4): if Hockett, SinL 12, speaks of sound change (phoneme replacements in morphs) as a machinery for phonemic change (typological change of the phonemic system), it is also a machinery for the preservation of phonemic systems, paradoxical as that may sound. In general, see chaps. 8 ff.

[15] Bloomfield, Language 436.

change has had a sweeping effect on the grammatical build of many Indo-European languages in which final syllables were merged with each other (sometimes with complete loss); since a majority of Indo-European words were inflected by suffixes, suffixation was thoroughly transformed, simplified, or radically abolished.[16] Particularly difficult problems are raised when a small class of phonemes makes up a restricted and special class of morphemes, as happens with the junctures, stresses, quantities, and pitches of some languages; here it becomes often impossible to distinguish between loss through sound change and morphological loss of a morpheme.

The following review of the entire framework of linguistic change is intended to elucidate further some of the relations between sound change and morphological change.

5.6. Review

At the outset we distinguished between amorphous (pseudo-) change and change proper. AMORPHOUS "change" is little more than the normal behavior of morphemes and morpheme combinations as they enter into new environments (within established constructions) or disappear from the language along with disappearing discourses. Change proper is a matter of more or less well-defined REPLACEMENT of losing morphs by gaining morphs in what thereby remain definable as the "same" discourse-long environments; as the gaining morph occupies a multiple or a subdivision of the environment of a given predecessor morph, the existing environment classes undergo relatively simple developments of merger or split or both. These rearrangements may preserve the contrasting (morphemic) character of a given morph with regard to other given morphs (changing only the extent of contrast or its location within a hypothetical table of all the contrasts in the language) (SEMANTIC CHANGE); they may preserve the non-contrasting (allomorphic) nature of a given set of morphs (ANALOGIC CHANGE, insofar as the boundary line between allomorphs within the morpheme is shifted); they may transform allomorphs into members of different morphemes (doublets and differentiation) or contrasting morphs into allomorphs (suppletion and syncretism). Finally, new morph boundaries may be created

---

[16] Martinet, *Économie* 170, suggests as a possibility that typological trends in morpheme structure may work against suffixation and that this, in turn, may facilitate the appropriate sound change. As in so many cause-and-effect controversies, there are as yet no criteria to decide this. The argument that the evidence for the morphological trend goes beyond the cases leading to sound change could not be used, since the reverse is certainly true: the sound change takes place "regularly" (i.e., in many instances in which it does not benefit the morphological drift; the latter is only supposed to have triggered it). See 8.3.

through the introduction of new morphemes elsewhere in the corpus, or old boundaries may be abolished by the disappearance of segments except in one mutual construction.

The replacing and the replaced forms may stand in some kind of formal relationship. Sets of replaced-replacer pairs may exhibit phonemic regularity; this is typical in two circumstances: where one of two morphophonemically related allomorphs is extended at the expense of the other and where a borrowing from a sister language takes the place of an indigenous form. Total borrowing such as it is not unreasonable to consider normal between very closely related (even only subphonemically different) types of speech within a community will lead to total morph replacement by phonemically corresponding morphs (SOUND CHANGE). It is precisely through (conditioned) sound change that morphophonemically related allomorphs (which may or may not subsequently replace each other within the morpheme) come into being. Moreover, sound change creates homonymy, that is, a special kind of semantic or analogic change, including homonymy with nil (i.e., shortening of a sequence by one morph).

In the extreme case, the loss (amorphous or in replacement) of forms means the total disappearance of morphs from the language (OBSOLESCENCE). Conversely, existing forms in new discourses or forms entering existing environment classes may add these wider distributions to others which they already have, or they may leave the old while entering the new distributions; they may or may not themselves consist of new combinations of constituents down to morph length; and they may, in the limiting instance, contain entirely new morphs, created by BORROWING, through isolation or back formation as described above or rarely through invention.

6. DETAIL

The foregoing pages are meant to convey a picture of the effects of change on that rough scale to which the fragmentary nature of our material —fragmentary even in the most fully documented fields and periods—is likely to limit us. Close-range, minute investigation of idiolects and sub-dialects, of population movement, bilingualism, and conscious and unconscious attitudes toward bilingualism are among the studies needed to know more—but such studies are few and far between even for contemporary language communities, and they are by necessity altogether absent for the periods of past history which furnish our information at least for "earlier stages" in change. The crucial zone where synchronic variability and diachronic changeability meet must be approached by interpolation and extrapolation from the accidentally spaced data vouchsafed us.[1]

6.1. Productivity: Analogic Creation

In synchronic study (precisely the kind of study applicable to such a question) it may be considered that amorphous extension in the distribution of a form in new utterances (3.6–3.7) is carried out along lines which are preformed in the existing corpus. Suppose, for instance, that the existing corpus contains the following constructions:

puppies grow				*sell puppies*	*young puppies*
debts grow					
apples grow	*apple juice*	*rotten apple*	*ripe apple*	*sell apples*	
pears grow		*rotten pear*	*ripe pear*	*sell pears*	
oranges grow	*orange juice*	*rotten orange*	*ripe orange*	*sell oranges*	
		rotten wood		*sell wood*	*young wood*

Suppose, also, that the phrases *papaya juice* and *papayas grow* (or *papaya* in classes of new environments all characterized by —— *juice* and —— *grow*) are introduced. The chances that *rotten papaya, ripe papaya, sell papayas* will also appear are considerably greater than those for the appearance of *young papayas*, and it is not inconceivable that a full tabulation of all morphemes and their environments, or a proper sample tabulation thereof, would make possible a numerical expression of those probabilities.

---

[1] With regard to the details of the analogic process see Kuryłowicz, *AL* 5, and (with important applications) Kuryłowicz, in *Accentuation*, and in *Apophonie* (esp. 5–23). On the other hand, see Watkins, *Lg.* 34.393.

The criterion would seem to be that *apple, orange,* and *pear* have a common characteristic environment class (formed by the overlap of their individual characteristic environments). It is this principle which is responsible for the term "analogic" creation.[2] A popular expression of it is the proportion, say, *apples grow : oranges grow : papayas grow :: apple juice : orange juice : papaya juice :: ripe apples : ripe oranges : x; x = ripe papayas.* If it is said that a valid proportion requires both formal perfection and semantic closeness, we may recognize the formal counterpart of this last-named quality in the requirement that, in order for a set of forms to favor the creation of another form, its initial common characteristic environment class must be considerable. The analogic creation may be a back formation (3.7); thus, when *chauffeur* was new in English, the proportion *driver : drive :: chauffeur : x;* produced an *x = chauffe.*[3] Presumably, the common characteristic environment class for *driver* and *chauffeur* was especially well filled—the other existing agent nouns in /-ər/ may have mattered very little in comparison.

If an amorphous widening into new environments is thus preformed in the existing corpus, it can be carried out over and over again by speakers. It is impossible to tell whether in saying *ripe papayas* a speaker says what he has heard or is making up the phrase for the first time.[4] Another way of stating this is that the construction is PRODUCTIVE; the meaning of the form (i.e., its distribution in discourse-long environments) can be predicted inasmuch as it differs from the distribution of *papayas* or of *rotten papayas* by a class of environments which includes the overlap of the environment ranges by which *ripe apples* differs from *apples, rotten apples* and *ripe oranges* differ from *oranges, rotten oranges.* Just because it is a productive construction, the inference is just as valid from the longer form to the shorter as it is between forms of equal length or from the shorter to the longer: the meaning of *papayas, apples, oranges* is predictable from *ripe papayas,* etc.

6.2. Disturbances in the Productive Pattern

By contrast, a form which figures in a productive pattern may go through a distributional change of its own; for example, it may change its meaning (by a replacement process), or it may be lost (say, in a replacement process). This may destroy the productive pattern; or it may give rise to the development of a new pattern, which may then compete with the old. The de-

---

[2] All extensions are analogic CREATIONS; an extension which replaces an allomorph within a morpheme is an analogic CHANGE of the morpheme (or of constructions involving the morpheme). See 4.6.4, and Greenberg, *Essays* 22.

[3] I.e., a *chauffe* extended to environments other than before {-er}.

[4] See Hockett, *Course* 425.

tailed formal analysis of these processes is a highly complicated task; but, in qualitative, meaning-content terms, examples are familiar enough.[5] When Lat. *validē*, the adverb of *validus* 'healthy', extended its meaning to 'very' (and, in addition, suffered sound change to *valdē*), the predictability of its meanings from *validus* was disturbed. One of two things may happen in such a situation to restore predictability: either a new *validē* 'healthily' may at any time be formed (it was, and its emergence can be dated as having taken place after the sound change which made the older *validē* into *valdē*), or a new *validus* 'of a strong degree' (after the sound change: **valdus) could be created. This second possibility did not materialize. Of course, the phrase "a new *v.*" is arbitrary or at least expresses historical hindsight only. The synchronic result is that such a *validus*, at most, has two meanings, possibly recognizable as two by a clustering in the distributional picture (Fig. 5). An English parallel to the latter possibility is the history of *fast*, originally only 'firm', with an adverb *faste* 'firmly'. The adverb goes through a semantic change; it comes to mean 'rapidly'. After that, *fast* 'rapid' appears, filling the productive pattern from the shifted adverbial starting point. Characteristically, the "new" *fast* and the old, with their almost opposite meanings, have been competing with each other across the gulf in the clustering table of *fast*. Schematically, what happened was this:

$$\begin{array}{ccccc}
fast & \longrightarrow & faste & \text{'firmly'} \\
\diagdown\!\!=\!\!\diagdown & & \downarrow & \\
fast & \longleftarrow & fast(e) & \text{'rapidly',}
\end{array}$$

with *faste* in the meaning 'firmly' quite lost at the time of the change. Items like *fast* 'firm' or *valdē* 'very' may be called ISOLATED.[6]

6.3. Productivity of Allomorphs

The morpheme that is being extended into new discourses may be an alternating one (the particular instance of its developing alternation in the

---

[5] One of the most familiar aspects of such disturbance in languages with extensive derivative suffixation is the isolation of suffix sequences. Latin adjectives in *-tōrius* (with verb stems underlying) are to begin with adjectives in *-ius* from nouns in *-tor*, which, in turn, were from verb stems. But there are in historical Latin adjectives in *-tōrius* either without nouns in *-tor* or with a special meaning which is missing for the noun in *-tor*. What is more, the adjectives in *-tōrius* form part of a quasi-transformational system whereby *-tōrius* is tied to *-tiō* and other suffixes (see Leumann, *Lat. Gr.* 213). The learned vocabulary of English is full of such examples of Latin derivational suffixes.

[6] See Stern, *Meaning* 216. On the whole, productive processes have the property of changing the terms which govern the quasi-transformations of the language (Harris, *Lg.* 33) or of turning quasi-transformations into true transformations.

very act of extension may be left aside). Which allomorph will represent it in the extension? Here, too, common characteristic environment with other, existing morpheme combinations appears to be the central factor. One trivial side of this is seen where the common characteristic environment is defined by a phonemic feature in the near environment, that is, where the allomorphs are regular (chap. 10). The choice may be so clear cut as to be determined by phonemic structure itself (automatic [chap. 10]); supposing that the singular of *photostat* came into English before the plural, the form *photostats* represents an extension (without replacement) of the plural suffix morpheme. Automaticity excludes the allomorph /-z/ (/-tz/ does not occur in the phonemic system); the existing regularity vastly favors /-s/ over /-iz/, /zero/, /-in/ (*bushes, sheep, oxen*). The allomorph /-iz/, in addition, is disfavored by the fact that it, in turn, is limited "regularly" to a characteristic environment that can be formulated phonemically. But one could construct the overriding factor favoring /zero/ and /-in/; if *photostat* had a characteristic environment range in common with *sheep, fish,* or *ox,* the analogical creation involved in making up its plural for the first time might very well result in the addition of /zero/ or /-in/. A new animal name coming in by borrowing might easily be given an endingless plural.

Similarly, assuming (in a somewhat simplified manner) that gender difference in German is allomorphic (say, *-er / -ie / -as* after *d-*, determined, on the whole irregularly, by the noun), the introduction of a new noun will lead to new environments for the alternating morpheme. The treatment of loanwords (e.g., from English) can be said in part to illustrate the workings of the principle of a common characteristic environment: a loan like *Groom* (E *groom*) will share the environments characteristic of nouns and noun phrases denoting holders of male professions (say, G *Lotse* 'pilot', *Arzt* 'physician', . . .) all of which select *-er* as the allomorph to follow *d-*. Also (to stay with the same example), while gender is in part irregular, it is not entirely so; the listing of noun morphemes by gender can in fact be shortened by including some such statement as that nouns in *-us* take *-er;* hence a noun like E *caucus* when borrowed into German will be a masculine so long as this mild regularity is not overridden by special distributional affinities (e.g., a class meaning "female", i.e., the occurrences characteristic thereof). These examples are trivial; they have interest only because of the larger context into which they fit.

As usual, replacement processes are more to the point. We turn first to analogic change (as distinct from analogic creation itself, which may or may not be associated with replacement). When a speaker says *ripe papayas,* it is impossible to tell whether or not he has carried out an extension of the morphemes involved or is repeating a complex form which he has heard. A speaker (i.e., "the first speaker") saying *roofs* (extending the morph *roof-* into the environment in which *cliff-*, *hat-*, *wave-*, *bush-* occur likewise) will also produce an utterance which is morphemically like one that exists already, *rooves*.[7] Allomorphically, however, this utterance is different. (When *rooves* is lost, the analogic CHANGE is complete.) Here, too, as in the above instances, one must take into account the whole of the productive constructions into which *roof* enters. The distributional affinities of *roof* to such items as *scarf*, *leaf*, *knife* (all of which have -*v*- allomorphs in the plural) are probably not significant enough to outweigh those to other nouns in general or perhaps to some individual nouns; hence a proportion like *ceiling* : *ceilings* :: *floor* : *floors* :: *roof* : *x* will produce $X = roofs$. It is often stated that the decisive factor is the simplification of the paradigm, that is, the reduction of morpheme alternants per se: paradigms allegedly tend to be regularized, and the redundancy involved in having a formal (allomorphic; i.e., phonemic) difference which does not serve contrastive purposes tends to be eliminated. True, many instances of analogic change are of this sort. This is so where the background for alternating morphemes is generally one of non-alternating morphemes belonging to the same morpheme class and even to quasi-subclasses of morphemes defined by similarly clustering individual distributions. Different language structures must necessarily present very different conditions; but, even where allomorphic variety is moderate, there are areas in grammar where alternants are created rather than eliminated by analogic change; we may refer to the occasional spread of "strong" verb conjugation in English (Fig. 14).

Lastly, the productive, that is, proportionally created new formation may serve to replace other forms in the various patterns of semantic change discussed earlier (chap. 4).

6.4. Reinterpretation of Dialect Borrowings as a Mechanism of Morphological Change

Not every superficial alteration is a structural change, inasmuch as it may leave the environment classes intact. Where serious change does take place, its fundamental mechanism is often one of MERGER to which split may be secondary. This is true in connection both with semantic change and with the special variety of replacement change known as sound change (5.4). Apropos of the latter, it was suggested that complete dialect borrowing (dialect learning) may eliminate phonemic contrasts. The phonemic substitution which leads to the merger of phonemes might be labeled, somewhat naïvely, "misunderstanding". It is worth noting that such "misunder-

---

[7] The allomorphs of the SUFFIX are disregarded.

standing" seems to be a factor in the wider category of semantic change itself.[8] In some cases it can certainly be shown that the replacement goes forward roughly in the following fashion. A dialect has two contrasting morphs or morph sequences, (A) and (B). Another dialect has (A) but not (B)—the chances are that the environments of (B) are simply filled by a physically different morph or morph sequence. The second dialect borrows predominantly from the first. When (A) is encountered, it presents no difficulty. The form (B) may be encountered in an ambiguous (i.e., a non-characteristic) environment and therefore be interpreted ("misunderstood") as the elegant equivalent of (A). G. Stern's famous example is a good model: *premises*, in the "dialect", perhaps, of lawyers, meant (in accordance with its etymology) 'the above-mentioned things'.[9] Ordinary speakers of English were likely to encounter it in lease contracts and the like, where it was ambiguous and could therefore be interpreted as merely a technical, hence desirable, equivalent of 'buildings' or 'land with buildings'. The result is a "change of meaning" if the dialect difference is ignored and the form as such is considered (a plausible procedure especially after *premises* in the meaning 'aforesaid things' was more or less lost in technical language afterwards). It is a merger from the point of view of the source dialect in the sense that one of its semantic distinctions is not recognized. Lat. *quare* 'why' becomes (as F *car*) 'for, because', through "misunderstanding" of sequences like *vēnī. quare? aegrōtus eram.* 'I came. Why? I was sick'.[10] The discrepancy here is subtle; it exists between two dialects one of which (the "borrowing," i.e., the changing, one) has, say, a phonemically or perhaps only phonetically (5.3) different pitch pattern characterizing self-questioning or possesses a syntax from which rhetorical sequences of question and answer are absent. To doubt the wider validity of this machinery for semantic change on the ground that "misunderstandings" are "abnormal" is to be misled by a term: subtle discrepancies between local, and particularly between social, dialects in matters of vocabulary are surely perfectly normal things in the life of a language community. Sometimes, no doubt, the reinterpretation openly serves a purpose: the use of *Coast* for *West Coast* (4.3.4) perhaps duplicates a possible "misunderstanding" rather than constitutes a real one; while a Californian in the East would use *West Coast* and *coast* in contrast, his imitator, by substituting *Coast* as it were for both *coast* and *West*

---

[8] Note that the "contrastive" environment, at least in homonyms (3.2, 3.5), may also be characterized as an AMBIGUOUS environment.

[9] Stern, *Meaning* 358.

[10] The classical article on this subject is Leumann, *IF* 45, from which some of our examples are taken.

Coast, conveys the illusion of being in a situation (in this case, in physical proximity to the Pacific) where the simple *coast* with its contrastive meaning is the proper term of reference. The recent or current substitution (not complete) of *home* for *house* is similar.[11] The essential formal point is that these replacements require as a pivot a reinterpreted utterance or set of utterances from the non-characteristic ("I") environment class. It may be suspected that obsolescence in the characteristic environments is a contributing factor, but there is little evidence that one may hope to find except in extreme instances where nearly obsolete words are in some literary or otherwise semiartificial way interpreted "wrongly" on the bases of a few archaic occurrences.[12]

6.5. Taboo

Taboo is a case in point. Euphemistic paraphrasing as such, to be sure, should not be confused with true replacement. Calling the bear 'honey-eater' (as some Indo-Europeans apparently did) probably did nothing to make the "real" name of the animal obsolescent so long as the taboo was a living practice; the hardiness of tabooed words is proverbial. But there are later forms of Indo-European, the Slavic languages, in which 'honey-eater' (Old Church Slavic *medvědĭ*) is the ordinary name. If anything, the replacement is connected with the LOSS of the taboo; it would seem to require a misinterpretation on the part of those who had no native equivalent to the difference between tabooed term and euphemism and to whom 'honey-eater' was simply a word for bear—encountered in one context and therefrom extended into another.[13]

When the replacement has run its course, the net structural result is either nil (as in the case of *ēam* : *uncle* [see 4.1.3]) or a relatively simple merger or split, the latter often along lines already adumbrated in the occur-

---

[11] Bloomfield, *Language* 441.

[12] Gk. *stētē* 'woman' in Theocritus, *Syrinx* 14 is distilled out of Homer, *Il.* 1.6: *diastētēn erisante* 'both fell out quarreling', misread *dià stētēn erisanto* 'they quarreled about X'. X = 'woman' is supplied from the context. The process presupposes the obsolescence of the dual morpheme which is represented in the endings of *diastētēn* and of the original *erisante.*

[13] Just as *pea* from *pea(-)s* is plausible because of the fact that the plural was probably more frequently heard than the singular (see 4.4). Whether this "misunderstanding" of the euphemism for the central term is part of the Indo-Europeanization of substratum speakers or of a later dialect borrowing cannot be known. The two other northeastern Indo-European languages, Baltic and Germanic, have also used taboo terms as replacements (Lithuanian *lokȳs* 'he who licks[?], bear'; OE *bera* 'bear' [originally 'brown']). See Havers, *Sprachtabu* 35; Emeneau, *Lg.* 24; Smal-Stocki, *Lg.* 26.

rence pattern at the earlier stage (3.5). Isolated instances in otherwise abandoned territory may continue to exist, hence *meat and drink* and *sweet-meats;* the compound as a whole functions in a semantic category (i.e., shows environmental overlap) with other nouns not necessarily complex (e.g., other designations of food). In fact, *-meat* in *sweetmeats* (if at all identifiable as a morph) is in a sense merely homonymous at the later stage with *meat* elsewhere (4.5).

The impression that the phonic material of the language moves in and out of a rather permanent framework (4.1.3, 4.6.1) is heightened by an occasional glimpse of the state of affairs which exists while the replacement is carried out. Generally, it is not so much that the replaced form in some of its "lexical" meanings (i.e., in a subclass of its distribution, formally recognizable at short range) is affected first, with the remainder to follow. The competition between the old and the new form is rather quite typically an example of dialect or STYLE rivalry, with both dialects or styles having essentially congruent boundaries between environment classes and, hence, neatly translatable forms. In other words, *ēam* and *uncle* may be expected to have had two kinds of characteristic discourse environments: one close range, or "referential", associated with differences in family relations as known to Englishmen and to Frenchmen, represented largely by increases and obsolescences in the use of *ēam* and *uncle* in new types of discourses; the other marked by other factors in the wider environment, such as the occurrence of other French loans, etc.

The ultimate replacement may be looked upon as a further reinterpretation under changed circumstances, this time on the part of speakers to whom the difference in style is meaningless and who therefore treat the stylistic variants as interchangeable.

6.6. Phonemic and Other Hyperforms

A little more is known about contact between forms of speech where two contrasting entities, A and B, in one area (a) are matched by only one entity, C, in another area (b)—owing, perhaps, to replacement change having taken place earlier. If (b) borrows from (a), A and B are likely to merge, no matter what their physical relationship with C. If (a) and (b) are closely similar dialects, its C may be phonemically "identical" with one of the forms in (a), say, A:

$$(a) \quad A \quad \text{x} \quad \text{x}$$
$$B \quad \text{x} \qquad \text{x}$$
$$(b) \quad \text{``}A\text{''} \ \text{x} \quad \text{x} \quad \text{x},$$

and the result of the borrowing may be

$$(b) \quad \text{``}B\text{''} \ \text{x} \quad \text{x} \quad \text{x},$$

i.e., a "hyperform"; or else *A* and *B* will be redistributed on an allomorphic basis if a background of morpheme alternation exists. In South German, *ich habe getragen* 'I carried' corresponds both to the homophonous (i.e., morphically identical) form of standard German and to *ich trug*, which differs from the latter in aspect meaning. But in the speech of many persons, and under conditions in which familiarity with the standard language is affected, *ich trug* is said as a translation of both *ich habe getragen* and *ich trug*. It is important to realize that the effect of borrowing is merger in either case; only the morph content differs.[14] Likewise with sound change: if we modify our earlier example (Figs. 43 and 44) of sound substitution among dialects by positing that the initial phoneme is the same in /tem/ and /tcl/ in (*b*) and by introducing a third original entity, "/r/" (represented by a form "/ren/", and preserved unchanged in (*a*)), we obtain Figure 45. In (*b*) there will be

| (*a*) | [tem] | [del] | [ren] |
| (*b*) | [tem, tel] | [den] | |

· · · · · · · · · · · · ·

FIG. 45

created, by dialect borrowing, an elegant variant, /del/, which is phonemically "possible" because of the presence of /d/ in /den/. Hence the proportion:

local /tel/ : elegant /del/ : : local /tem/ : elegant *x;*
   x = /dem/

Should the "elegant" replacement from (*a*) once again be "total", thus duplicating the process which had resulted in the merger of (*b*) /tem, tel/ in the first place, the effect, though phonetically drastic, will otherwise be minor. In either case: sound change to a common /t/ or "hyperform" in the guise of a common /d/ (provided the distinction is at all defensible phonemically after the total borrowing), the forms represented by (*a*) *tem* and *del* have merged in (*b*).[15]

---

[14] This example differs from 6.4 in two respects: (1) the environment of "*B*" (earlier: of "*A*") in (*b*) roughly equals the combined total of the environments of *A* and of *B* in (*a*), instead of equaling the environment of *A* only; (2) *A* and *B* form a close-knit paradigm—often (as in this case) with some morphic resemblance—rather than a mere lexical contrast.

[15] Analogic change has created (Fig. 14) a stylistic quasi-allomorph (6.5), *dem.* See also 8.1.3.

7. RECONSTRUCTION OF GRAMMATICAL AND SEMANTIC FEATURES

"Reconstruction" in historical linguistics refers traditionally to procedures whereby the phonemic shape of morphs is recovered from later evidence (chaps. 10 and 12). Those procedures are indeed more workable than any that can be applied to the reconstruction of morph changes. Yet some types of morph changes yield results which are typical enough to permit inferences. The following is a brief review of morph changes, this time from the point of view of possible reconstruction, insofar as it is not too deeply involved with the procedures for the subgrouping of language families (chap. 13).

7.1. Internal Reconstruction

Some fairly obvious conclusions are possible from morpheme alternants. Morphophonemically related morpheme alternants normally go back to sound change (5.5); hence their further utility in the reconstruction of sound change (chap. 10). Suppletive allomorphs, on the other hand, are likely to represent syncretism; whether the morpheme is "grammatical" or "lexical", "free" or "bound", matters little: both *go/wend* and IE *-ay/-i* are open to the same interpretation (4.2.4). Doublets contrasting by members of morphophonemes (*honor:honōs*) reflect the superaddition of analogic change over the effects of sound change; so do, in a less clear fashion, differentiated paradigms (on both, see below, chap. 10).

Doublets contrasting otherwise (Ital. *plębe:pięve*) reflect dialect borrowing (5.2). Note that the decision concerning the nature of the doublet is eased decisively if more than one set of different but matched phonemes occurs in the morph (or even in the form as a whole; in the last-named case, *l/i* and *b/v*, neither of which figures in complementary allomorphs).

Isolation is an important but difficult criterion (6.2). Uniquely occurring morphemes (like *brunt*), virtually limited to constructions with *bear the* ——, are very generally the work of obsolescence. An earlier wider distribution may be inferred, partly (obsolescence often being a phase of culture change [see 3.6]) from non-linguistic data, partly by finding other forms with which the form in question shares characteristic environment classes; thus it might be surmised, among other possible guesses, that *brunt* meant

—or was largely interchangeable with—*assault*, by observing that *bearing the brunt* and *bearing the assault* are near-synonyms.[1]

In Indo-European languages in which derivative suffixation and word compounding lead to very regular productive patterns (*luck*:*lucky*:*luckless*::*air*:*airy*:*airless*:: . . . ; or: [*stand in good*] *stead*:*steady*:*steadfast*:*bedstead*:*instead*) between unaffixed and affixed stem forms, the occasional lack of an unaffixed term in a proportional expression (*x-*:*happy*:*hapless*; *x*: *steady*) is commonly considered sufficient justification to reconstruct it, although sophisticated workers will add the caution that, once it (*hap, stead*) had disappeared, or nearly disappeared, as a "free" form, it could have at any time been remade by back formation (3.7).

Homonymy (3.5) due to loss from some environments ("semantic change" or simple obsolescence, as in the "various meanings" of E *board* 'plank; committee; food; . . .'[2]) and spotty survival in others, homonymy from analogic re-creation after semantic change elsewhere in the distribution of the form (E *fast*), and, finally, homonymy from borrowing (3.9) or sound change are often difficult to distinguish. The first two may be recoverable by finding that filling up the missing distribution (the lost connecting meaning) in a semantically coherent way (i.e., by positing "one" meaning or its distributional counterpart) produces a normally distributed item, that is, one of which the characteristic environment class overlaps reasonably well with those of other items in the same substitution class. Homonymy through borrowing or sound change, on the other hand, is semantically only an accident, so that in most cases the "filling-in" would have to range over the entire table of meanings (to fill in the gap between *mead* 'a beverage' and *mead* 'meadow', one would have to combine distributions which are not typically combined in the distribution of other nouns; hence one would conclude, even if no other information were available, that *mead* and *mead* are homonyms from sound change).[3]

7.2. Sets of Correspondences: Comparative Method

Much better opportunities for reconstruction exist where the older stage can be triangulated from two or more independent later stages into which the speech community has separated. This is often not easy to analyze in

---

[1] See P. Thieme's example in 13.4.3, where the reasoning is partly internal, partly comparative. Henning, *TPS* 1948, found in Iranian the Indo-European word meaning 'palm' which had long been postulated as the missing singular to match the unmistakable dual which constitutes the Indo-European numeral "eight" (*$ok'tōw$). See also Benveniste, *Word* 10.

[2] Bloomfield, *Language* 432.

[3] See above, Fig. 5.

detail. But one reason for the greater efficacy of a "comparative" attack (the term is extended from the analogous, but far better controlled, procedure as applied to the phonemes of reconstructed morphs) is that the essence of morphological change is merger. For instance, if we take the above (6.6) relationship between two sister dialects

$$
\begin{array}{llll}
(a) & A & \text{x} & \text{x} \\
    & B & \text{x} & & \text{x} \\
(b) & A & \text{x} & \text{x} & \text{x}
\end{array}
$$

or, for that matter,

$$
\begin{array}{lllll}
(a) & A & \text{x} & \text{x} \\
    & B & \text{x} & & \text{x} \\
(b) & M & \text{x} & \text{x} & \text{x}
\end{array}
$$

(as would occur increasingly as (a) and (b) have become less similar to one another), the chances are that the common ancestor of (a) and (b) possessed the distinction between the two environment classes and that they simply continue to exist in (a). It is not implied, of course, that all that happens in language history is a consistent merging of distinctions. But, by and large,

	(I)	(II)	(III)	(IV)
(LATIN)	"Genitive"	"Ablative"	"Ablative"	"Dative"
(GREEK)	"Genitive"	"Genitive"	"Dative"	"Dative"

FIG. 46

it is the mergers which the "comparative" method catches; the splits take their place as features of the merger to which they are incidental (as the split of 'living animal matter' and 'edible animal matter' is incidental to the merger of the latter with 'food'—taking *meat and drink* seriously for the sake of simplification [see 4.5]). Just what the phonemic shape of the ancestor form was it is impossible to know from the matching process itself; the object of the reconstruction in this case is the environment class or the morpheme or morpheme sequence defined as filling it but not the morphs that make it up.[4] Thus it is sometimes possible to reconstruct the meaning but not necessarily the phonemics of Athapaskan kinship terms.[5] Or, in two Indo-European languages, case morphemes are aligned in translation (i.e., in this case, in largely congruent environments) as in Fig. 46. Three Latin

---

[4] Precisely as the primary goal of ordinary phonological reconstruction is the phoneme, not the phone (12.8.2).

[5] See Hoijer, *A A* 58 ("Kinship Categories Represented", p. 309); in particular, the entities reconstructed for 'older brother, younger brother' (p. 315). His data are less conclusive, since there is only a variety of irreconcilable morphs but no significant excess of sets over monolingual contrasts. See also Hymes, *Word* 11; and, in general, below, chap. 13.

morphemes (G A D) correspond to two Greek morphemes (Γ Δ)— the use of the same terms would at this stage only be misleading. For the common ancestor, Indo-European, four morphemes ("four cases"), one for each numbered SET OF CORRESPONDENCES, are postulated. This is corroborated by suppletive alternation in the Latin ablative and in the Greek dative, a sign of syncretism (4.2.4). Confirmation comes from other sister languages, like Indic and Slavic, in which there is not only contrast of more than three morphemes (Fig. 47) but which also have the very morphs that are supple-

	(I)	(II)	(III)	(IV)
(LATIN)	G	A	A	D
(GREEK)	Γ	Γ	Δ	Δ
(OTHER)	"genit."	"ablat."	"loc."	"dat."

FIG. 47

tive in Latin A or in Greek Δ contrast as "ablative", "locative", and "dative" morphemes. In a broad typological view one might judge that some Indo-European languages underwent a structural change in the direction of a lesser case system.[6] Since the way in which Latin, on the one hand, and Greek, on the other, reacted to that pressure was not the same, the matter is reconstructible. Whether or not the merger leaves in each descendant language an objectively recognizable trace in the shape of a semantic (in this instance: syntactic) subdivision into "ablative of separation" and "locative ablative" and the like is very doubtful.

---

[6] See Meillet-Vendryes, *Traité* 556. For the phonological counterpart see 12.1 and 12.7.1. Actually the matter is more complex, due to the presence (not reconstructible from Latin and Greek), in some sister languages as well as in the ancestor language of an additional "instrumental" morpheme. It is also less complex in that Latin as well as Greek preserves a few contrasting remnants of the locative.

8. SOUND CHANGE: PRELIMINARIES

As implied before (5.4), mere alteration in the physical properties of phones does not constitute sound change in the technical sense except minimally. The term is used where the later (i.e., replacing) morphs are in some way phonemically different from the earlier (replaced) ones.[1] Phonetic alteration per se is largely lost to us, owing to the phonemic or quasi-phonemic nature of the syllabic and alphabetic script in which our direct records are written (chap. 2) or to the phonemic nature of our reconstructions (see 12.8.2); only scattered evidence from secondary transmission (chap. 2) will furnish occasional information.

The replacement pattern which characterizes a sound change is the basis of the comparative method; it will be investigated in detail in the chapters which follow (9–12). Aside from it, sound change may also be classified, and has many times been classified, by the phonetic relationship which exists between the replaced and the replacing phone. This method of classification will be briefly sketched in the next few sections.

8.1. Phonetic Properties of Sound Change[2]

8.1.1. Alleged Gradual Character of Phonetic Alteration

It has been said that any sound can change into any sound, but it has also been added that this is true only if a long enough lapse of time is allowed.[3] The shorter the period, the greater the physical similarity. This has led to the view that sound change is a gradual matter; in this view, sound change proceeds in small "imperceptible" steps so long as no contrasts are imperiled or other structural changes are called for. When these things do happen, gradual subphonemic alteration "becomes" phonemic. In the almost total absence of large-scale, questionnaire-supported observations which would have to be extended or repeated over generations of speakers in a community, such a picture can be only guesswork. Among its

---

[1] That is, either in the sense that the correspondence is not one to one or, at least, that the one-to-one correspondences link typologically different entities.

[2] This subchapter may be said to correspond to 5.1–5.3, where formal affinities between replacing and replaced MORPHS are treated.

[3] See Austin, *Lg.* 33, with further important contributions to the subject. The whole question ought also to be posed from the point of view of acoustic phonetics and in terms of a segmentation derived from acoustic phonetics.

weaknesses is the fact that, in spite of an appearance to the contrary, it fails to explain the phonemic reinterpretation of the lexicon material which makes a change proper out of the alteration and which is by nature sudden (since phonemes are discrete entities): no matter how gradually the [k] in *knot* vanished, the act of letting *knot* become homonymous with *not* has nothing gradual about it. Another difficulty has to do with a class of sound changes (e.g., metatheses, certain dissimilations; the—largely subphonemic —replacement of lingual by uvular *r* in many European languages) for which a continuous articulatory shift cannot well be imagined, but many of which occur nevertheless with the same regularity that characterizes other sound changes. On the other hand, viewing sound change as a special case of (total) dialect borrowing (5.4) does no such violence to these facts; it accounts both for the suddenness of phonemic change and for its regularity and requires few particular assumptions beyond that of the existence of subphonemic variation in the speech community—an assumption in perfect keeping with observed data. The phonetic similarity between antecedent and outcome in sound changes with a reasonably short time lapse is then due not to gradualness but to the role which phonetic similarity plays in sound substitution in general (3.9). The absolute datum that *k* (in *knot*) was or became very similar to ø is less relevant than the relative datum that the phone representing /k/ in one subdialect was MORE similar, in the other (surviving) subdialect, to ø than to the phone representing /k/ there —however difficult it may be to gauge these similarities except circularly by the outcome of the change itself.[4]

8.1.2. Types of Conditioning: Ease of Articulation

A phonetic comparison between earlier and later forms in sound change very often, perhaps generally, suggests a rationale: simplification in the articulatory movements. A given phone is replaced by one which resembles the phones that precede or follow (not necessarily immediately) or which for some anatomical reason combine more easily with surrounding phones or represent a less taxing combination of distinctive features. Thus sound change is frequently CONDITIONED: the positional allophones grouped into one phoneme change in different ways, governed by the very similarities with neighboring phones (e.g., in terms of shared distinctive features) which are likely to determine their phonetic differentiation in the first place. Conversely, if the historian finds that a phoneme has been split by conditioned change, he will conclude that allophonic variation has preceded it. These changes, known as assimilations, take many shapes. Frequently, they may

---

[4] The doctrine of gradual phonetic change may turn out to be a remnant from pre-phonemic days.

be looked upon as replacements of one distinctive feature by another (identical with a portion of the surroundings in the flow of speech, thus creating distributional limitations or long components; e.g., an *mt* yielding to *nt* with the dental component extended over both segments). The result may be a geminate cluster (Lat. *ct* > Ital. *tt*) or loss of a phone from the sequence ("assimilated", in initial or final position, to the stretch of silence which precedes or follows or generally simplifying the articulation of a sequence of segments, as in E *softening* with *ftn* > *fn*). On the other hand, there are sound changes which add a segment to a form (at least phonemically speaking [see 9.1.4.3]). They, too, may be said to "simplify" articulation; if *nr* > *ndr*, the physical change, if any, may be one from a sequence in which the abandonment of two component articulations (viz., nasality and full apical contact), instead of having to be timed to coincide exactly, proceeds one by one: first, the velum is raised (end of nasality, beginning of segment [d]); second, the tongue is brought into trill position (end of segment [d]). Assimilation may be mutual, as in Skt. *ṣṭ* from *śt* with the palatal *ś* and the dental *t* meeting halfway at the retroflex point of articulation. If so, two segments may be telescoped into one (*sk* > NE *š*). Assimilation may also take place between features within a segment, as when the Indo-European voiced aspirates (assuming that they did indeed involve a "difficult" or unstable combination of features, viz., voice and breath)[5] become simply voiced stops (*dh* > *d*) in a number of Indo-European languages (Iranian, Slavic, Germanic, Celtic, and others).[6] Such sound changes, if formulated (as is customary) for the segment-sized phoneme rather than for the component, are often UNCONDITIONAL (in our example, inasmuch as all occurrences of *d* + breath are affected).

8.1.3. Phonetic Plausibility and Hyperforms

There are other widespread types of sound change which may be presumed to contribute to so-called ease of articulation. Thus nasalization and lack of stress seem to be unfavorable to the production (or to the perception) of vowel contrasts; typically—at least in some language structures which are well studied—unstressed vowels tend to be centralized or lost,

---

[5] See Jakobson, *Eighth Congress;* Martinet, *Économie* 115.

[6] Such statements are precarious, as most typological generalizations are (see Hoenigswald, *Lg.* 33). As for this particular example it must be pointed out that the deaspiration of IE **dh* in Iranian, Slavic, and Celtic involves a merger with **d*, while in Germanic it does not (see 12.7.2.1, 13.4.2.2). For a classification of sound changes by phonetic features see Grammont, *Traité;* Bloomfield, *Language* chap. 21. Certain types of change which seem to be typical enough in non-European languages, like fluctuations between tones and glottal phones, are often overlooked.

and nasalized vowels tend to be lowered or backed. In certain cases the repetition of the same segments seems to be a difficulty and to call for the remedy of dissimilation; laterals and trills (more often when separated by vowels than when in contact) are frequently so treated. No generalization on these matters has so far been satisfactorily free from glossocentric bias or at least from the unavoidable typological restriction imposed by the fragmentary nature of known historical and reconstructed material. Yet, despite this necessary proviso, considerations of phonetic plausibility such as they are act as a powerful and important check on the possibilities left by the procedures of reconstruction based on contrast per se. Of this, hyperforms furnish an instructive illustration. Of the two possible "regular" developments envisaged above (6.6, end) for one of two dialects related as indicated in Figure 45, only one ($d > t$, $t > t$ merging in dialect (b)) need carry any phonetic plausibility. If it does, the other (hyperform) alternative (apparent $d > d$, $t > d$ in the same dialect (b)) will run precisely counter to such plausibility. This is a valuable indication of the true historical state of affairs. In some types of Italian there are enough instances of an apparent change of pretonic $o > i$ before m (Lat. *domesticus* > Ital. *dimestico* 'pertaining to the house') to suggest regular sound change. But the phonetically expected development would be the opposite—assimilatory lip-rounding before the labial m. Other information makes it certain that forms like *dimestico* are indeed hyperforms, secondary to a sound change, whereby pretonic e, i before labials went to o (*de post* > *dopo* 'after', *de mane* > *domani* 'tomorrow') in the phonetically expected fashion.[7]

8.2. Replacement Pattern in Sound Change

8.2.1. Regularity

The replacement pattern of sound change—as distinct from its physical content—is the crucial factor in structural phonological change; by the same token, its analysis provides the tools for phonologic reconstruction. There are significant parallels to be drawn between the major patterns of morph replacement as studied in chapter 4 above and the patterns of replacement in phonology as sketched in this section and studied more fully in the chapters which follow. The parallelism reflects the overriding importance of contrast as a principle of analysis both in grammar and in phonolo-

---

[7] As E. P. Hamp points out (privately), the difficulty lies in judging what is typologically plausible in a given language. Outside of Italian (or of the wider area to which Italian belongs), absorption of lip-rounding by the following m might have been the "expected thing", at least as a matter of phonemicization if not of physical alteration. It is also possible that the prefix *di-* had a hand in the process.

gy. The differences are no less significant; perhaps the most clearly recognizable among them is the absence, in sound change, of anything paralleling the environment class labeled "I" in our discussion of morpheme split (4.3.1); for the discourse *This is meat* there is in the later language (a) *This is flesh*, but also (b) *This is meat*—according to "meaning".[8] In the case of phonemes there are no such bifurcations; the set of all discourse-long environments in which a phoneme occurs splits up into subsets such that the replacement for the phoneme in each subset is a different phoneme at the later stage and such that the subsets do not overlap: at the time when some instances of E *k* go to *k* (*clip* > *clip*) and others go to ϕ (*knot* > (*k*)*not*), there are no environments whatever in which the outcome is, at the given time and place, ambiguous; sound change is, in this sense, entirely REGULAR. In a somewhat different way this has already been said above (8.1.2), where it was pointed out that phonemic split affects positional allophones; synchronically (here with reference to the earlier stage of a change), any environment, even if minimal, determines a definite positional allophone or range of positional allophones.

8.2.2. *Reduction and Redistribution of Contrast*

The replacement patterns studied below (chaps. 9 ff.) may in a preliminary fashion be described as follows: the circles at each stage represent phonemes; their segments, allophones; vertical alignment is to be taken as an indication of phonetic similarity between the earlier and the later allophonic ranges for each phoneme (or, in the case of parallel changes, each distinctive feature); lines symbolize sound change in replacing morphs.

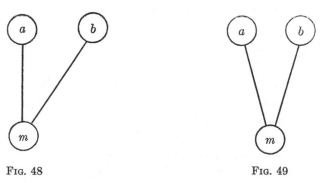

FIG. 48   FIG. 49

---

[8] The reason for this lies in the fact that in one sense *This is meat*, as a complete discourse, cannot be called a "replacement" of either *This is meat* or *This is flesh* any more than a phoneme by itself (i.e., outside its environment within a morph), in sound change, can be called the replacement of another phoneme. But the utterance *This is meat* occurs, and this fact is important.

As implied before (5.4 and later), merger is the central process in sound change. If merger is unconditional, we find the patterns shown in Figures 48 and 49, according to the relative location of *a, b* (members of the phonemic system of the earlier stage) and *m* (part of the phonemic system of the later stage) on an imaginary phonetic scale. Other possible types are left aside.

Merger may be associated with split in two ways: the merging phone may itself be the one which by the very fact of its merger with an outside entity splits off from its former co-allophones (PRIMARY SPLIT) (Fig. 50), or else a sound difference becomes phonemic in one other way: the phonemic distinction between the two kinds of environment in which each of the different phones occurs may disappear in a merger; if the phones remain distinct, their difference is no longer (that is, no longer entirely) predictable and therefore has become phonemic (SECONDARY SPLIT).[9] One may also say that sequences as wholes (consisting of phones and environments) have remained phonemically distinct, the merger having merely brought it about that the contrast lodges in another segment. Thus IE *k^we and *k^wo with contrasting vowels have become Indo-Iranian *ka* and *ča* with contrasting consonants due to vowel merger; see Figure 51. The difference between

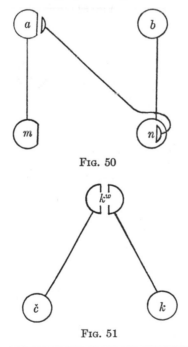

FIG. 50

FIG. 51

---

[9] Jakobson's "Phonologisierung", *TCLP* 4; see also Hill, *Lg.* 12 (=*Readings in Linguistics* 82).

primary and secondary phonemic split reflects our practices of segmentation. Both have in common the important fact that they cannot occur spontaneously—that, in fact, they are only corollaries of merger processes.

8.2.3. Phonetic Alteration: Effects Other
than Reduction of Contrasts

The phones making up a phoneme may be replaced in part or entirely by phones whose distinctive features do not bear their former relationship to one another. Thus a replacement may be represented as a movement of a phone from one phoneme to another even without merger. Such phones

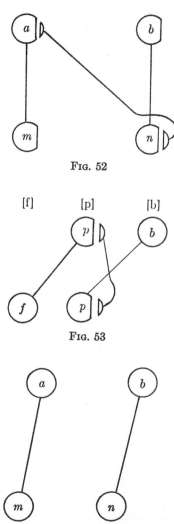

FIG. 52

FIG. 53

FIG. 54

continue to be in a position where a contrast is neutralized; it is their "phonetic similarity" which suggests a change in assignment, that is, an association with new co-allophones, as in Figure 52. Whether the extent of alteration is greater in the REASSIGNED or in the contrasting position is irrelevant: if location on a horizontal axis expresses phonetic characteristics, the picture might also be as shown in Figure 53, which depicts a phase of the Germanic consonant ("Grimm's") shift; the reassigned fragment, which probably remained more or less the same physically, occurred after $s = [s]$.

If there is no reassignment, the phonetic alteration disturbs neither existing contrasts nor existing morphophonemic relationships (Fig. 54). It may have typological interest (see below, 8.4).

8.3. Replacement Pattern and Predictability of Sound Change

Even if all sound change could be made out to simplify articulation (8.1.2), this cannot claim to be a causal explanation, since the particular segments which are simplified, the particular direction in which they are simplified, and the particular time and dialect in which the segment, sometimes after millennia of undisturbed existence, is altered, all remain unpredicted. That articulations which have been eliminated from a phonemic system impress later speakers acting as (naïve) observers as especially difficult and therefore naturally exposed to replacement is beside the point. At any rate, it is interesting to note that articulations lost by sound change are frequently reintroduced by another sound change within a short period of time. The argument from "ease of articulation" is weak and, at best, serves to narrow down the possibilities of change.

The replacement pattern of change—or of the hypothetical replacement pattern of changes which have not occurred—may itself be looked upon as another factor favorable or unfavorable to sound change. Merger creates homonyms and thereby endangers communication. It is reasonable to look for an inverse correlation between the incidence of merger and the amount of real homonymy which it has, or would have, created; if a particular contrast is little used in the language, its elimination will do less harm than the elimination of a contrast with a high functional load.[10] The older idea that sound change is inhibited in the particular forms in which homonymy results but goes ahead unchecked in other cases has turned out to be untenable.[11] Not only do we fail to find speech "spotted over with all sorts of

---

[10] One would expect reassignments of "neutralized" phones to be more frequent than they are.

[11] Rather, some analogical creations LOOK like forms untouched by sound change (see 10.2.2.1).

queer deviant sounds in forms which had resisted sound change",[12] as we would expect to do, but the famous studies of Gilliéron and others have shown how homonymy can be dealt with by orthodox means:[13] one of the newly created homonyms (i.e., the new morph or morph sequence in that part of its environment which is equal to the earlier environment of one, but not the other, of the two source forms) is replaced by a neologism or a borrowing of some sort (as when all kinds of paraphrases, near-synonyms, etc., take the place of Lat. *gallus* 'rooster' precisely in that area [in southwestern France] in which *gallus* and *gattus* 'cat' would have become the same). But it is entirely conceivable that threatened homonymy should also be considered as counteracting the forces of "articulatory ease" in holding back an entire merger process and in preserving a phonemic contrast even where it is not minimal. The enormous difficulty in gauging functional load even in living languages, let alone in extinct ones, has prevented going beyond speculation on this point.[14] It is also possible to look upon phonemic systems as tending toward a state of balance unfavorable both to extremes of frequency of occurrence and to lack of symmetry insofar as the privileges of occurrence (clustering) of phonemes or of distinctive features ("gaps in the system") are concerned. One may point to the fact that many Indo-European languages have, by means of one sound change or another (and by other processes, such as borrowing, as well), given normal frequency to the sound type *b* which was extremely rare at the earliest attainable stage or to the fact that the Romance languages possess initial *dr-*, a combination which is not natively Latin. It is certainly impossible to overlook the importance of this factor in judging the mechanics of phonemic substitution in borrowing (5.4). It is sometimes said that unconditioned (or nearly unconditioned) sound change takes place in stages, in the sense that a primary split occurs first in one definite environment (perhaps in one lexical item?) and then spreads. There seems to be no indication that this is generally true.[15] Certainly, some sound changes give the impression of working toward a well-characterized typological goal precisely by being, and remaining, conditioned. If the proto-Algonquian vowels are lost in final position in

---

[12] Bloomfield, *Language* 356.

[13] E.g., *Pathologie*. "Or homonymy simply stands, as in Scottish Gaelic *húg . . . jíi* 'gave to her; took off her' " (E. P. Hamp [privately]).

[14] Hockett, *Manual* 215. If human speech is generally characterized by "50 per cent redundancy", this would constrain the effects produced by change. See Hockett, *Course* 89.

[15] Greenberg, Osgood, Saporta, in Osgood and Saporta (eds.), *Psycholinguistics* 148. More below, chap. 11.

Menomini (thereby setting up a rigid structural mold for Menomini words) there is no reason to suppose that this has made it easier for vowels to be lost in other surroundings as well. Languages observed in the field show great statistical and distributional disparity of phonemes and distinctive features, and there is little to indicate that these disparities are merely transitory.

Causality and teleology aside, there are great advantages to be derived from any view of phonemic change in which all its so-called effects, that is, all its distributional properties beyond those affecting the immediate binary relationship between two merging (or otherwise linked) phonemes, are considered. The fact that an IE *k' ("palatal") before u (more properly, before a syllabic /w/) seems to go to s in Hittite is in itself merely an example of primary split through merger (of *$k'u$ with *su). Phonetic parallels (from Oscan, Japanese, English, etc.) may be found to make the process plausible. What is more interesting is that the split does not leave a true gap, since, while *$k'o$ and *$k'e$ appear as ka and ke, there is also a "new" ku representing a non-palatal *ku; this "pure velar" *ku had been either allophonically or morphophonemically related with a *k^w (or *kw) occurring before o, e, etc., but not before u. Whether *ko, *ke had also existed is uncertain; in any event, *ku had been more frequent, and the movement of $k'u$ in the direction of su may well be looked upon as saving the important contrast between IE *$k'u$ and *ku from merger. Why the merging of k' and s before u was easier to tolerate would still have to be shown (Figs. 55 and

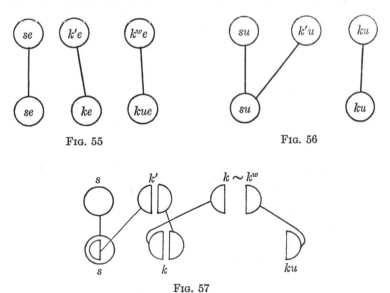

Fig. 55   Fig. 56

Fig. 57

56; for a combined picture see Fig. 57, where the left semicircle indicates occurrence before *u*, and the right semicircle, occurrence before *e*).[16]

8.4. Convergence Areas and Change, Especially Sound Change

Language traits—morphemic or phonetic-phonemic—are sometimes characteristic of well-defined geographic areas. All over India, for instance, we find a syntax "in which verb stems or nonfinite verb forms are strung together in series which are closed by a finite verb form (or other predicate-ender)".[17] Near the southern tip of Africa clicks are part of the sound system.[18] The various languages spoken in the Balkan Peninsula share a number of grammatical and phonological features.[19]

The languages which resemble each other in this fashion are often unrelated or only distantly related. As can be shown either from records or through reconstruction, their areal characteristics are acquired through change, presumably as a result of contact with their neighbors. The adaptation process is no doubt connected with bilingualism and language learning in the border zones or in the path of a language which spreads at the expense of another; we may picture it as a process akin to that which produces loan translations. While imperfectly understood in detail, there is no doubt that areal trends are among the major factors which influence the direction of change and detract from its randomness. Unlike the other two factors which we have discerned at work in sound change, viz. phonetic plausibility, and internal structural pressures, areal tendencies are specific and link language with historical accident rather than merely with presumed universals.

Areal type itself is of course not immutable. It may alter in the sense that the member languages, related or not, alter their structures in a parallel manner. Such a typological transformation is on the whole a slow process. A prevailing areal type, and hence a fortiori the structure of a given language, unless it is exposed to new surroundings, possesses great stability. And in some ways, phones and phonemes under change behave much like morphs

---

[16] Goetze, *Lg.* 30. The theory of "drag-chain" and "push-chain" combinations of sound change has been expounded particularly by Martinet, *Économie passim;* see also Joos, *Lg.* 28 (=*Readings in Linguistics* 372); Twaddell, *For Roman Jakobson;* Moulton, *Lg.* 30; Ruipérez, *Word* 12; Haudricourt and Juilland, *Essai;* and many other recent studies.

[17] Emeneau, *Lg.* 32.9, perhaps the most lucid account of a convergence area and of the principles. For a further history of the concept see the bibliographical references assembled by Emeneau, and Weinreich, *Word* 14, who proposes the term "convergence areas".

[18] Westermann, *Berlin Sitzungsberichte* 1948:1.

[19] Sandfeld, *Linguistique balkanique.*

and morphemes (6.4). Phonemic systems before and after even an entire complex of changes are often descriptively unaltered; it is only that in a given set of morphs a given phoneme is replaced not by the phoneme occupying the corresponding place in the later, but structurally identical, phonemic system, but instead by a phoneme occupying a different place. Because of this remarkable stability, it has been possible to say that, between two stages, "*b* 'remains' *b*" while "*p* 'becomes' *f*", even though, strictly speaking, the phonemes at each stage can be defined only by all other phonemes at the same stage. The persistent identity which is implied is not only the physical identity of phones (which cannot by itself be relevant in any event) but rather homologous position in a permanent or at least much more slowly altering phonemic system. In the following chapter we shall, generally, not make use of this semipermanency, mainly so as to avoid begging any questions. But it should be kept in mind that change as we normally think of it may or may not result in a new typology and also that the same new typology may be brought about through different individual changes. This is easiest to observe in the history of one language family; here a number of "daughter languages" (chap. 12) share the same starting point (the same ancestor language) and may from the final result be judged to have responded, in their separate development, to the same typological trend— be it because the areal type has indeed gone through one of its slow changes or because of common outside contacts.[20] Yet that development—that is, the set of particular changes utilized, as it were, for the attainment of the final result—has been truly separate. The Indo-European languages have largely reduced their case categories (same typological result); but different languages have achieved this by merging different pairs of case morphemes (separate development) (see 7.2). Or, to come back once more to sound change, several Indo-European languages have developed a multiplicity of spirants and sibilants where the proto-language had only one *s*; and this is done by means of a most bewildering variety of split processes from a number of different sources (e.g., morphs with *s* split *s* into *s* and *z* in Germanic; after *z* merges with *r* in most Germanic dialects, the split is repeated; in a number of Germanic dialects *sk* is replaced by *š*; in Slavic, *s* splits into *s* [Polish *s*, *ś*], *š*, *z* [Polish *z*, *ź*], etc., while *k'* gives *s*, *g* gives *z*). It is of course possible, and under certain circumstances probable, that two daughter languages yield to the same pressure also in exactly the same way:

---

[20] That is the difficulty with Hockett's requirement (*Course* 506) of "realism" in reconstruction. It is not necessarily true that "the parent language should be expected to be somewhat more like each of its descendants than they are like each other".

such "duplicate" change creates one of the major difficulties for the comparative method of reconstruction (chap. 13).

It should be made clear, however, that contact does not generally produce the effects which common descent produces. In common descent different replacement changes affect the same morphs (those of the ancestor language) in the different subdivisions of the speech community as it breaks up.[21] The result, as will be shown in detail (chap. 12), is a recurrence of phonemic correspondences in the "same" morphs of the daughter languages: Lat. *u* > *o* in Italian; > *u* in Rumanian; hence some occurrences of Ital. *o* correspond to some occurrences of Rumanian *u*. This is so regardless of whether these phonemes are members of typologically similar or dissimilar phonemic systems. On the other hand, Armenian and Georgian, unrelated, are neighbors with very similar phonemic systems.[22] Yet, borrowings aside, no correspondences between phonemes of the two languages recur in any way.[23] It is only in the case of rather closely related dialects that secondary contact may take on the characteristics of original relation, thereby wiping out differences between the dialects which had existed previously.

The case of Armenian is instructive in another way. While the phonemic structure, at least in inventory, resembles strikingly that of its unrelated neighbor, there are relatively few Georgian loanwords in the language. By contrast, it is all but overwhelmed with loanwords from Iranian. The Iranian languages are, as it happens, Indo-European and hence related to Armenian; that is, phonemic correspondences between them and the non-borrowed residual core of the Armenian lexicon recur. But they are correspondences between elements of very differently constructed systems: except possibly for Ossetic, an isolated Iranian speech community now part of the Armenian-Georgian language area, typical Iranian structure shows few of the special traits of the latter. One is inclined to see in this a reflex of the relationship between the speech communities and of their external history. Armenian represents Indo-European as it spread to a border area, perhaps Indo-European as "learned" by speakers of languages of the type still represented to us by Georgian; as an "upper" language it has relatively few out-

---

[21] Trubetzkoy, *AL* 1, refuted in great detail by Thieme, *Heimat*, wanted to show that a language family like Indo-European might be the result of convergence rather than split. See also Weinreich, *Word* 14.

[22] Deeters, *Caucasica* 3–4; Vogt, *Word* 10. Welsh has a somewhat "English" phonemic system (/θ, ð/, central vowels, diphthongs, stresses), while its close relative, Breton, shows "French" /z, š, ž/, front rounded vowels, elimination of diphthongs, /ñ, λ/, and appropriate stresses and superfixes. (E. Hamp.)

[23] On maximum borrowing and "basic vocabulary" see chaps. 6 and 13.

right borrowings from the "lower" language.[24] With regard to Iranian, however, Armenian had acted as the "lower" language, although without succumbing to the "upper" language (i.e., without the speakers "learning" it). Like English after the Norman period, or like Urdu in northern India after the high tide of Persian-Hindi bilingualism, the surviving "lower" language shows the marks of the struggle in the shape of borrowed vocabulary.

Similar indications exist elsewhere. Most languages of India have a set of retroflex stops in contrast with dentals. In Indo-Aryan (i.e., in the principal form of IE represented in the area) this is an innovation accomplished mainly by secondary split (see below, 9.2.1). In Dravidian

it is a matter of the utmost certainty that retroflexes in contrast with dentals are proto-Dravidian in origin. . . . In Southern Dravidian, moreover, several languages have three phonemic series in the front of the mouth—dental, alveolar, retroflex. . . . The comparative evidence looks to similar distinctions in Proto-Dravidian. This being so for Dravidian, it is beyond doubt that even where Indo-European material yields Sanskrit retroflexes, pre-Indo-Aryan and pre-Dravidian bilingualism provided the conditions which allowed pre-Indo-European allophones to be redistributed as retroflex phonemes. Certainly as time went on, Middle Indo-Aryan showed more such phonemes than Old Indo-Aryan, and in consequence Modern Indo-Aryan does so, too. This is a clear instance of Indianization of the Indo-European component in the Indic linguistic scene.[25]

It should be added that southern Dravidian is farthest removed from the zone of contact between Dravidian and Indo-Aryan and that the northeasternmost form of Indo-Aryan, Assamese, where there is contact with yet another language family (viz., Tibeto-Burmese), fails to exhibit the contrast; it is also alien to Tibeto-Burmese (see 2.3). Considerations of this sort play an important part in the determining of language relationship (chaps. 12 and 13).

---

[24] Bloomfield, *Language* chap. 26.
[25] Emeneau, *Lg.* 32.7. See below, Fig. 78.

9. PATTERNS OF SOUND CHANGE

In the discussion which follows we shall employ the two-dimensional notation of chapter 4 to record a change and to represent its phonemic effect (8.2),[1] as in Figure 58. *Read:* At the older stage, phoneme *a* occurs in en-

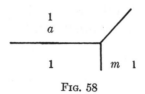

FIG. 58

vironment 1 (horizontal axis). At the later stage, phoneme *m* occurs in environment 1 (vertical axis). The sound change in question consists in *a* being replaced by *m* in environment 1 (intersection). The term "environment" will be explained later. More simply and directly we shall also write the notation given in Figure 59. (*Read: a* becomes *m.*)

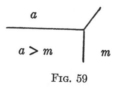

FIG. 59

---

[1] Compare the morph charts in chap. 4. Since the phonemes at different stages can be the "same" only in the sense that they are homologous in the system (8.4), it would have been more consistent to rename not only the phonemes (*a, b* at the earlier stage; *m, n* at the later stage) but the environments as well. Thus Figure 58 should really read:

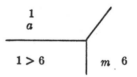

This is in fact necessary in the case of secondary split (9.2). The term 'phoneme' is used here for the sake of brevity—in many of the examples which follow, the pattern applies to a set of phonemes (as when, in 'Grimm's Law' the various voiceless stops are treated in a parallel fashion)—i.e., to a distinctive feature. We have here no more than a special application of the principles that synchronic analysis must precede historical study and that phonemic solutions are not unique. See, e.g., 9.1.1 and the discussion under 8.1.2.

9.1. Types of Sound Change in Constant Environments

First, supposing that the environments of the older stage remain distinct at the later stage, we may distinguish four types of sound change according to their effect on the system of phonemic contrasts in the language.

9.1.1. Absence of Phonemic Change

In Figure 60, a and b have one environment class (1,2) in common (they contrast); in addition, a occurs in a second environment class (3,4), b in a third (5). It is always to be assumed that there is a fourth (unmarked) in which neither a nor b occurs. This is the general type of mutual distribution existing between two phonemes. The array of numbers above "a" and "b" on the horizontal axis expresses graphically both the extent of

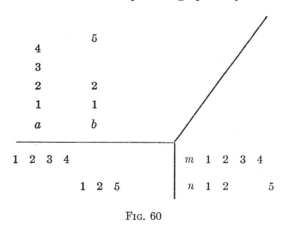

Fig. 60

contrast and the significance of the numbers themselves. At the intersections the chart indicates that a in all its environments goes to m, and b in all its environments to n, with the result (stated by the adscript numbers in the vertical column) that m has the former environment of a, n the former environment of b. It is implied (I) that there are no other sources for m and n and (II) that the numbered environments have remained mutually exclusive. Environments may be thought of as stated in terms of entries in a chart extended to show the changes that have affected all the phonemes of the language between the older and the later stage. Thus, "5" may include "occurrence before $c > o$", which would mean that the sequence bc of the older stage appears as the sequence no at the later stage.[2] This type of relation between two phonemes each at two stages has no effect on contrast. To the extent that the allophones of a and m and those of b and n are physically different ("shifted"), the phonetic alteration may

---

[2] See n. 1.

be worth noting, especially when it leaves traces in script history (chap. 2) or when new combinations of distinctive features arise (Fig. 61). Proto-Semitic *p*, reconstructed phonetically as a bilabial stop, is in Arabic replaced by a labiodental spirant, *f*. This alteration has left all contrasts intact, and it has not introduced new contrasts. A distinctive feature analysis of both phonemic systems may, however, reveal that the combination of labiality with stoppage was replaced by a combination of labiality with spirant articulation.[3]

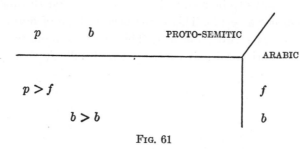

FIG. 61

9.1.2.1. Split from Reassignment of Non-contrasting Phones

In Figure 62 the starting point (horizontal axis) is the same as in the preceding case. However, the one phone occurring in environment 4 ceases to be an allophone of $a > m$ and becomes an allophone of $b > n$. This reassignment must be justified from the phonetic facts in the separate synchronic phonemicizations. Roughly, the phone in question must have become "more similar" to the other allophones in n than it used to be to those in a. This

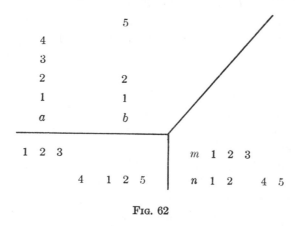

FIG. 62

---

[3] This would make an instance of reassignment (9.1.2) out of the present case.

Hereafter, the asterisk (*) characterizing reconstructed phonemes or forms will be omitted except when explicitly needed.

may be the effect of a physical alteration in the phone itself or in each or both of the other sets of phones concerned or in all three. This type of change, like the preceding, has no effect on the number of contrasts in the language. While the preceding type of change may affect the combinations of distinctive features, the present type changes the inventory of phonemic sequences (clusters), a result which is more generally reflected in script and also in the customary elementary phonemicizations. The use of long components or archiphonemes will often relegate this type to the status of the preceding (Fig. 63). In reconstructed Indo-European words p, but not b,

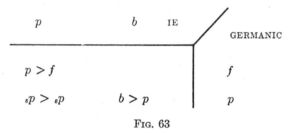

FIG. 63

occurs after s. In Proto-Germanic, IE b goes to a new p, and p (except for the allophone after s) generally to f. The allophone occurring after $s > s$ is reassigned from the old p to the new p. It may be supposed that sp did not change its pronunciation much, whereas the other phones were shifted (as suggested by the choice of the letter "p" to fill the places of a and n [not $m!$], respectively).[4]

9.1.2.2. Split from Twofold Reassignment

Twofold split without merger may have consequences like those illustrated in Figure 64. The phone which replaces a in 2, 5 is assigned, on a phonetic basis, with the phone which replaces b in 3, 7. It will be characteristic for the distribution of m, n, and o that there is no environment in which all three phones contrast. Lat. n, g, $ŋ$ may be in this position: before n, ("2,5"), [ŋ] contrasts with [n] (*aŋnus*, spelled "agnus", 'lamb' : *annus* 'year') and is complementary with [g]; before g and other velars ("3,7") it contrasts with [g] (*aŋgor*, spelled "angor" 'anguish' : *agger* 'dam') but not with [n]. In the former case it replaces an earlier g, etc.; in the latter, an earlier n. Similarly, in Tavda Vogul, a new $ē$ is created from two reassignment processes: $ir > ēr$ and $jē̮ > jē$.[5]

---

[4] See Fig. 53.

[5] Steinitz, *Geschichte* 188, 218. In descriptive work, considerations of economy and the morphophonemic ties which may link the descendants of each earlier phoneme often lead investigators to ignore what phonetic similarity there is between the two portions of o and to allow "intersection"

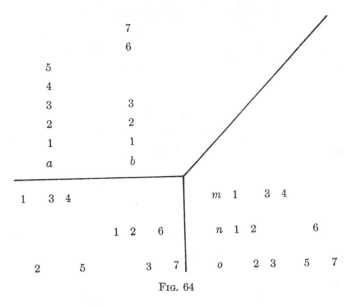

FIG. 64

9.1.3.1. Unconditional Merger

In Figure 65 the starting point is once more the same as in the two previous classifications. In the present instance, *a* and *b* merge where they have contrasted (environment class 1,2), owing to a phonetic alteration in *a*, in *b*, or in both. As a result, *a* in the environment class 3,4 and *b* in 5 become mere co-allophones regardless of whether or not the phones involved undergo physical change. The phoneme *m* now occurs in the combined environments of the former *a* and *b*. That environment class in which *a* and *b* overlapped, and in which there are two different etymological sources for *m*, is here underlined.

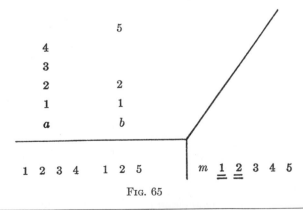

FIG. 65

between an *m* (in 1,2,3; 4,5) and an *n* (in 1,2,3; 6,7), with neutralization (or continued reliance on greater similarity) in 4,5,6,7. This, of course, amounts to "no change". See 12.7.2.2 and Hockett, *Course*, 466.

In Figure 66, Proto-Semitic ꜥ and γ (if rightly reconstructed) have fallen together in most Semitic languages (e.g., Hebrew). Phonetically (as indicated roughly by the choice of symbols), the phones of γ changed in the direction of the phones of ꜥ.

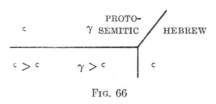

FIG. 66

9.1.3.2. Unconditional Loss

Figure 67 illustrates a somewhat special case. Old Latin *h* was lost in later Latin, so that, for example, *hortus* 'garden' became homonymous with *ortus* 'origin'. ∅ ("nothing")—in fact, any conveniently assumed number of ∅'s—may be posited as occurring between any two segmental phonemes found in sequence. Thus the environment of ∅ in English includes *t*——*i*, # —— *t*, but not # —— ŋ.

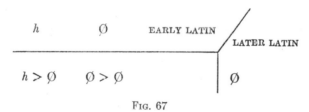

FIG. 67

9.1.4.1. Conditioned Merger with Primary Split

In Figure 68, *a* and *b* are distributed as before. The contrasting portion of *a* splits: some allophones (*a* in environment class 2) merge with the allophones of *b* in the same environment class. The resulting phone is assigned to either *m* or *n* (*n* in Fig. 68) for structural or phonetic reasons other than

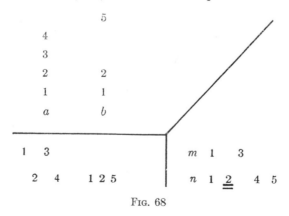

FIG. 68

contrast—in short, because of greater "similarity". The same is true of the non-contrasting phones surviving from *a* in the environment class 3,4. It is here assumed that some (*a*-in-3) are assigned to *m;* the others (*a*-in-4) to *n.* Contrast between *m* and *n* exists in environment class 1 only.

In Figure 69, in older Latin *s* and *r* contrast between vowels as well as

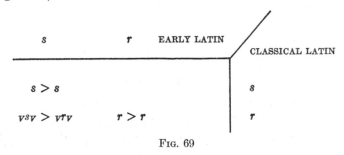

FIG. 69

in other environments. In early historical times the allophones of *s* between vowels (with the second vowel not followed by *r*) merge with those of *r,* the phonetic result being on the whole like the erstwhile *r.* In other positions contrast continues. There is a residual phoneme *s.*

9.1.4.2. *Conditioned Loss with Primary Split*

In Figure 70, one allophone of earlier modern English *k* merges with *ø,* or "initial *kn* yields *n*".[6]

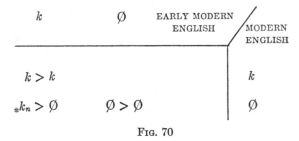

FIG. 70

9.1.4.3. *Conditioned Increment with Primary Split*

ø may appear on the horizontal axis to express the trivial[7] relationship "*ø* > *ø*" (on the whole, where there is nothing between two phonemes at

---

[6] Often it is physically arbitrary to decide which segment of a phoneme sequence has been replaced by *ø*: when *sk* > *š* in a number of Germanic dialects, this can be entered as *s* > *š, k* > *ø*, or as *s* > *ø, k* > *š.* Neither describes the event very concretely. If it were found that *s* > *š* in environments other than before *k* as well (during the same time interval), the first solution would be somewhat more elegant. The validity of the operation is of course not affected by the arbitrary character of this decision. The corresponding comment holds for 9.1.4.3; consider diphthongization of (long) vowels or the like.

[7] See, however, 4.2.3.

the older stage, there will be nothing at the later stage), which has figured above as a goal toward which merger may be directed (9.1.3.2) in instances of loss. The example given in Figure 71 shows the reverse process. In IE *sr* contrasts with *str*, or $\emptyset$ contrasts with *t* in the environment *s*——*r*. In Slavic both IE *sr* and IE *str* appear as what can phonetically and phonemically only be described as the triple cluster *str*.[8]

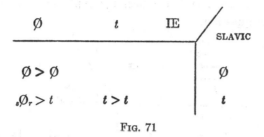

FIG. 71

9.2. Secondary Split, etc.

9.2.1. Secondary Split

So far it has been assumed that the environment classes relevant to the behavior of two phonemes remain distinguishable (even mutually exclusive) during the period of change. This is not always the case. It is therefore necessary to investigate the situation in which a change elsewhere in the system will turn the allophones of one phoneme into distinct phonemes.

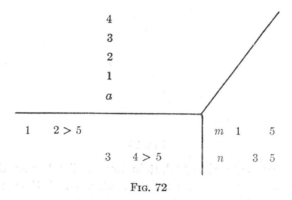

FIG. 72

In Figure 72 let there be, at the older stage, a phoneme *a* occurring over the range 1,2,3,4. Furthermore, let there be a merger such that two portions out of this range, say, 2 and 4, fall together, thereby creating a new environment class, 5. If the allophones of *a* in 2 remain physically different

---

[8] It should here be added that increment may also be due to secondary split of the type taken up in the next section. If the older stage has /sr/ [str], and if another sound change creates an [sr] (say, /sir/ > /sr/ [sr]), then, phonemically, /sr/ > /str/ without physical change in the morphs.

from those in 4 after 2 and 4 have merged, the two different phones now contrast in environment 5: *a*-in-2 has become *m*-in-5, and *a*-in-4 has become *n*-in-5. The erstwhile *a* in 1,3 will take its place with *m* or *n* in the usual fashion. In the more general case, some allophones (*a*-in-1) are more similar to *a*-in-2 > *m*; others, more similar to *a*-in-4 > *n*. More briefly, allophones become phonemes when part or all of their determining environments fall together without at the same time canceling the phonetic difference between the allophones in question.

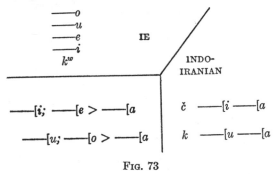

FIG. 73

In some types of Indo-European, *k*ʷ may be thought to have had pala-talized allophones before *e* and *y* (*i*) and unpalatalized allophones before *o*, *r*, (*w*), and in other positions (Fig. 73). In Indo-Iranian, IE *e* and *o* are

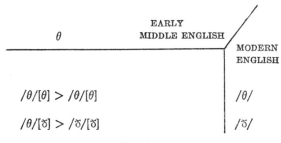

FIG. 74

merged into *a* not only after *k*ʷ but in almost all other existing environ-ments. As a consequence the palatalized contrasts with the non-palatalized stop before *a*; *k* and *č* have become phonemes. The phoneme *k* occurs also before *r*, etc., and *č* also before *i* and *y*.

In early Middle English [θ] and [ð] must have been complementarily dis-tributed: [θ] (roughly) word initially and finally, [ð] between vowels (Fig. 74). The later loss of final unstressed syllables put many instances of [ð] into word-final position. This has been one of the sources of phonemic status for /θ/ and /ð/.

9.2.2. Split through Merger, without Residue

Changes in which more than two phonemes are involved may be viewed as combinations of the individual processes studied here. Occasionally, these combinations have noteworthy characteristics. For instance, our examples of conditioned split through merger of an allophone with another phoneme (9.1.4.1) may be extended as shown in Figure 75. In this case three

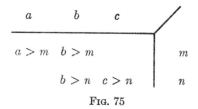

FIG. 75

phonemes have been reduced to two, and there is no residual phoneme (i.e., no phoneme having only one antecedent phoneme).

IE *p* before *t* appears in Old Irish as *ch* (IE *k* in this position gives the same result); in other environments it is lost (or merges differently) (see Fig. 76).

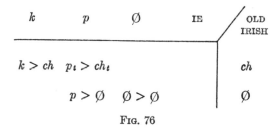

FIG. 76

9.3. Appendix

9.3.1. Sample Chart of Interlocking Changes

In theory, changes affecting an entire phonemic system can be charted in this fashion. Actually, limitation to certain sectors of it, as well as other simplifications, are usually necessary. The examples given in Figure 77 illustrate the manner in which parallelisms and other systemic affinities between phonemes and phoneme changes find graphic expression.

The older stage is Indo-European; the later, Latin. The fact that it may be possible to reconstruct intermediate stages (chap. 11) does not matter here. Changes may be formulated for any two stages belonging to one line of descent. Note that three of the four "aspirates" divide up into a word-initial and a word-medial allophone each, the former merging with each other, the latter merging separately with the homorganic voiced non-aspirate. Note further the other factors which detract from symmetry. Lat. f is characterized as residual (9.1.4.1) by its severely limited distribution.[9]

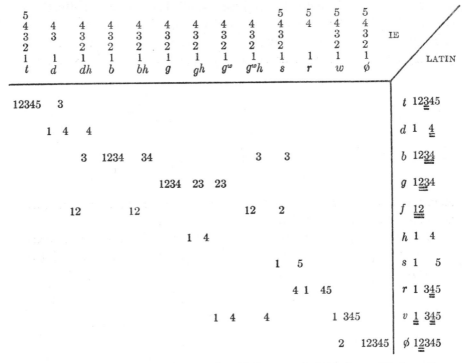

FIG. 77.—1;2 initially; 3;4;5 after vowel; 1;4 before vowel; 2;3 before r; 5 before others

9.3.2. Borrowed Phonemes

It is sometimes asserted that borrowing under conditions in which sound substitution (3.9) is not carried out completely "causes" an enlargement of the phonemic possibilities. It is useful to distinguish some types of foreign influence. (I) In Lifu p, t, and s occur indigenously; b has been added in borrowed words. As has been pointed out, this may be interpreted as the rise of a new combination of existing distinctive features. The new b may play a role in a later phonemic change as a goal of merger.[10] (II) In Latin, loan-words from Greek add scl to the list of other triple s-clusters like scr, spl, spr with sc, sp, cr, cl, pr, pl also existing); this changes the statements on environment (esp. on the immediate environments of s, c, l). (III) In

---

[9] It is true, however, that the other two voiceless spirants of Latin each have peculiar weaknesses of distribution: s is later lost intervocalically (and, at different times, in a number of clusters), while h since proto-Italic times occurred only in #——V and in V——V.

[10] Lenormand, *Word* 8.

IE →	$:$	s	t	d	dh	k'	ksw	SANSKRIT
	$i:d > i:d$ $isd > i:d$ $i:dh > i:dh$ $isdh > i:dh$							$:$ after i....
		$ast > ast$ $\#s > \#s$						s after a, $\#$
		$ist > ist$ $i:st > ?st$				$ik't > ist$ $i:k't > i:st$ $ak't > ast$	$\#ksw > \#s$	$ṣ$ after i, $i:$, a, s, $\#$
			$i:t > i:t$ $ast > ast$ $\#t > \#t$					t after i, $i:$, a, s, $\#$
			$ik't > ist$ $i:k't > i:st$ $\#kkʷ > ist$					t after $ṣ$
				$i:d > i:d....$				d after i, $i:;(a ...)$
					$i:dh > i:dh....$			dh after i, $i:;(, a ...)$
				$isd > i:ḍ$				$ḍ$ after $i:$
					$isdh > i:ḍh$			$ḍh$ after $i:$

FIG. 78

English, *v* is introduced in French loanwords in positions in which it contrasts with *f*. The voiced intervocalic allophone of *f*, [*v*], therefore, had to be reassigned to a new, foreign phoneme *v*.

Consider the development in Sanskrit illustrated in Figure 78. This diagram shows how *ḍ* and *ḍh* developed contrast with the other stops through obscuration of their environment (9.2). The contrast is very limited (only after certain long vowels). In indigenous material *ṭ* does not contrast with *t*. Whether or not it is set up as a phoneme depends on the weight given to pattern congruency or on the degree to which distinctive features are recognized as central entities. Certainly, without *ṭ* we have a gap: *p b bh*, *t d dh*, *-ḍ -ḍh*, etc. Dravidian and other non–Indo-European borrowings provide (I) instances of *ḍ* and *ḍh* in many other positions than those in which contrast had developed through sound change from IE *d* and *dh* and (II) instances of /ṭ/.

10. ALTERNATIONS

In another context (5.6) we discussed the effect of morphological change on the internal (allomorphic) properties of morphemes. We made a distinction between suppletion and morphophonemic alternation. In English, *go* and *wend* (in *wen-t*) are suppletive allomorphs; their membership in one and the same morpheme is the outcome of a morphologic change (4.2.4). On the other hand, *roof* and *roov-* (in *rooves*) are in a morphophonemic relationship: they even "resemble" each other in sharing a number of phonemes, and they differ in that one has *f*, the other, *v*—a difference which recurs in many other morphemes (*knife/knive-*, *life/live*, *sift/sieve*). The dividing lines, and therefore the reliability of reasoning backward, may become somewhat blurred for several reasons: (I) morphological change may by lexical accident involve morphs that happen to contain morphophonemes or (II) an alternation, while resulting from phonemic split, may, in addition to being unique in itself (5.6), fail to be associated with other recurring morphophonemes in the same morpheme.[1] It is obvious that both sources of error are particularly serious in morphemes with morphs too short to allow much scope for observation.[2]

10.1. Morphophonemic Consequences of Phonemic Split: Internal Reconstruction

Our first task is to examine the morphophonemic consequences of sound change. One thing is immediately clear: processes of merger as such—and merger is the central type of sound change—leave no such consequences at all. Instances of unconditioned disappearance of phonemic contrast, whether between two phonemes or between one phoneme and its absence (9.1.3.1–9.1.3.2), lead to no grammatical complication. Of course, the resulting phoneme, *n* (or the resulting *ø*), has the combined frequency of occurrence of both of its sources in the environment classes in which they previously contrasted $(\underline{1},\underline{2})$, which may or may not, according to the initial frequencies of each, lead to a telltale rise in frequency. Thus in a universe of "10,000 sounds of continuous text in 10 different [Sanskrit] passages, of 1,000 sounds each" *a* occurs with a frequency of 19.78 per cent, while the next ranking segmental phoneme occurs less than half as frequently.[3] The phoneme *a* has

---

[1] See 5.1.

[2] On this and the following see Marchand, *Lg.* 32.

[3] Whitney, *Sanskrit Grammar* §25.

at least five different and once widely contrasting sources (IE *a *e *o *n *m [perhaps also *ə in diphthongs]). It is possible that later changes in the language tend to equalize such uneven distribution, although in the case just quoted it has existed throughout Indo-Aryan. The lack of other than uncertain statistical evidence in phoneme occurrence both textwise and listwise must be kept in mind when the credibility of reconstructed phonemic systems with apparently "too few" phonemic distinctions is challenged. Those who have reconstructed only one vowel for pre–Indo-European will admit that this particular feature may hide a variety of contrast which was lost without a split, or without the favorable morphological conditions, to be examined presently, which make internal reconstruction feasible.

What has here been said about unconditional merger (and loss) is also true for that portion of the more complicated patterns of sound change which consists of merger. On the other hand, phonemic SPLIT in several of its varieties leads to morphophonemic alternation, provided that morph boundaries fall between[4] the conditioning and the conditioned phoneme or phonemes and provided that the same phoneme in the same morph thus comes within the range sometimes of one, sometimes of the other, type of conditioning phoneme or phonemes. The terms of the conditioning are often such that it does not extend beyond certain junctures which happen to function as morph dividers at the same time. The rise of morphophonemic variety is therefore subject to many different elements in the language structure. Furthermore, after an alternation comes into existence, not only is it subject to subsequent sound change but its continuation is threatened by analogic change (4.1.4). The following paragraphs deal with some typical phases of morphophonemic history.

10.1.1. Alternations from Primary Split

We shall first consider the case in which an allophone merges into another phoneme, thereby splitting off from its earlier fellow allophones (primary split [see 9.1.4.1–9.1.4.2]). We assume that a morph containing a occurs in constructions such that a comes to stand in environment classes 1,3, as well as in others, such that a comes to stand in environments 2,4. At the later stage such a morph will appear in the shape of two allomorphs: one with m in 1,3, the other with an alternating n in 2,4.

This alternation (or morphophoneme m/n) has characteristic properties. In the earlier diagram (Fig. 68) the total distribution of m and of n (vertical column) appeared as shown in Figure 79, where 2, 4, and 5 mark three mutually exclusive environment classes distinguished on historical grounds

---

[4] "Between" must be taken to refer to suprasegmental phonemes as well as segmental phonemes in the environment.

(2 from a contrasting with b, 4 from a not contrasting with b, 5 from b).
Synchronically, however, the three are indistinguishable. The later stage
has simply n and m in a normal contrastive distribution (see 9.1.1), with one
overlapping ("1") and two distinctive environment classes ("3" for m, and
"2,4,5", without any phonological criterion for subdivision, for n). The
observable alternations are, therefore, those marked by double lines in
Figure 80. In other words, n in its non-contrasting position alternates with
m in its non-contrasting (3) and with m in its contrasting (1) position; n in
contrasting position is not involved. Such alternations are called AUTO-
MATIC: the phase involving m-in-3 is BILATERALLY AUTOMATIC, while that
involving m-in-1 is UNILATERALLY AUTOMATIC with the m-allomorph as a
BASE, in the sense that the n-allomorph occurs in its stead where, and only
where, the phonemic system precludes the m-allomorph.

Under favorable circumstances it is further possible to discover that the
environment class 2,4,5, however homogeneous phonologically, can yet be
subdivided according to the morphophonemic behavior of some instances

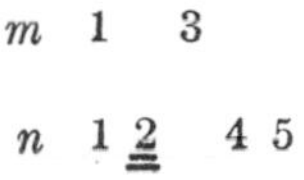

m 1   3

n 1 $\underline{2}$ 4 5

FIG. 79

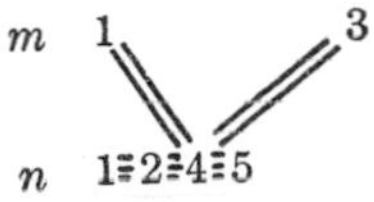

m 1$\diagdown$ $\diagup$3

n 1$\equiv$2$\equiv$4$\equiv$5

FIG. 80

of n occurring within it. It must be remembered that—under such favorable
conditions—the later stage will also contain non-alternating morphemes
showing n both in environment 1 and in environment 2,4,5: these are the
b's of the earlier stage (9.1.4.1), marked $\equiv$. By construction, then, the n's
occurring in 1 are either non-alternating or indeterminate (the latter if the
morpheme does not happen to recur in the language in such a way as to
place n in 2,4,5). Position 2,4,5, however, will fall into up to four parts:

   (A) One in which n is non-alternating or indeterminate.
   (B) One in which n is alternating or indeterminate.
   (C) One in which n is alternating, non-alternating, or indeterminate.
   (D) One in which n is indeterminate.

Clearly, this subdivision reflects the environment classes 2, 4, and 5 as defined by the terms of the sound change (9.1.4.1). The n's in 5 come from b,
which was never affected by split and can therefore never result in an n
that alternates (A). The n's in 4 all come from a in 4; since a in 1,3 went to
m, an n in 4 will never be a non-alternating n (B). In environment 2, old
a's and old b's have merged into n, so that both alternating and non-alternating n's occur in 2 (C). Finally, there may be subdivisions of 2, 4, and 5
each, in which n is always indeterminate with regard to alternation (owing

to the fact that the morpheme does not enter into sequences which would ever bring *n* into 1; (D)).

Unless other processes are found to yield the same result, the foregoing reasoning may serve as a procedure for reconstruction. To recapitulate: If two phonemes, *m* and *n*, occur in automatic alternation with *m* functioning as base, *m* goes back to *a*, and *n* goes back in part to *a* and in part to *b*: to *b* in its contrasting environment and in that part of its non-contrasting environment occupied by non-alternating or indeterminate instances of *n*; to *a* in that part of its non-contrasting environment occupied by alternating or indeterminate instances. In that portion of its non-contrasting environment which includes all three kinds of *n*, non-alternating, alternating, and indeterminate, *a* and *b* have merged. The environment where *n* is always indeterminate does not lend itself to reconstruction of this sort. This is an

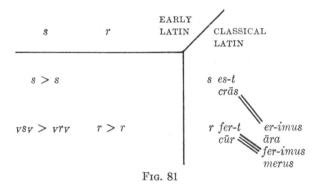

FIG. 81

important limitation of internal reconstruction. According as morpheme boundaries occur in the crucial places our knowledge of what was included in the factors that conditioned a phonemic split is more or less full, but it will not be exhaustive.

For Figure 81 see above (9.1.4.1). Only environments 1 (syllable-final) and 2 (intervocalic) are represented. *es-(t)* 'he is' ~ *er-(imus)* 'we shall be' is alternating; *fer-(t)* 'he carries' ~ *fer-(imus)* 'we carry' is non-alternating; *crās* 'tomorrow', *cūr* 'why', *āra* 'altar', and *merus* 'pure' are indeterminate; as it happens, *āra* has old *s*, *merus* has old *r*.

10.1.2. *Alternations from Secondary Split*

Split due to merger in the environment (secondary split) may likewise lead to alternation. If *m* and *n* in their entirety are former allophones of *a* (9.2), *m* may be expected to alternate with *n* to the extent that morphemes with *a* occurred in constructions such as to place *a* in some or all of the relevantly different environments (see Fig. 82).

Thus Skt. *ci, ca* (representing Indo-Iranian **či*, **ča*) alternates with *ku,* *ka* (9.2). In part these alternations have properties resembling those treated in the preceding section. Where the older stage had morphemes in which *a* occurred sometimes in 1 and sometimes in 3 (IE $*k^w$-*i* $*k^w$-*u*, the later stage has a bilateral automatic alternation *m*-in-1 $\sim$ *n*-in-3 (Skt. *c-i; k-u*). An *a* in 1 recurring in 4 (IE $*k^w$-*i* $*k^w$-*o*) becomes a unilateral automatic *m*-in-1 $\sim$ *n*-in-5 with *n* as base (Skt. *c-i; k-a;* base *k*) and vice versa, *a* in 3 recurring in 2 (IE $*k^w$-*u; *$*k^w$-*e*) appears as a unilateral automatic *n*-in-3 $\sim$ *m*-in-5 with *m* as base (Skt. *k-u; c-a;* base *c*). In addition, however, if *a* recurs in 2 and 4, *m*-in-5 will alternate with *n*-in-5. As Figure 82 indicates, this alternation is NON-AUTOMATIC (obviously neither *m* nor *n* are excluded from 5 by the rules of the phonemic system) and IRREGULAR in the sense that the morphs containing the factor 5 (Skt. *-a* . .) must be either listed or suitably identified by a morphophonemic notation (e.g., Skt. ▾*a* in *ca* versus ▫*a* in *ka*).

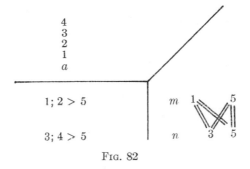

FIG. 82

It may of course be that morphemes with *a* do not occur in constructions that expose *a* alternately to 2 and to 4 (i.e., k^w- alternately to *-e* and to *-o* in our example). In some morphemes *a* may recur in 1, 3, and 4, while in others it may recur in 1, 3, and 2 (respectively, k^w-*i*, k^w-*u*, k^w-*o* versus k^w-*i*, k^w-*u*, k^w-*e*). This results in merely automatic alternations between *m* and *n* ("Skt." *c-i, k-u, k-a*, with base *k; c-i, k-u, c-a*, with base *c*); the fact that both *m* and *n* function as bases still distinguishes this case sufficiently from the very different case discussed earlier. But the data may be even weaker: if *a* recurs in 3 and 4 in one class of morphemes, in 1, 3, and 2 in another class of morphemes (k^w-*u*, k^w-*o* versus k^w-*i*, k^w-*u*, k^w-*e*), we shall obtain *m* and *n* in automatic alternation with only *m* as a base ("Skt." *k-u, k-a* versus *c-i, k-u, c-a*, with basic *c*), or, in other words, a non-alternating *n* ("Skt." *k*) and an alternating *n*. It will still be true, however, that the environment 5 in the non-alternating paradigm and the environment 5 in the alternating paradigm will not belong to the same morpheme, since, while in the former 5 goes back to 4 (*-a* goes back to *-o*), in the latter 5 goes back to 2 (*-a* to *-e*). By contrast, automatic alternation of the type studied earlier (i.e., representing split from primary rather than from secondary merger [10.1.1]) typically provides the same morphemes—not merely the same phonemes—as part of those environments in which the alternating and the non-alternating morphemes differ phonemically (e.g., Lat. *es-t* [morpheme {*es; er*}] and *fer-t* [morpheme {*fer*}] and with the same morpheme *-t* '3d sg').[5]

10.1.3. Summary

To summarize graphically: If in at least one morpheme *a* is exposed to all four relevant environments, *m* and *n* alternate as illustrated in Figure 83.

If *a* recurs in some morphemes in 1, 3, and 2 and in other morphemes in 1, 3, and 4, we obtain Figure 84.

If *a* recurs in 1, 3, and 2 (or simply in 3 and 2) in some morphemes and in 3 and 4 in others, we obtain Figure 85 or 86, always with the proviso

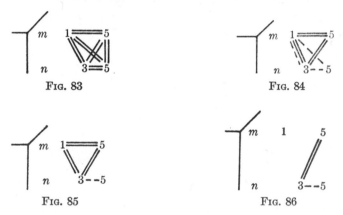

FIG. 83   FIG. 84

FIG. 85   FIG. 86

that the 5 in which *m* occurs must be morphologically different from the 5 in which *n* occurs. Note that, once the common descent of *m* and *n* from *a* is established, the validity of internal reconstruction is not limited by the extent to which alternations occur: the indeterminate ("isolated") cases are as useful as the alternating and non-alternating ones for the purpose of defining 1, 2, 3, and 4.

10.2. Effects of Concurrent or Subsequent Change on Alternations

These morphophonemic relationships prevail, under the favorable circumstances stated, as the immediate outcome of one or the other type of phonemic split. They are, however, subject to alteration through concurrent or subsequent change, (*a*) phonemic or (*b*) morphemic. The initial stages of such change are not necessarily fatal to the possibility of internal reconstruction.

---

[5] Unless *fert* is from **bhereti* with syncope of the second vowel.—It should be emphasized that the preceding data are somewhat simplified. The reconstruction *kʷu* is probably not in this form valid (see 8.3, end).

10.2.1. Further Sound Change

This is particularly true of concurrent or subsequent sound change of the sort that partly or wholly restores to a phoneme the missing portion which it had either lost through the splitting-off of a class of allophones (Lat. *s*) or which it lacks because it used to be in complementary distribution with a fellow allophone and is still in near-complementary distribution with another phoneme (Skt. *k* $\sim$ *c*). If only the gap, or part of it, is restored, the additional sound change is a case of reassignment without merger (9.1.2). If the sound change extends to other positions, it does constitute merger. For our present purpose this makes little difference. What is important is that the new instances of the phoneme in question change the phonemic system without, per se, altering the existing alternations which go back to the earlier change.

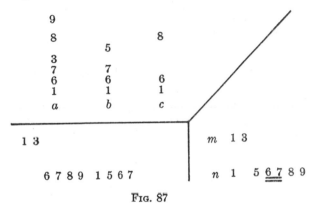

Fig. 87

Suppose that our starting point is a phonemic contrast and a set of alternations between *m* and *n* such as results from primary split. We elaborate on the original diagram (9.1.4.1) by recognizing two subclasses each in the environment classes labeled 2 and 4 (i.e., those in which *a* had merged with, or had been assigned without merger to, *b*). We replace 2 by 6,7; 4 by 8,9. A third phoneme at the older stage, *c*, occurs in 6 and 8, and, furthermore, say, in 1 and possibly in a non-contrasting environment, here disregarded (Fig. 87).

The phones constituting *c* in 6 and *c* in 8 now contrast only with *n*, not with *m*. If, on the basis of the standard procedures (relative "similarity," etc.) they can be assigned to *m*, we obtain (I) Figure 88 or (II) Figure 89, according as *c* in 1 has or has not merged with *m* in 1. In either event, the alternations existing between *m* and *n* (10.1.1) have changed one of their properties. They are still REGULAR inasmuch as all morphemes with *m* in 1 (II)—or at least all morphemes with alternating *m* in 1 (I)—have *n* instead of *m* if the segment in question is exposed to 6, 7, 8, or 9: no list of morphemes, only an identification of phonemic environment, is required. On the other hand, this regular alternation is automatic for 7 and 9 only; for 6 and 8 it is NON-AUTOMATIC, since the phonemic structure permits m in 6 and 8. By the same token, if c and a did not merge in environment class 1 (II), m in 6,8 and m in 1(,3) will never belong to the same morpheme. If there was merger of c and a in 1 (I), there will be two kinds of m (in addi-

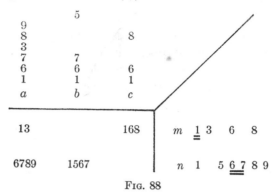

FIG. 88

tion to indeterminate m): non-alternating (representing the erstwhile c) and alternating such that n replaces m in 6,7,8,9 (representing a). In other words, a non-automatic but regular alternation may be regarded as revealing two processes: insofar as it is regular, it reflects split through condi-

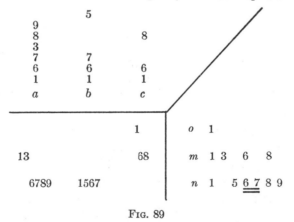

FIG. 89

tioned merger—$b > n$ in 6,7,8,9; insofar as all or part of it is non-automatic, it reflects a reassignment (II) or second merger (I)—$c > m$ in 6,8 (see Fig. 90).

Compare 9.1.4.1 and 10.1.1. Note that, in addition to the indications above, $s > s$ before an r in the following syllable so that *passer* 'sparrow' and *miser* 'wretched' contrast. In the written records s appears instead of ss several generations after s between vowels and not preceding r had merged with r.

It goes without saying that the automatic and regular phases of alternation through merger in the environment (10.1.2) may be similarly affected.

The assumption of concurrent or subsequent sound change which has been made above requires some further discussion which will be offered later (chap. 11).

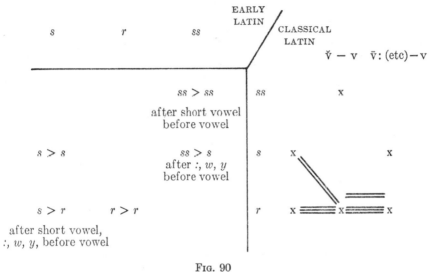

FIG. 90

10.2.2. *Further Morphological Change*

The further changes capable of modifying existing alternations may themselves be morphological rather than phonemic in nature. When new utterances—or even new types of utterances—give new occurrences to old morphemes, the phonemes that made up their morphs will not in general be provided with significantly new phonemic environments across the morpheme boundaries. But the appearance of altogether new morphs in borrowing (3.7), and still more the play of allomorphs within morphemes in analogic and related processes (4.1.5), is likely to have certain effects. We begin with the latter.

10.2.2.1. *Analogic New Formation*

In analogic processes allomorphs expand or lessen their distribution— often at each other's expense—with total disappearance and fresh emergence as extreme instances. It might be thought that the phonemic system constrains analogic new formation; that, in other words, an allomorph will not spread in such a way as to produce phonemically prohibited utterances (any more than a new sequence made up of existing morphemes can be said to violate the prevailing phonemic structure). This can, however, only be a matter of degree: if "permitted" means "occurring", and if the length of the stretch over which occurrence is considered is not arbitrarily restricted, no new utterance would be permitted except one phonemically homonymous to an existing utterance. We shall here nevertheless distinguish between processes which create or would create new phonemic sequences over relatively short stretches (and might, therefore, be expected to find "resistance") and processes resulting in "permitted" sequences.

A given primary split creates two parallel classes of morphemes: one non-alternating (having n in 1,2 [see 10.1.1]), the other showing regular and, at least to begin with, automatic alternation (m in 1 $\sim$ n in 2). Immediately after such a split allomorphs may widen their distribution in one of the following two ways:

(I) n-allomorphs (non-basic allomorphs) of alternating morphemes may be extended into the contrasting environment class (1—where n is not phonemically compulsory). Or (II) non-alternating morphemes may develop m-allomorphs (basic allomorphs) in the contrasting environments (1).

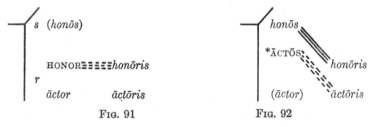

FIG. 91   FIG. 92

The first-named process (I) is known as analogic LEVELING, as when in Latin the allomorph *honōr-* (by sound change from *honōs-* before vowel in *honōs-is honōr-is* genitive singular or the like) is extended to position before pause (where it then competes as an endingless nominative singular with the original *honōs*). The latter process (II) is probably on the whole less common (6.3), depending on the morphological structure of the language. If on the model of *honōs* nom.: *honōr-is* gen. Lat. *āctōr-is* gen. (always an r-stem) and generated a new nom. **āctōs*, we would have the counterpart (II) to what actually happened (I). Great relative frequency of the type *honōs:honōris* as compared with *āctor:āctōris* might have favored such a development (Figs. 91 and 92).

As long as the alternation between m and n is regular and automatic, with m as base, leveling to m encounters the resistance of a phonemic system which does not provide m-in-2. Thus the *honōs-is* lost by sound change could not, strictly speaking, be "restored" analogically until ss had become s after long vowel or diphthong and before vowel (10.2.1),[6] thus making the

---

[6] In this connection Hockett (*SinL* 12) speaks of phonemic change by analogy. The role of juncture in sound change and in other change processes is badly in need of more investigation. For a problem connected with that role see Hockett, *IJAL* 22.

alternation of *s* and *r* non-automatic, that is, in general formulation, until *m*-in-2 is reintroduced, at least in part, by a change *c* > *m*. At that point, certainly, *m*-allomorphs of formerly alternating morphemes can be extended to environment 2 without thereby changing phonemic structure (III). This will have the effect of giving the morpheme the phonemic shape which it had before the sound change. The morpheme has been leveled back. Furthermore, a morpheme which has become alternating through analogy (II; type *actōs:actōr-is*) might be leveled in the direction of *m* (*actōs:*actōs-is*).

At the stage where *m* and *n* still alternate automatically, the extensions of allomorphs treated under (I) and (II), in order seriously to interfere with the reconstructability of the sound change, would have to be complete in two senses of the term. First, ALL alternating morphemes (in the case of I) would have to be leveled, or ALL non-alternating *n*-morphemes (in the case of II) would have to develop *m*-allomorphs. As long as only some do while others retain their status, the primary phonemic split which had led to the alternation remains recoverable as such to the degree outlined above (10.1.1); only the phonemic shape of specific morphemes would be reconstructed incorrectly. From *honor:honōr-is* it is impossible to find that the word is an old *s*-stem, but the remaining alternating paradigms (e.g., *flōs: flōr-is* 'flower', *est:erimus*) are still available to attest to the sound change as a sound change. Second, within each morpheme the extension must be total: *honōr-* was extended to the endingless nominative singular, but in *hones-tus* 'honorable' the basic *s*-allomorph is still there to give away the alternating nature of the stem morpheme. Moreover, *honōs* and *honor* existed, for a while at least, side by side as nominatives (DOUBLET). The relationship existing between *r*- and *s*-allomorphs in the phonemically contrasting environment (here: non-intervocalic, such as final or before *t*) could be described as an irregular alternation. It differs, however, from the irregular alternation which is the immediate result of secondary split (10.1.2) in that the appearance of one as against the other allomorph is not predictable from the nature of the morphemes in the environment (as it is in the case of the Sanskrit suffixes with palatalizing *a* versus those with non-palatalizing *a* [see 10.1.2]). Before the zero (or absence of) suffix in the nominative singular *flōs* 'flower' (gen. *flōr-is*) has *s*, while honor has *r*. What is more, "one and the same" morpheme has both *s* and *r* in *honōs* and *honor*. The further analogical possibilities envisaged under III complicate the picture but do not change it radically.

The morphologically determined but phonemically irregular alternations resulting from secondary split naturally lend themselves to leveling in either direction. Even immediately after the sound change *m*-allomorphs in position 5 (9.2) can always replace *n*-allomorphs and conversely. The non-alternating models for such leveling are furnished by parallel morphemes which have $b > o$ (no split) instead of $a > m$, $a > n$ (see Figs. 93 and 94).

Thus Sanskrit "roots" ending in $c \sim k$ have been leveled extensively before the suffixes and suffix groups beginning in -a (in part former -o, in part -e) which predominate in verb paradigms. From *lewk^w-e . . comes Skt. loca . . , from *lewk^{w}o- . . , loka . . (e.g., locati 'he shines': lokanti 'they

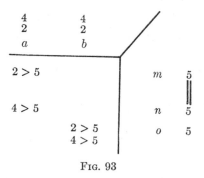

FIG. 93

shine'); this paradigm, as it happens, is leveled both ways: locati, locanti and lokati, lokanti become near-synonyms, or doublets. (See 4.3.3.) The non-alternating model for these levelings exists in examples like bharati, bharanti (<bhereti, bheronti) 'he carries, they carry'.

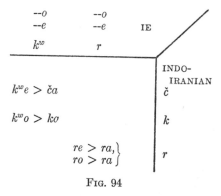

FIG. 94

If analogic new formation is carried out uniformly and completely (both for all morphemes and for all occurrences of their allomorphs), the effects of the sound change may become completely obscured. Thus, if the replacement of non-intervocalic s-allomorphs in Latin had gone farther than it did (adding, e.g., *flōr nom. sing. and also *honertus), s would seem to have been changed to r unconditionally. As was pointed out above, so-called sound changes may indeed include such misinterpreted analogical extension. This uncertainty not only threatens internal reconstruction but may make difficult even an analysis of change where the older and the later stage are known (through records or from the comparative method). To decide a dilemma (e.g., did non-intervocalic Lat. *s* become *r* or *s?*), the following considerations are available. (1) Indeterminate occurrences show the effects of sound change but are never analogic creation; *crās* 'tomorrow' shows that *flōs* is phonologically correct (i.e., not analogically replaced), while *honor* is an extended allomorph. A few cases, even one indeterminate case, will thus outweigh a whole set of analogical replacements. (2) Doublets and doublet paradigms (*rocati/rokati*) are likely to show the phonologically original phoneme in competition with the replacement. A morphological or lexical study of the doublets may reveal that one (*honor* nom. sing.) forms a more productive paradigm with other occurrences of the morpheme (*honōris*) than does the other doublet (*honōs* archaic nom. sing.; *hones-tus* derivative of a nearly unproductive type). That doublet is then the replacement. Since most replacements are levelings, we are more likely to find the non-alternating doublet in this role. (3) For this very reason, even where there are no doublets, evidence from alternating morphemes (*flōs* ∼ *flōr-*) has precedence over data from non-alternating morphemes (*color* 'color' ∼ *colōris;* historically from -*s*(-), but with no surviving *s*-alternants). The order or trustworthiness then is: indeterminate morphemes ("isolated forms"), doublets, alternating morphemes, non-alternating morphemes.

10.2.2.2. Borrowing

Borrowings are normally adopted with sound substitution (3.9). As in the case of extended allomorphs, it is difficult to predict the amount of resistance against new phoneme sequences or new phonemes (i.e., new combinations of existing distinctive features, as when the emergence of medial *ḍ* and *ḍh* in Sanskrit makes the adoption of initial *ḍ* and *ḍh*, as well as that of initial and medial *ṭ*, in loanwords possible [see 9.3.3]). But it is true that distributions of phonemes imported with borrowings may transform automatic alternations into non-automatic ones. E *θ* and *ð* became phonemic largely through secondary split, with final position as part of the contrasting environment (*wreath:wreathe*) and a unilateral automatic relationship between, say, *wreath(ing)* and *wreath* (base *θ*). The borrowing of such items as *ether* would have made this alternation non-automatic (*θ* now also internally) even if analogical extensions (*pithy*) had not done the same.

For the relation between dialect borrowing and sound change see 5.4.[7]

---

[7] It should be added that sound change may have a further effect, not listed above (10.2.1): it may merge morphophonemically connected phonemes and thereby eliminate the alternation (see Hockett, *Course* 388).

11. RELATIVE CHRONOLOGY

Sometimes, either through written records or from reconstruction, we command more than only two successive stages of "one language". This raises the question of possible formal relationships between successive sound changes (RELATIVE CHRONOLOGY). In particular, it must be asked under what conditions intermediate stages can be reconstructed if the initial and the final stages are given. The present discussion will be limited to three stages (initial, intermediate, final) and to the two periods of change between them. Some effects of "concurrent or subsequent change" have already been briefly dealt with (10.2).

11.1. Widened Conditioning

a) First, we consider a case which is said to be empirically frequent or typical: the gradual transformation of a narrowly conditioned to a more

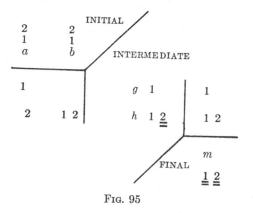

Fig. 95

widely conditioned or, as below, of a conditioned to an unconditioned sound change (8.3). This may, for instance, be viewed as an expression of drift, or as an areally conditioned response to typological pressure, in the direction of a smaller phonemic system. Stripped of irrelevant features, the development is shown in Figure 95.[1]

Omitting the intermediate stage, we get the result given in Figure 96. There is clearly nothing in the later stage that would justify inferring the preceding, or any other, three-stage picture. The alternations (if any) exist-

---

[1] Since the intermediate stage is "earlier" with regard to the final, and "later" with regard to the initial, stage, the diagrams are tripartite. In the right-hand quadrant split now figures as a row (not as a column) of entries, etc.

ing between g-in-1 and h-in-2 at the intermediate stage are lost by the merger of g and h.

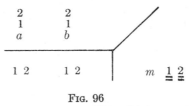

FIG. 96

Consider, for instance, Figure 97.[2] The phoneme w disappeared gradually. At the intermediate stage one allophone was lost (no metrical effect of w- before o in Homer), another had become p (after $k' > p$, as in *hippos* 'horse'), and a third continued in existence (say, *we-*). By the time of the

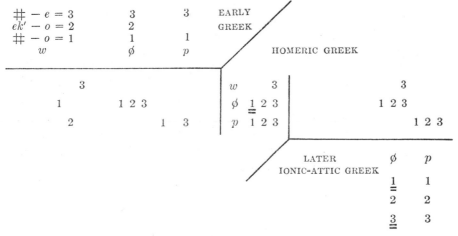

FIG. 97

final stage, $w(e)$- has joined the former $w(o)$-: both are now $\emptyset$. The net result is shown in Figure 98.[3]

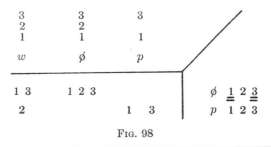

FIG. 98

[2] For the present purpose, Homeric Greek is treated as though it were the "ancestor" of Ionic-Attic. (See 13.1.1.)

[3] Laryngeals in the environment such as may possibly have to be reconstructed in some of the relevant examples are here disregarded.

11.2. Split without Residue

b) Second, it might be supposed that the primary split without residue considered above (9.2.2) took place in the two separate developments which that two-stage picture seems to combine. In this case we would have either Figure 99, with a temporary residue from IE p in position other than be-

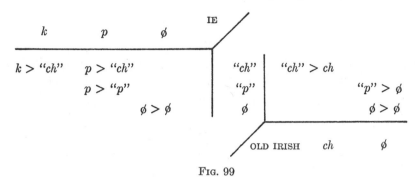

Fig. 99

fore t (later merged with ϕ), or else Figure 100, with a temporary residue from IE p before t (later merged with earlier k before t). But neither is cogent. Preference for one or the other would depend on such factors as phonetic plausibility or one's typological presuppositions. In the present instance the second alternative (with a highly restricted p) seems weaker than the first (with a lightly restricted p); yet there happens to be good independent evidence in favor of it.[4]

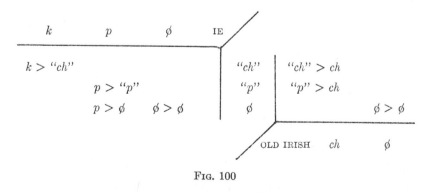

Fig. 100

---

[4] Hamp, *Lochlann* 1. How persuasive a combination of phonetic and typological reasoning can be is best illustrated with an extremely simple instance like the following: IE . . *aso* . . > Attic Gk . . *ō* . . . An intermediate . . *ao* . . is set up. The argument is based on the fact that *s* > ϕ not only between *a* and *o* but generally between vowels (some of which remain in hiatus; e.g., . . *eso* . . > . . *eo* . ., under certain conditions); that . . *ao* . . if made plausible as an intermediate stage from another source (e.g., > . . *ayo* . .) is treated in the same fashion (> *ō*); and that . . *ao* . . is physi-

11.3. Split of a Merged Phoneme: "Rectangular Pattern"

We now consider the three-stage picture illustrated in Figure 101. At the intermediate stage a and b have yielded g and h by a typical change involving both split and merger. The merger in particular is represented by h-in-2,6, the earlier so labeled subenvironment "2" (9.1.4.1) being renamed "2,6". At the third stage, h has been split in such a way as to bring part of h-in-2,6 (namely, h-in-2) into n, the remainder (h-in-6) into o. It is unimportant just how h in the other environments has been treated (in the figure it is shown as remaining with h-in-2). It is also understood that o has other sources causing it to contrast with m and n.

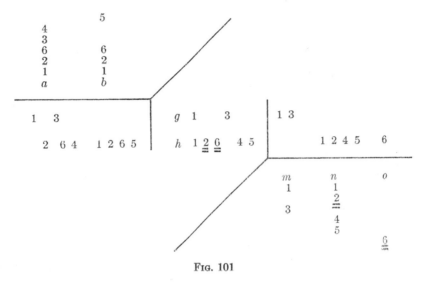

FIG. 101

The two-stage record, with the intermediate stage suppressed, is given in Figure 102. Now, it is characteristic of the origin of this figure that one of its rows (the n row) should have one environment index (2) recur in the same columns (the a column and the b column) in which another row (the o row), too, shows a recurring environment index (6) (see Fig. 103). When this rectangular pattern is found, a resolution into two successive changes yields the most economic and therefore in many cases the most probable solution: a and b were merged first into h (Fig. 104), and then h was split into n and o (Fig. 105). The alternative would be to suppose that a and b broke up independently but along precisely the same positional lines.

cally plausible both as a development from . . *aso* . . (> . . *aho* . .) and as an antecedent of $\bar{o}$. It is then asserted, again not entirely without plausibility, that $s > \emptyset$ IN GENERAL, i.e., including . . *eso* . . > . . *eo* . ., antedates the contraction . . *ao* . . > . . $\bar{o}$ . . .

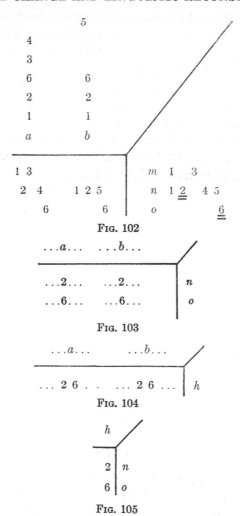

Fig. 102

Fig. 103

Fig. 104

Fig. 105

An example of this is found above (Fig. 77). The rectangular recurrence especially of "2", "3" in the *b* and *f* rows suggests that *sr* and *dhr* merged with one another (and with *bhr* and *gʷhr*) and that the result ("*fr*" for phonetic plausibility) was split into #*fr* and . . . *br* (Fig. 106).

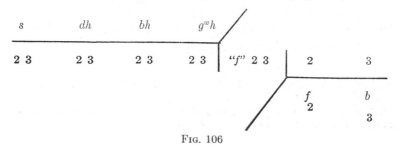

Fig. 106

11.4. Irreversibility of Merger

If contrasting phones of the initial stage (e.g., *a*-in-1 and *b*-in-1 [Figs. 101–2]) are replaced, in corresponding morphs, by (i.e., "go to") phones which still contrast at the final stage (*m*-in-1, *n*-in-1, respectively), there can never have been an intermediate stage at which the contrast was lost through merger, only to be reversed through split. Once phones merge (e.g., *a*-in-2,6 with *b*-in-2,6 into *h*-in-2,6 [Fig. 101]), their subsequent phonological history is for all times identical; sound change can split them only by positional allophones (*h*-in-2 of whichever provenience > *n*-in-2, *h*-in-6 > *o*-in-6) but not in such a way as to separate out the morphs with original *a* and those with original *b*. In this sense merger is irreversible.

On the other hand, the typological effect of a merger can be undone by a subsequent split. This is not only possible but frequent; it is one of the mechanisms whereby phonemic systems maintain their character while contrasts between morphs are redistributed. A representative example is given in Figure 107, where *E* is the non-low front vowel in a four-vowel

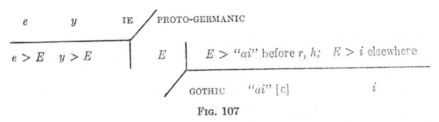

FIG. 107

system; Gothic "*ai*" and *i* have become phonemic through borrowings, creating instances of "*ai*" before consonants other than *r* or *h*. The split has restored a contrast between mid-front and high-front short vowels to the phonemic system, but both Gothic "*ai*" and *i* occur in morphs which had IE *e* and in those which had IE *y*.

11.5. System Stability and Relative Chronology

Consideration of the irreversibility of merger can be decisive in a complex picture. Short vowels in medial open syllables in Latin are subject to two kinds of treatment, for example, **reddatus* > *redditus* 'given back', **caputis* > *capitis* 'of the head' (by "weakening"), but **conquatis* > *concutis* 'you shake (tr.)' (by "syncope" with syllabification of the semivowel). Positing the weakening as taking place first, we obtain the simple picture shown in Figure 108. In the first phase (earlier to intermediate) the *a* of **reddatus* and **conquatis* and the *u* of **caputis* merge with the *i* of *concito* 'I drive'. In the second phase, the *i* of **conquitis*, is syncopated away after the semivowel /w/ (written "*u*"), with the effect of changing /w/ to /u/. This solution has the advantage of picturing the change as going on within one and the same phoneme inventory (. . /a, i, u, w/ . .) and with only minor ups and downs in phoneme distribution: in the first phase, contrasts in medial open syllables are largely eliminated (in other syllables they continue to exist, e.g., *capitis* with *a* in the first syllable). In the second phase, such a contrast is restored in compensation for the disappearance of /w/

EARLIER STAGE:	*concito*	**reddatus*	**caputis*	**conquatis*
INTERMEDIATE STAGE:	*concito*	*redditus*	*capitis*	**conquitis*
LATER STAGE:	*concito*	*redditus*	*capitis*	*concutis*

FIG. 108

from one of its positions. If, on the other hand, we imagine that syncope was earlier than weakening, we find that we need a temporarily increased list of contrasts at the intermediate stage. To set up the sequence given in Figure 109 is to leave unexplained why *concutis* did not go to **concitis* when

EARLIER STAGE:	*concito*	**reddatus*	**caputis*	**conquatis*
INTERMEDIATE STAGE:	*concito*	**reddatus*	**caputis*	*concutis*
LATER STAGE:	*concito*	*redditus*	*capitis*	*concutis*

FIG. 109

*caputis > *capitis*. The events simply tell us that *capitis* and *concutis* never rhymed at any time in their antecedent history. In order to save the implications of Figure 109, one might, for instance, have to (1) set up a fourth vowel (say, "*ü*") to accommodate *caputis/concütis* and to (2) state that this vowel (in *concütis*) remained uniquely unweakened in the second phase of change. This or any other similar solution would be uneconomical and typologically improbable.[5]

---

[5] Another approach to relative chronology is implicit in the procedure outlined in 13.1.1. See also Goetze, *Indog. Forsch.* 41; Leumann, *Lat. Gr.* 81–95. Whether or not **reddatus*, etc., went through a stage with medial *e* is unimportant.

   We append an example of the kind of relative chronology which is beginning to be better appreciated thanks to Kuryłowicz' detailed study of the analogic process (6, n. 1). Certain Indo-European present-tense stems show alternation between a form with -*e*- (some singular forms, etc.; "full grade") and one without -*e*- (some plurals, etc.; "zero-grade"): **ə₁es-ti* 'he is', **sty-steə₂-ti* 'he places', **ə₁s-mes* 'we are', **sty-stə₂-mes* 'we place' (the reconstructions are in an early form). Similarly, some verbs have -*new-ti* : -*nw-mes*. The Greek forms are, in part: . . . *hí-stā-ti* (Att. *hístēsi* 'he places'): *hístamen*, with regular sound change, *eə₂* > *ā*, *ə₂* > *a;* also -*numen* (*deíknumen* 'we show') in the plural (regular), but -*nūti* in the singular (*deíknūti* 'he shows') instead of the expected -*neuti*. It is clear that the sound change has made the analogy possible: once *eə₂* > *ā*, *ə₂* > *a*, the singular is descriptively derivable from the plural no longer "by adding -*e*-" (the old formula) but "by vowel lengthening"—the exact morphemic formulation does not matter. Compare n. 4 above, and 12.8.32. See also Harris, *Development*.

12. COMPARATIVE METHOD

When different changes, including different sound changes, affect different parts of one speech community (language split), we are faced with one earlier stage (ANCESTOR or PROTO- language) and two or more later stages (DAUGHTER languages, or, with regard to each other, SISTER languages). The procedure whereby morphs of two or more sister languages are matched in order to reconstruct the ancestor language is known as the COMPARATIVE METHOD.[1]

12.1. Sets of Correspondences

In the figures which follow, the phonemes of the ancestor language are entered, as heretofore, on the horizontal axis. The vertical axis, upward and downward, respectively, contains the phonemes for each one of two daughter languages.

If a phoneme a of the ancestor language in a given environment class (1) appears as m in one daughter language and as t in the other daughter language, corresponding morphs in the two sister languages will be matched in such a way that m in one answers t in the other. Such a pair of phonemes, one in the first language and one in the second, is a SET OF CORRESPONDENCES, written t/m (see Fig. 110).

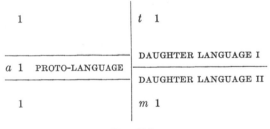

FIG. 110

A given phoneme in a sister language may appear in more than one set; in addition to t/m, there may be u/m and t/n.

These three sets will arise, for instance, from three proto-phonemes and two mergers, one each in each daughter language (see Fig. 111).

The three sets t/m, u/n, and t/n all occur in the same environment, "1/1", hence they are in contrast with one another.[2] In the following sections sets

---

[1] See 7.2 on the comparative method in morphology.

[2] One numeral ("1") is used to denote corresponding environment classes in three languages (see n. 1 of chap. 9).

and their distributions as they arise from sound change in sister languages will be examined. First we shall deal with a limiting case (12.2), then with cases in which one daughter language remains unchanged (12.3–6), and then with change in both daughter languages (12.7).[3]

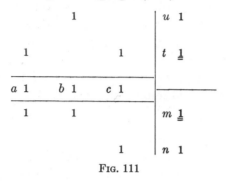

Fig. 111

12.2. Correspondence Sets in Phonemically Unchanged Daughter Languages

In the minimal instance neither language changes phonemically (see Fig. 112).

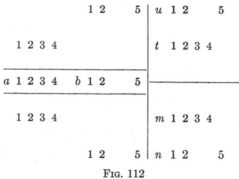

Fig. 112

As a result these sets exist:

t / m in environment 1/1 2/2 3/3 4/4
u / n in environment 1/1 2/2   5/5 .

Clearly, each set in each subenvironment represents a phone or an aggregate of phones of the proto-language. If the environments are assumed to be stable (9.1), hence distinct (as "1", "2", "3", "4", "5") in the proto-language, there were at least two contrasting phones in 1,2 and only one in 3,4,5. The phone represented by t/m may then be rewritten *a; that represented by u/n, as *b even in the environments 3,4 and 5, respectively.

---

[3] "Unchanged" in respect to the segments in question. (See 13.1.1.)

Since *t*-in-3,4 is assigned to the phoneme *t*, and *m*-in-3,4 to the phoneme *m*, presumably on phonetic grounds, it is simplest to infer that the antecedent of *t/m* in 3/3,4/4 was more "similar" to **a* than to **b*. Conversely, *u/n* is to be assigned as a descendant of **b* rather than **a*.

12.3. Correspondence Sets from Sound Change in One Daughter Language

Reassignment without merger (see 9.1.2) in one daughter language (II)

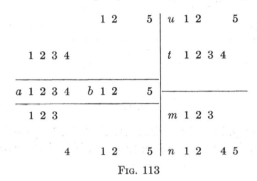

FIG. 113

(Fig. 113) produces these sets:

$$t \ / \ m \text{ in } 1/1 \ 2/2 \ 3/3$$
$$t \ / \ n \text{ in } \qquad\qquad\qquad 4/4$$
$$u \ / \ n \text{ in } 1/1 \ 2/2 \qquad\qquad 5/5$$

Again, in 1,2, **a* and **b* may be reconstructed by observing *t/m* and *u/n* in contrast and by extending the reconstruction to *a* in 3 and *b* in 5 on the same grounds as before. There is, however, a third set, *t/n*, in a non-contrasting position (viz., 4). The proto-phone which it represents was, then, distributed complementarily with the phones already assigned to **a* as well as with those assigned to **b*. The sister languages give no clue as to which of the two it resembled more.

12.4. Unconditional Merger in One Daughter Language

If language II goes through an unconditional merger (see 9.1.3.1) (Fig.

```
            1 2      5 | u  1 2      5
      1 2 3 4           | t  1 2 3 4
   ───────────────────  ─────────────
   a 1 2 3 4   b 1 2   5 |
     1 2 3 4     1 2   5 | m  1̲ 2̲ 3 4 5
```

FIG. 114

114) we obtain:

$$t \,/\, m \text{ in } 1/1 \; 2/2 \; 3/3 \; 4/4$$
$$u \,/\, m \text{ in } 1/1 \; 2/2 \qquad 5/5$$

or two PARTIALLY LIKE sets (as t/n was partially like the other two sets in the last example) in normally contrasting and non-contrasting environments. Each set may be taken as continuing one proto-phoneme, *a and *b. Specifically, the merger of *a and *b in environment 1,2 has been retrieved.

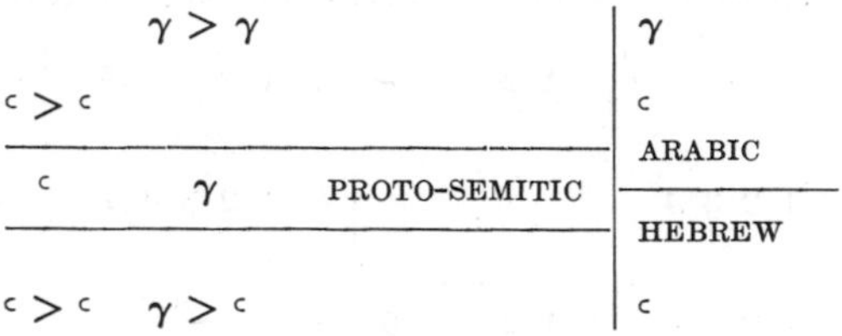

$$\gamma > \gamma \qquad\qquad \gamma$$

c > c				c
				ARABIC
c	γ	PROTO-SEMITIC		
				HEBREW
c > c	γ > c			c

FIG. 115

Thus sound change in Hebrew (see 9.1.3.1) (Fig. 115) produces these set of correspondences between (unchanged) Arabic and Hebrew

$$^{c}/^{c} \text{ in most positions}$$
$$\gamma/^{c} \text{ in most positions}$$

and hence allows us to reconstruct proto-Semitic $*^{c}$ and $*\gamma$.

12.5. Sets Resulting from Conditional Merger with Primary Split in One Daughter Language

This is the most general instance of phonemic merger (see 9.1.4.1) (Fig. 116).

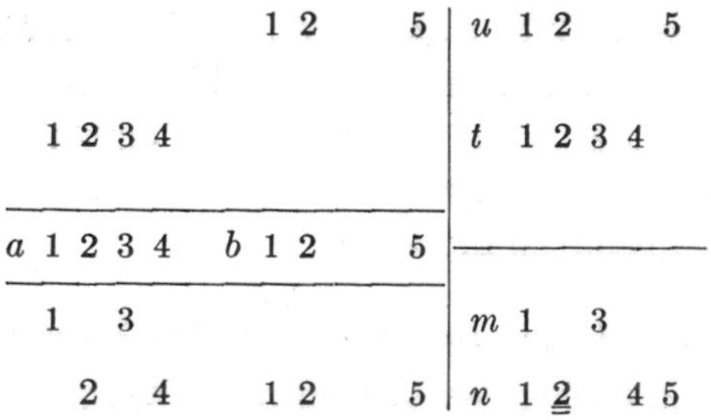

	1 2		5		u	1 2	5
1 2 3 4					t	1 2 3 4	
a 1 2 3 4	b 1 2		5				
1	3				m	1 3	
	2	4	1 2	5	n	1 2	4 5

FIG. 116

The resulting sets are:

$$t \,/\, m \text{ in } 1/1 \qquad 3/3$$
$$t \,/\, n \text{ in } \qquad 2/2 \qquad 4/4$$
$$u \,/\, n \text{ in } 1/1 \; 2/2 \qquad\qquad 5/5$$

The sets t/m and t/n are complementary; in addition, they are partially alike, which means that they may be taken as continuations from a proto-*a with split in language II. The set u/n contrasts with both t/m (in 1/1) and t/n (in 2/2) and hence represents a proto-*b: contrasting phones, even if "similar", are assigned to different phonemes. This is not binding for t/n in 4/4; this phone could be reconstructed equally well as belonging to *a or to *b.

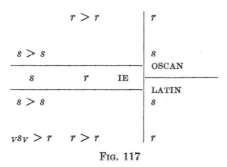

Fig. 117

Thus, in Oscan and Latin, IE (or proto-Italic) s and r have developed, as illustrated in Figure 117. These sets obtain:

s/s not between vowels ———
s/r ——— between vowels[4]
r/r in all positions

for example, Oscan *pis*, Lat. *quis* 'who'; Oscan *aasa*, Lat. *āra* 'altar'; Oscan *-r*, Lat. *-r* (mediopassive ending).

12.6. Sets Resulting from Secondary Split in One Daughter Language

In secondary split (see 9.2) environments are merged as shown in Figure

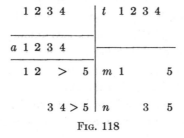

Fig. 118

118. These sets ensue:

t / m in 1/1 2/5
t / n in   3/3 4/5

---

[4] This also includes position after semivowels and after vowel length; compare Figs. 81 and 90.

The two sets are complementary and partially alike and are therefore to be reconstructed as erstwhile allophones of one $*a$. Thus, from the secondary split of IE k^w into Indo-Iranian $\check{c}$, k, we have Figure 119. Correspondence

$k^w > k$	k
	LITHUANIAN
k^w IE	
	INDO-IRANIAN
$k^w i,\ k^w e > \check{c}i,\ \check{c}a$	$\check{c}$
$k^w r,\ k^w o > kr,\ ka$	k

FIG. 119

sets arise between Lithuanian and Indo-Iranian as follows:

	before i/i	before r/r	before e/a	before a/a
$k/\check{c}$	x		x	
k/k		x		x

Their distribution is, in other words, complementary, and one phoneme ("k^w") may be reconstructed.

12.7. Correspondence Sets from Sound Change in Both Daughter Languages

The preceding discussion suggests that allophones survive as complementary and partially like correspondence sets if one daughter language stays unchanged. Sound change occurring in both languages may jeopardize our chances to reconstruct.

12.7.1. Merger in Each Daughter Language; Different Sets Resulting

As Figure 111 shows, merger in each language need not, however, interfere with reconstruction. The problem summarized there has great importance in comparative work: it involves two phonemes in two sister languages forming three contrasting sets, leading to the reconstruction of a proto-language with three rather than two contrasts, or with a more elaborate phonemic structure than either daughter language (insofar as that particular sector of the phonemic system is concerned). Thus, if proto-Semitic were reconstructed from any two Semitic languages other than South Arabic, there would be sets of correspondences between sibilants, up to three in each language, for example, Akkadian $\check{s}$, s, North Arabic θ, s, $\check{s}$, and Hebrew $\check{s}$, $\acute{s}$, s. If certain pairs of daughter languages are chosen, there are altogether four sets, for example, North Arabic/Akkadian: $\theta/\check{s}$, $\check{s}/\check{s}$, $s/\check{s}$, s/s. In South Arabic there actually exist all four contrasting sibilants which represent the otherwise reconstructable proto-Semitic phonemes.[5]

---

[5] Bergsträsser, *Einführung* 4.

Similarly, Arapaho confirms, with its own $\theta:t:l:n$, the reconstruction of proto-Algonquian $*\theta:*t:*l:*n$, which could have been arrived at from such sets as Fox/Cree n/t, t/t, n/y, n/n.[6]

12.7.2. Multiple Origin for One Set

The same set may arise from more than one source. Here two rather different contingencies must be considered. The former (12.7.2.1) is less favorable to reconstruction: the latter (12.7.2.2), a more complicated process, leaves open certain possibilities. Under (12.7.2.3) both are confronted within one framework.

12.7.2.1. Duplicate Merger

The environments in which the same set arises overlap: two originally contrasting proto-phones merge (Fig. 120). (Note that here, and under

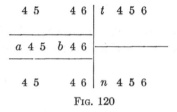

$$
\begin{array}{cc|l}
4\ 5 \quad\quad 4\ 6 & t & 4\ 5\ 6 \\[6pt]
\hline
a\ 4\ 5 \quad b\ 4\ 6 & & \overline{} \\[6pt]
4\ 5 \quad\quad 4\ 6 & n & 4\ 5\ 6
\end{array}
$$

Fig. 120

12.7.2.2, index numbers and phoneme symbols are chosen so as to make the examples fit into the more general formulation below.) There is no trace of the twofold origin of the set t/n (or Slavic d / Iranian d) (Fig. 121). It

$$
\begin{array}{ccc|l}
d > d \quad dh > d & & & d \quad \text{SLAVIC} \\[6pt]
\hline
d \quad\quad dh & & \text{IE} & \\[6pt]
\hline
 & & & \text{IRANIAN} \\[4pt]
d > d \quad dh > d & & & d
\end{array}
$$

Fig. 121

might in fact be inferred that the common source of daughter languages I and II (of Slavic and Iranian) had only one, not two, phonemes.

Of course the merger of a and b into t and n, respectively, need not be unconditional. If the total picture were as shown in Figure 122, it would

$$
\begin{array}{cc|l}
4\ 9\ 5\ 0 \quad\quad 4\ 9\ 6 & t & 4\ 9\ 5\ 6\ 0 \\[6pt]
\hline
a\ 4\ 9\ 5\ 0 \quad b\ 4\ 9\ 6 & & \overline{} \\[6pt]
4 \quad 5 \quad\quad 4\ 9\ 6 & n & 4\ 9\ 5\ 6 \\[6pt]
9 \quad 0 & o & 9 \quad\quad 0
\end{array}
$$

Fig. 122

---

[6] Bloomfield, *Linguistic Structures* §6; Gleason, *Introduction* 341.

still be true that *t/n* is found to occur in 4,9,5,6, with no possibility to distinguish *a* (4,5) from *b* (4,9,6) or to establish complementary distribution of *t/o* with that part of *t/n* which comes from *a*.

12.7.2.2. Composite Sets

The environments in which a set arises from one proto-phoneme are different from those in which the same set arises from another proto-phoneme (two originally complementary proto-phones are reassigned [see 12.8]), as shown in Figure 123. In this figure *t/n*-in-3 comes from *a*; *t/n*-in-2, from *b*.

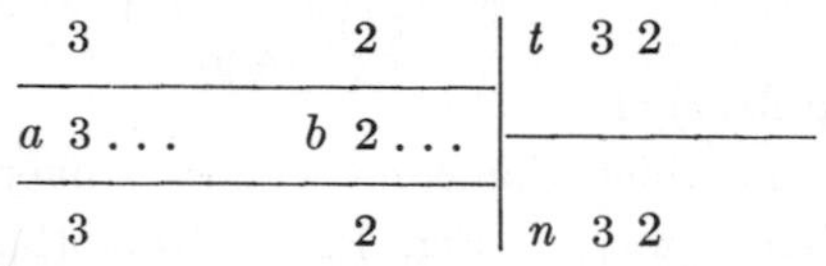

FIG. 123

For fuller discussion we single out the example in Figure 124; the conditioning of the mergers which provides the background for the complementarity of the two parts of the set is also represented. The set *d/d* arises twice: from **lþ* > E *ld* and from **nd* > G *nd*.

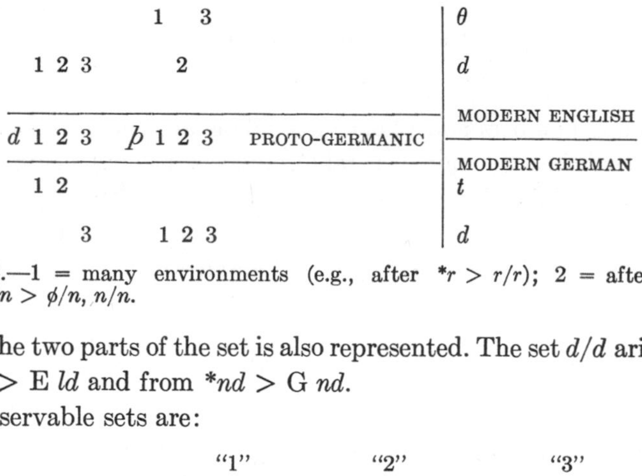

FIG. 124.—1 = many environments (e.g., after **r* > *r/r*); 2 = after **l* > *l/l*; 3 = after **n* > *ø/n*, *n/n*.

The observable sets are:

	"1"	"2"	"3"
d/t:	after *r/r*, etc.	after *l/l*	——
θ/d:	after *r/r*, etc.	——	after *ø/n*
d/d:	——	after *l/l*	after *n/n*

Examples are: E *sword*/G *Schwert-*, *hold/halten; hearth/Herd-*, *mouth/Mund-; gold/Gold-*, *bind/binden.*

This array contains indications of its historical origin. First, in no environment are there more than two contrasting sets. This suggests that there were never more than two phonemes involved. In analogy to synchronic procedure, it may be asked if one set cannot be treated as an 'overlapping' phone and be divided into two parts: one part complementary with one remaining set, the other part complementary with the other remaining set.

Now, clearly, the third set, d/d, which is partially alike with both the first (same English component) and the second (same German component) sets, is the most promising candidate for such a division. Hence d/d after l/l may be assigned with θ/d; d/d after n/n, with d/t. This amounts to reconstructing two proto-phonemes: $*\flat$ ($>$E θ, but after l, $>$E d; $>$G d) and $*d$ ($>$E d; $>$G t, but after n, $>$G d), and that, as we know, is the correct solution. In fact, the older German texts write "nt" in words like *bintan* 'bind'; the records change to *binden* in Middle High German times.

12.7.2.3. General Formula

An extension constructed upon the last example will furnish a more general formulation. If there had been further environment classes—for example, one ("4") in which both $*d$ and $*\flat$ had occurred originally and had both yielded d/d, or one each ("5", "6") in which only $*\flat$ or only $*d$ had occurred and yielded d/d—the first observation (with regard to there never being more than two sets contrasting) still holds. But as d/d-in-4,5,6 is complementary with both d/t and θ/d, its prehistory is indeterminate, except for the possibilities offered by internal reconstruction.

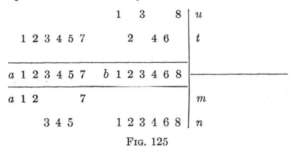

FIG. 125

In Figure 125 we consider two proto-phonemes, a and b (taking the place of Germanic $*d$ and $*\flat$ in the last example). They contrast in the environment classes 1,2,3,4; only a occurs in 5,7; only b occurs in 6,8.

The following sets ensue:

t/m in environments 1/1 2/2   7/7
u/n 1/1   3/3   8/8
t/n 2/2 3/3 4/4 5/5 6/6

The three sets are nowhere in full contrast. Therefore, one set may be broken up and divided between the two proto-phonemes needed; t/n, which is partially like each of the other two, is selected for that role (see above).[7] Thus t/n-in-2/2 is grouped with u/n ("$*b$", split in daughter language I); t/n-in-3/3 is grouped with t/m ("$*a$", split in daughter language II). The origin of t/n-in-4/4, 5/5, 6/6 remains undetermined.

---

[7] Compare the breaking up of o in Fig. 64.

12.7.3. Split in Both Daughter Languages

If two daughter languages let the same phoneme split up, the feature of partial likeness between resulting sets is endangered.

12.7.3.1. Split with Intersecting Conditioning

Consider the following: In Indo-Iranian, IE $s > s$ (after e . .) and $> ṣ$ (after u (*/w/) . .); r generally $> r$ (Fig. 126). Altogether there are four relevant environments for IE s: after e, before consonant ("1"); after u,

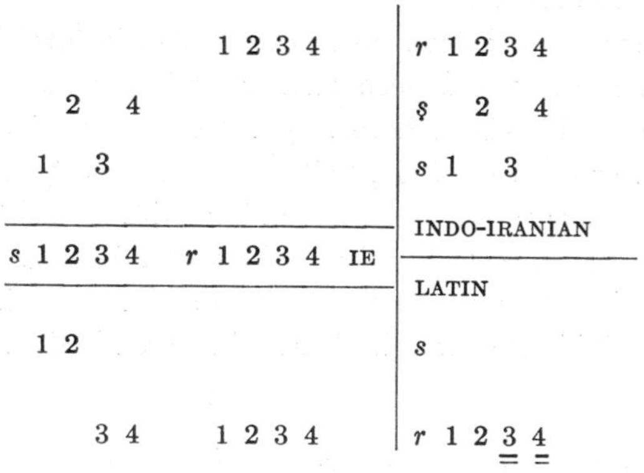

FIG. 126

before consonant ("2"); after e, before vowel ("3"); and after u, before vowel ("4") (Fig. 126). As a result, Indo-Iranian and Latin correspond thus:[8]

> s/s in 1/1 ("asp/esp")
> $ṣ/s$ in   2/2 ("uṣp/usp")
> s/r in   3/3 ("asu/eru")
> $ṣ/r$ in   4/4 ("uṣu/uru")
> r/r in 1/1 2/2 3/3 4/4

The first four sets are still neatly complementary with regard to the surrounding sets. Each, however, is partially like only two out of the other three complementary sets (thus s/s is partially like $ṣ/s$ and also partially like s/r but unlike $ṣ/r$). The fifth set, r/r (added for fuller background), contrasts, of course, with the first four. As a result, IE *s (from the first four) and IE *r may still be reconstructed as contrasting proto-phonemes.

---

[8] It is of course an impressive physical fact that the environments which stay together share phonetic features: 1 and 2 = non-intervocalic, 3 and 4 = intervocalic; 1 and 3 after e . . , 2 and 4 after u . . . In other words, the conditioning is phonetically "simple" in both languages. (See 8.1.2.)

12.7.3.2. *Duplicate Split*

The chainlike relation between the first four sets obtains if the conditions for the split in each language are independent and therefore intersecting (in Indo-Iranian: after *u*, etc.; in Latin: between any two vowels). But if the same allophonic division which has been made distinctive in one daughter language also operates, wholly or in part, in the other, sets without par-

$$
\begin{array}{cc|l}
2\ 3 & & u \\[1ex]
1 & & t \\[1ex]
\hline
a\ 1\ 2\ 3 & & \overline{} \\[1ex]
1 & & m \\[1ex]
2 & & n \\[1ex]
3 & & o
\end{array}
$$

Fig. 127

tial likeness will result. For instance, Figure 127 (with an allophonic difference between 1 and 2,3 leading to duplicate split) implies these sets:

$$t/m \text{ in } 1/1$$
$$u/n \text{ in } \quad 2/2$$
$$u/o \text{ in } \qquad 3/3$$

that is, three complementarily distributed sets of which one (*t/m*) is totally different from the other two. So long as the split-off phones do not MERGE in duplicate fashion as well (12.7.2.1), their distribution remains indicative of their origin. Figure 128 (with legend) is an illustration. The sets from **dh*, viz., *d/t* before, say, *h/k^c* in the next syllable and *dh/t^c*

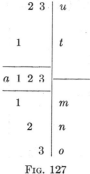

Fig. 128.—2 = before a following syllable beginning with an aspirate; 1 = otherwise. IE **dh* splits along the same lines in Sanskrit and in Greek, but in Sanskrit it splits by merging with IE **d;* in Greek, by merging with IE **t*. **t* in 2 was rare.

before, say, j/g in the next syllable, are unlike (owing to duplicate split) but complementarily distributed (owing to mergers in different directions and hence to continuing recognizability of the conditioning environments).

12.7.3.3. Primary Split Based on Duplicate Merger

If the process of merger which at the same time constitutes a ("primary") split in each daughter language is duplicated from one daughter language to the other, the split itself is lost (i.e., it can be reconstructed only as having

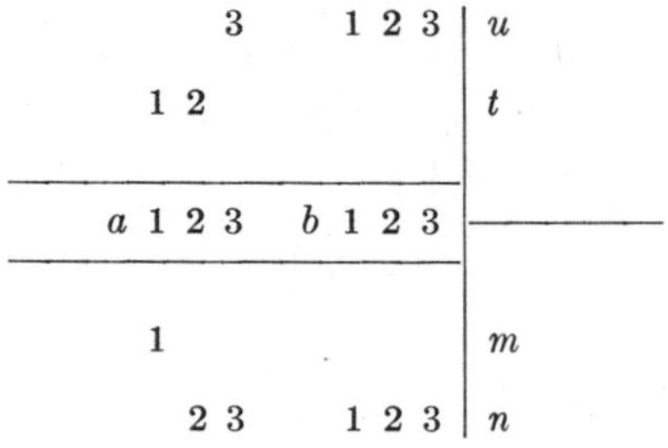

$$
\begin{array}{ll|l}
\quad\quad 3 \quad\quad 1\ 2\ 3 & u \\
1\ 2 & t \\
\hline
a\ 1\ 2\ 3 \quad b\ 1\ 2\ 3 & \rule{1cm}{0.4pt} \\
\hline
1 & m \\
\quad\quad 2\ 3 \quad\quad 1\ 2\ 3 & n
\end{array}
$$

FIG. 129

taken place before the dialect division). If the changes are like those shown in Figure 129, with a-in-3 and b-in-3 merging in each language, the sets are:

t/m in environment 1/1
t/n 2/2
u/n 1/1 2/2 3/3 .

There is no indication (outside of morphophonemics) that u/n-in-3/3 contains a proto-phone which had split off from a. The split itself in this example is non-duplicate (12.7.3.1). If there is duplicate split (12.7.3.2; i.e., if there is no relevant environment class 2), we obtain

t/m in 1/1
u/n in 1/1   3/3 ;

that is, the sets are unlike.

12.7.3.4. Secondary Split Based on Duplicate Merger in Environment

Next we consider the effects of secondary split, that is, of merger in the environment such that former allophones come to stand in contrast (see 9.2). As the discussion in 12.6 shows, this is not fatal so long as it takes place in one daughter language only; it simply leads to what are in effect partially like (but still different) environment sets (2/5 and 4/5 in Fig. 118) as settings for partially like sets of phonemes (t/m and t/n). Evidently, once the same environmental distinctions which are obscured in daughter language II are partly or wholly obscured in daughter language I as well, the merger, along with the secondary split associated with it, can no longer be retrieved without the help of internal reconstruction. A proto-a may split as shown in Figure 130. The two daughter languages agree in (1) assigning a-in-1,2 and a-in-3,4,6 to different phonemes and in (2) merging 2 and 4 themselves. In addition, 6 is merged with 2 and 4 in daughter language I

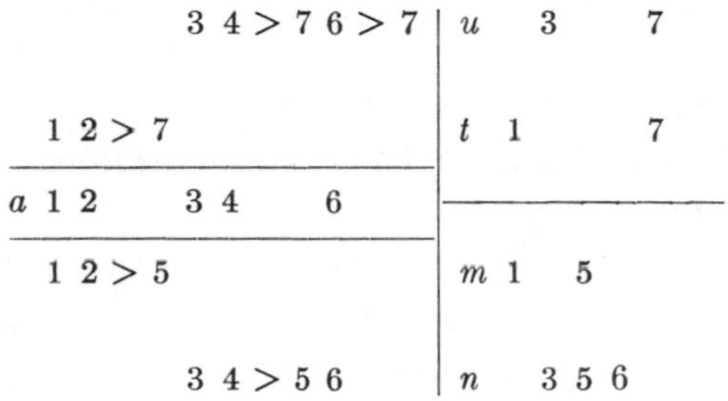

$$
\begin{array}{l|lll}
3\ 4 > 7\ 6 > 7 & u & 3 & \quad 7 \\[4pt]
1\ 2 > 7 & t & 1 & \quad 7 \\
\hline
a\ 1\ 2\quad 3\ 4\quad 6 & & & \\
\hline
1\ 2 > 5 & m & 1\ 5 & \\[4pt]
\qquad 3\ 4 > 5\ 6 & n & & 3\ 5\ 6
\end{array}
$$

FIG. 130

(the resulting environment class is labeled "7"), while it remains distinct in II (although, of course, simply as part of the environment—3,6—in which n does not contrast with m). The daughter languages correspond thus:

$$t/m \text{ occurs in } 1/1\ \ 7/5$$
$$u/n \qquad \text{in} \qquad 7/5\ \ 3/3\ \ 7/6 \,.$$

To the extent that the environments have undergone duplicate merger (2 with 4 into 5 and the same 2 and 4 into 7), the two resulting sets contrast. In the present example the sets are unlike because the split itself was duplicate (12.7.3.2); if this had not been so, a chain of like sets would have arisen (12.7.3.1).

Umlaut, that is, a conditioned sound change turning fronted allophones of rounded vowels into phonemes due to merger in following syllables, occurs in various Germanic languages after their separation. The precise conditioning is not quite uniform. We compare (somewhat schematically) one daughter dialect (I) in which umlaut has been carried out in fewer environments (3, 6) with another (II) where it has occurred in more environments (2, 5 in addition to 3, 6); moreover, environments 4, 5, and 6 are merged, duplicate fashion, into "7" in both daughter languages (Fig. 131).

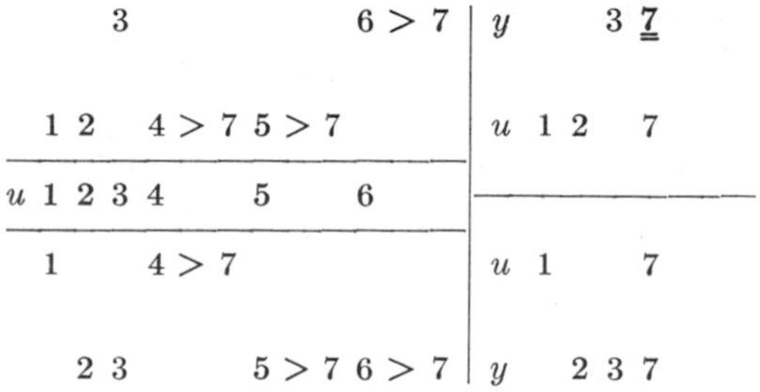

$$
\begin{array}{l|lll}
3 \qquad\qquad 6 > 7 & y & 3 & \underline{7} \\[4pt]
1\ 2\quad 4 > 7\ 5 > 7 & u & 1\ 2 & 7 \\
\hline
u\ 1\ 2\ 3\ 4\quad 5\quad 6 & & & \\
\hline
1\qquad 4 > 7 & u & 1 & 7 \\[4pt]
2\ 3 \qquad\quad 5 > 7\ 6 > 7 & y & 2\ 3 & 7
\end{array}
$$

FIG. 131

As a result, we obtain

$$u/u \text{ in environment } 1/1 \qquad 7/7$$
$$u/y \qquad\qquad 2/2 \quad 7/7$$
$$y/y \qquad\qquad\qquad 3/3 \; 7/7 \, ,$$

and we might erroneously reconstruct three phonemes, contrasting in 7/7.

12.8. Conclusion

12.8.1. Internal and Comparative Reconstruction: Merits and Limits

The merits and the limitations of the two standard methods for the reconstruction of the phonemic shape of morphs and for the reconstruction of sound change might be summarized as follows.

Internal reconstruction is based on the principle that phonemes which alternate represent, wholly or in part, former co-allophones. Internal reconstruction can recover processes of split, provided that morph boundaries occurred between the phone in question and the phone(s) making up the conditioning environment. It recovers processes of merger insofar as they are incidental to processes of split. The chances for successful internal reconstruction diminish as morpheme loss, analogic innovation, and further sound change overlay the effects of the split.

The comparative method is based on the principle that sets of recurring phoneme correspondences between two related languages continue blocks of positional allophones from the mother language; therefore, if such sets are subjected to the treatment accorded to phones in synchronic phonemics, a reconstruction is obtained. If split affects the same proto-phoneme in each daughter language, the partial likeness between the sets of correspondences is impaired, but their distribution remains intact. If merger affects the same proto-phoneme in each daughter language, it must not be duplicate merger, that is, the same set must not arise twice in the same environment, or the original contrast is beyond retrieval. It is evident that the strength of the comparative method rests on the fact that, once a merger has taken place, no subsequent event can have the effect of reconstituting the original distinction between merged morphs.

It would be possible to combine the procedures for internal reconstruction of each daughter language with the manipulation of the correspondence sets. For instance, in comparing Oscan and Latin (12.5), we might write our sets, instead of simply

OSCAN	s	s	r
LATIN	s	r	r

in this fashion:

OSCAN	s		s		r
LATIN	s	$\sim$	r		r

thus indicating that the particular instances of Lat. r which are matched
by an Oscan r are either alternating or indeterminate (10.1.1).

The combination of internal and comparative reconstruction is particularly enlightening in the recognition of composite sets. Our example above
(12.7.2.3) probably contains only indeterminate occurrences of proto-$(l)þ$
and $(n)d$, owing to the absence in sufficient strength of morpheme boundaries preceding the dentals. The following example, however, will serve:
in Greek, IE *t yields $t;$ in Germanic, it yields $þ$ initially and after accented
vowel, but d after unaccented vowel. However, IE *dh > Gk. t^c, except

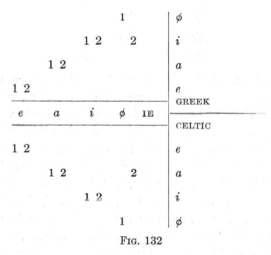

Fig. 132

>Gk. t if the next syllable begins with another aspirate; dh goes to d
generally in Germanic. Thus some instances of Gk. t/Germanic ("Gmc.")
d are from IE *$t;$ others are from IE *dh. Moreover, Gk. t < *dh is typically
initial and does not seem to occur in environments in which IE *t becomes
Gmc. d. Not only is it true, therefore, that the environment range of t/d
falls into two parts—one in which t/d is complementary with $t/þ$, the other
in which it is complementary with t^c/d—but there are also, among the d's
of the first-named range, near-instances of alternation with $þ$ (e.g., $patḗr/$
Gothic $fadar$ 'father', $p^c r\bar{a}t\bar{e}r$ 'member or a brotherhood'/$broþar$ 'brother'),
and corresponding instances of alternation of the Gk. t of the last-named
range with t^c (e.g., $trép^c\bar{o}$ 'I thicken', $t^c réps\bar{o}$ 'I shall thicken'/Gothic $drobjan$
'trouble').

The presence of alternation may decide questions in which mere complementary distribution admits more than one solution; what in synchronic phonemics can serve only purposes of elegance without being necessarily relevant is here an overriding factor, since alternations are normally the outcome of a split. This becomes strikingly clear where ϕ is in some way part of the picture (9.1.3.2).

According to one plausible interpretation of the data, Figure 132 summarizes the antecedents of parts of the Greek and the Celtic vowel system;[9] where 1 and 2 are certain interconsonantal environments, 1 includes VC——CV, 2 includes $\#C$——CC. Clearly, if ϕ were an ordinary phoneme, it would be said to have undergone duplicate split associated with non-duplicate merger. The result is as may be expected:

$$e/e \text{ occurs in } 1/1 \text{ and } 2/2$$

a/a	1/1	2/2
i/i	1/1	2/2
ϕ/ϕ	1/1	
i/a		2/2;

in other words, Gk. i, where it corresponds to Celtic a (as in *pítnāmi* 'I spread'), occurs only between consonants and consonant groups that do not themselves, in that environment, cluster with each other. The fact that ϕ in any language and the set ϕ/ϕ in any two sister languages have an enormous distribution is not really an obstacle to recognizing its complementariness with other phonemes or other sets, since the occurrence of ϕ or ϕ/ϕ can always be stated negatively. However, in this case alternation serves to throw the mutual exclusivity of ϕ/ϕ and i/a into relief, since the paradigm of Gk. *pítnāmi* (with i in environment 2) contains such forms as perfect middle *péptamai* (with "ϕ in environment 1"). Physically, the Indo-European source of the set i/a may be pictured as a non-phonemic vowel-like segment occurring in certain consonantal environments. It is traditionally represented by "*ь" ("shwa secundum").[10]

12.8.2. The Reality of Reconstructions

In a literal sense reconstruction procedures serve only to identify the number of contrasting entities in the proto-language. But actually they do

---

[9] Hoenigswald, *Lg.* 35.419.

[10] This amounts to reconstructing an allophone of ϕ (an automatic anaptyctic vowel). There is no compelling theoretical reason against the setting-up of such an entity. (See also 4.2.3.) The view of shwa secundum here represented is reported by Edgerton, *Lg.* 10.264 and more fully explained by Hoenigswald, *Lg.* 29. Celtic is named here because shwa secundum is plentifully attested in Celtic and Italic. Actually, evidence in a case like this must be pieced together from all over the Indo-European family.

much more: they furnish presumptions about the location of these contrasts in the sequence (i.e., about the order in which the reconstructed segments follow each other), and they give us information on the physical nature of the proto-phones and proto-phonemes. These indications depend to some extent on the physical consensus between the daughter languages (as distinct from recurrence of correlations in sets) and on certain considerations of phonetic and typological plausibility.[11]

Where there is consensus, that is, where the phones making up the phonemic correspondence set are phonetically similar, the proto-language may be thought, as a first approximation, to have had an equally similar phone. If the period of unity is relatively recent, the morphs of the daughter languages may be expected to resemble each other phonetically as well as to correspond to each other phonemically. But our examples in the previous chapters, with their implied or express phonetic comment, show that a great deal of phonetic similarity may persist, at least for some phonemes, for a very long time. The first step in recognizing common descent is usually the recognition of phonetic similarity (as in the early days of Indo-European studies the similarity of such etymologies as Skt. *mātr-*, Lat. *māter*, Old High German *muotar* 'mother', etc.). Later the more remote regularities are discovered, and in the event of conflicting correspondences, one of which involves relatively similar phones whereas the other does not, the search for doublets (5.2) may turn up proof which makes it certain that the two rival sets do not represent original contrast but contact under two separate sets of circumstances, or analogical new creation. Thus consensus, or similarity, is not only not needed for proof of relationship; where it cannot be expected considering the presumable time depth since separation, its appearance is suspect rather than welcome.

Even if true consensus exists, however, this does not necessarily mean that the ancestor language was identical with the daughter languages. Just as the comparative method sometimes leads to reconstructions (12.7.1) which are phonemically quite unlike either daughter language, and just as we know that some such developments are hidden from us because of duplicate merger, so there is no reason to suppose that consensus cannot be the result of duplicate development. If a typological change overtakes both daughter languages (8.4), the result may well be that they resemble each other, phonetically as well as in other ways, more than each resembles the mother language. Like duplicate merger, this may not be reconstructable. If more than two daughter languages are known, and if they may be treated as witnesses for the same reconstructed stage (chap. 13), there is often near-consensus on phonetic matters. The Indo-European stops show great

---

[11] See Bonfante, *Word* 1; 2.

similarity in Italic, Greek, Indic, Baltic, Slavic, and Celtic, with Germanic far apart (although the phonemic correspondences are extremely simple); this great majority alone, unless overridden by weightier areal or phonetic considerations, militates in favor of regarding the Germanic phones as secondary. Here the phonetic considerations, too, may be said to confirm the conclusions: much of the phonetic alteration which takes place in German, like the replacement of stops by spirants, is of a rather widespread type, familiar at least to observers of the better-known European languages.

If there is neither complete nor even majority consensus, the phonetic and typological probabilities provide the only support. For conditioned sound change valuable phonetic clues may be obtained from the surrounding segments, using the fact that conditioned sound change is largely assimilatory (8.1). Scholars have attempted to determine the phonetic nature of the laryngeals in older Indo-European by making inferences from the secondary split in the surrounding segments which accompanied the disappearance of the laryngeals from the consonant system. Thus the laryngeal labeled $ə_3$ (or γ) has been said to show "o-color" (if it is true that $ə_3e > o$, $eə_3t > o{:}t$) and voicing (if $pə_3 > b$).[12] Similarly, there have been efforts to reconcile (in a chronological sequence) the somewhat contradictory evidence which Germanic, on the one hand, and Greek and Vedic Sanskrit, on the other, contribute toward the determination of the nature of the Indo-European word-accent phoneme on whose phonemic presence or absence the three languages agree: the effects in Germanic (voicing of spirants after an unaccented syllable) and the complete absence of any such effects in Sanskrit and Greek combined with the consensus of these languages tell two conflicting stories: the former evidence points to stress, the latter to pitch, as the phonetic characteristic.

In judging the concreteness of a reconstructed stage, we should not forget that, quite aside from phonetic detail, duplicate merger is lost in the comparative method and that unconditioned merger is lost in internal reconstruction (12.8.1). It is therefore always possible that we have missed a contrast which actually existed. The indications that this is so, if any, are in some sense typological. Reconstruction of the Romance languages apparently results in the setting-up of nine vowels. It is probable that eight of these (four front and four back) may be paired as long and short on the basis of the occurrence of the word accent in penultimate syllables. But this dichotomy is marred by the presence of a lone ninth-vowel correspondence (by consensus low unrounded) which acts in some forms like a long vowel, in others like a short one, while many forms, with the ninth vowel elsewhere

---

[12] See 12.8.3.2.

than in the crucial type of penult, are indeterminate. The indications are, then, that the low vowel did at one time also occur either with or without following length and that a and $\bar{a}$ later merged unconditionally. The metrical evidence from recorded Latin (2.2) and the reconstructed earlier history of Latin itself both make it certain that a and $\bar{a}$ were in contrast; but, when dealing with material where we are not so fortunate as to possess these further controls, we cannot be sure. If it were true that language structure universally requires more than one vowel in a phonemic system, the fact that older Indo-European seems to reconstruct with only one vowel would be highly suspicious (the different character of the known Indo-European vowel systems from those in the later languages should, of course, not be used as an argument [8.4]).[13] If one shares the suspicion, one should seek indications of an early merger of different vowel qualities into the one reconstructable vowel—the unusual nature of the phonemic system would then have only been temporary. If the merger was truly unconditional, no indications of that sort may be hoped for.

The few instances in which reconstructions may be checked against recorded texts in the proto-language or a very close relative thereof (13.1) have shown, on the whole, that they are rather effective. This is more definitely true, at the present juncture, of phonological and morphophonemic structure than it is of the lexicon, and particularly of syntax.

12.8.3.1. Sample Reconstruction (I)

In conclusion, we offer two sample reconstructions. The first concerns a sector of Indo-European consonant phonemics from two daughter languages, Vedic Sanskrit and Germanic. It is understood that analogical disturbances and pseudo-sets resulting from borrowing (e.g., in Germanic by borrowing from another Indo-European language) have been previously eliminated.[14]

The sets are (Sanskrit/Germanic):

I	II	III	IV	V	VI	VII	VIII	IX	X	XI	XII
t/t	t/d	$t/\text{þ}$	d/d	d/t	dh/d	p/p	p/b	p/f	b/b	b/p	bh/b

---

[13] Jakobson, *Eighth Congress* 9; but there are Caucasic languages with one vowel phoneme and a consequently large allophonic spread (Allen, *Eighth Congress*, Discussion). Furthermore, the term "vowel" is not well defined: is a language which has syllabic (nuclear) allophones for certain of its phonemes, as Indo-European does for /y,w .../, typologically a "one-vowel" language?

[14] With permission from the editor of *Language* and from the American Council of Learned Societies, this section is based on the contents of an article published in *Lg. 26 = Readings in Linguistics* 298. The sample has been simplified by means of a few omissions.

In each language three dental and three labial phonemes are involved. In Sanskrit all are stops: *t* and *p* have voiceless unaspirated phones, *d* and *b* voiced unaspirated, and *dh* and *bh* voiced aspirated. In Germanic the main allophones are: voiceless stops for *t* and *p* (perhaps lenis after *s* and other spirants [?]), voiceless spirants for *þ* (interdental) and *f* (bilabial), and voiced stops and spirants for *d* and *b*. The phoneme inventory is thus somewhat similar in the two languages. If fuller data were given, this similarity would probably appear more pronounced.

Examples: I *ásti*:*ist* 'is';[15] II *pitár-*:*fadar* 'father'; III *bhrátar-*:*broþar* 'brother'; IV *dehí-* 'wall':*d(e)igan* 'knead'; V *véda*:*wait* 'I know'; VI *mádhya-*:*midjis* 'middle'; VII *spáś-* 'watcher':OHG *spehon* 'look out'; VIII *lip-* '(stick,) smear':*bi-leiban* '(stick,)stay'; IX (*see* II); X *bódhati* 'awakes, is attentive':*ana-biudan* 'charge with, bid'; XI *rámbate* 'hangs down':MG *lampen* 'droop'; XII (*see* III).

The following sets are partially alike:

I	II	III						share Skt. *t*
			IV	V				share Skt. *d*
					VII	VIII	IX	share Skt. *p*
							X XI	share Skt. *b*
	II		IV		VI			share Gmc. *d*
						VIII	X XII	share Gmc. *b*
I				V				share Gmc. *t*
					VII		XI	share Gmc. *p*

Sets IV and X occur when the next syllable begins with Skt. *h*/Gmc. *g*, Skt. *dh*/Gmc. *d*, or a few other sets; sets VI and XII do not occur in these environments. Sets II and VIII occur only after Skt. unaccented vowel/ Gmc. vowel with or without certain consonants intervening; sets VI and XII occur in this environment also, as well as in others. Sets I and VII are found after sets whose Germanic component is a spirant (e.g., after Skt. *s*/Gmc. *s*, or after *p*/*f*).

Possible applications of our procedure may, however, be in conflict. Let us examine the entire table of partially like sets (given above) for the distribution of the sets in various environments. Sets IV and V, as well as X and XI, are in contrast; for, in the few surroundings where IV and X are found, V and XI occur also. The same is true, as has been shown, for sets II and VI, and equally for sets VIII and XII, whose distribution is parallel to that of II and VI. No contrast can be established between any other two

---

[15] The Germanic examples are mostly Gothic.

partially like sets: they are all more or less obviously in complementary distribution. This leaves the following choices. Set I may be grouped together with III (and possibly II [see the next statement]), which would amount to reconstructing a single source for all occurrences of Skt. *t;* but also with V, which is one of the sources of Gmc. *t.* Set II may be grouped with I and III (all sharing Skt. *t*), but also with IV, though not with VI (both Skt. *d*). Set III is grouped with I and perhaps II (see above). Set IV cannot, as we have seen, be grouped with V (Skt. *d*); hence it can be grouped only with VI or perhaps II (Gmc. *d*). Set V can belong only with I (Gmc. *t*), provided I is not rather linked with III (and II), in which case V would stand alone. Set VI goes with IV but not with II. The relationships among sets VII and XII are parallel to those among sets I and VI; in what follows sets VII and XII will not be specially noted.

Examining the possibilities for economy, we find that two different choices will each result in three reconstructed phonemes for sets I and VI (and three more for VII and XII); no choice will yield fewer than three, and several others will yield more. The two possibilities of grouping sets as reflexes of only three phonemes in the proto-language are these: either I and V, II and III, and IV and VI or else V by itself, I and II and III, and IV and VI. In other words, the only question still unsolved is whether set I (*t/t*) should be derived from the common source of II (*t/d*) and III (*t/þ*), or from the source of V (*d/t*), that is, from **t* or from **d.* We note that set I occurs only after *s/s*, *p/f*, etc. (set VII probably only after *s/s*).

It may sometimes be irrelevant to decide the status of such a set as I. In some instances of ambiguity, both possible reconstructions may be equally effective. However, for set I (though not for VII) we can go a step farther. It is true that I (*t/t*) nowhere contrasts with II and III, or with V, since II, III, and V do not occur in the same environments as I (say, after *s/s*). But it is also true that V (*d/t*) occurs in at least one environment where II and III do not: after *y/s*, as in Skt. *meda-* 'fat':Modern German *Mast* 'fattening'. (Here Skt. *y* is seen in the second element in long *e.*) Upon further examination the set *y/s* is, in turn, found to occur only in positions from which *s/s* is barred; there is an equation *st = st* (*ásti:ist*) and an equation *yd/st* (*meda-:Mast*), but there is no *sd/st* and no *yt/st.* Consequently, the choice between the two possible assignments of set I (*t/t*) will affect also the status of the set *y/s*. As soon as set I is grouped with V (i.e., derived from **d*), the sets *s/s* and *y/s* must be said to contrast with each other before **d* of the proto-language, and we must reconstruct something like **sd* for *ásti:ist* and **zd* for *meda-:Mast.* But if set I is grouped with II and III (i.e., derived from **t*), we need to reconstruct only **st* and **sd.* The former grouping requires the reconstruction of a new Indo-European phoneme *z, of very limited distribution; the latter grouping requires only such Indo-European phonemes as have been reconstructed already on the basis of other evidence and at the same time gives them a more complete distribution (both *t and *d now occur after *s).

Thus considerations of economy have again decided the dilemma. On the strength of the general parallelism between the dentals and the labials, set VII (p/p) will now be grouped with VIII and IX rather than with XI.

To sum up, we have obtained the following reconstructions and sound laws: IE *t for sets I, II, and III; IE *dh for sets IV and VI; IE *d for set V; IE *p for sets VII, VIII, and IX; IE *bh for sets X and XII; IE *b for set XI; "Verner's law" for sets II and VIII; "Grassmann's law" for sets IV and X; and the treatment of *t and *p after a Germanic spirant for sets I and VII. Incidentally, we have also decided against the reconstruction of IE *s.

COLUMN 1	COLUMN 2	COLUMN 3	
		$bh > bh$	bh
	$b > b$	$bh \, . \, . \, (h) > b \, . \, . \, (h)$	b
$p > p$			p
			SANSKRIT
*p	*b	*bh IE	
			GERMANIC
$(s)p > (s)p$	$b > p$		p
$(\breve{V})p > (V)b$		$bh > b$	b
other $p > f$			f

FIG. 133

If we arrange the six labial sets in three columns, each representing one of the three reconstructed phonemes, we obtain the familiar-looking graphic expression of Figure 133,[16] and similarly for the three Indo-European dentals. It should be noted that the split of *bh in Sanskrit is a primary one (the new b and the old b merge). The "Verner" split of *p into f and b in Germanic is ultimately both primary (p after unaccented vowel merges with *bh after unaccented vowel) and secondary (since unaccented vowels and accented vowels merge, or /'/ merges with ø, *$\breve{V}$p yields Vb, while *$\acute{V}$p yields Vf, thus placing Gmc. b and f in contrast irrespective of the b < *bh). The "change" *sp > sp is merely a reassignment (see Fig. 53), although it follows from what was said above that the case of the parallel dental phoneme *t is different, since *st and *sd [zd] were in contrast, while there was no occurrence of *sb.

---

[16] $\breve{V}$ = unaccented vowel.

Finally, internal reconstruction confirms the splits. The past-participle morpheme alternates between *d* and *t* in Gothic: *salbod-* 'anointed' (after vowel):*hafts* 'fettered' (after Germanic spirant); since the split was primary, the alternation is automatic. The preterit singular had its accent on the stem syllable, and the preterit plural on the ending, hence Gothic *þarf* 'I need':*þaurbum* 'we need'; the split, partly secondary, left an irregular alternation.[17] In Sanskrit, reduplication, which generally consists of a prefix beginning with the first consonant of the stem (*pa-pat* . . , *da-da* . .), has *b, d* for stems beginning with *bh* . . , *dh* . . (*da-dh* . . etc.), still a near-automatic alternation in historical Sanskrit.

12.8.3.2. Sample Reconstruction (II)

The following is a summary of one of the phases of the so-called laryngeal theory for Indo-European. From the daughter languages (say, from Sanskrit, Greek, and Latin, in this order) these sets may be formed:

AFTER VOWEL[18] BEFORE CONSONANT	BETWEEN CONSONANTS
$y^{19}/i/i$	$i/i/i$
$n/n/n$	$a/a/en$
. .	

so that the first row yields a proto-phoneme $*y$, the second a proto-phoneme $*n$, occurring in such sequences as *teyp pyt* (presumably [pit]) $k^w ent$ *pnt*. There is, moreover, a widespread alternation $\phi \sim e$, with the result that morphemes have allomorphs such as *teyp* $\sim$ *typ*, *pent* $\sim$ *pnt*.

In the first position (V——C) there is also

$$:/:/: \text{ (vowel length) ("*:")}$$

complementary with these four sets (in C——C)

$$i/e/a \quad (\text{"}*\partial_1\text{"})$$
$$i/a/a \quad (\text{"}*\partial_2\text{"})$$
$$a/e/e \quad (\text{"}*e\text{"})$$
$$a/a/a \quad (\text{"}*a\text{"}) .$$

---

[17] Note that the comparative reconstruction does not get rid of the allomorphic variation. The stem morphemes are now reconstructed with variable accent rather than with variable stops. In other words, the proto-language had morphophonemes $\acute{V} \sim \check{V}$.

[18] That is, *e* or *a* (see below). The vowel *o* is left out of account (see n. 21).

[19] A phonemic expression of the second component of the Sanskrit "diphthong" *e*.

Vowel length, however, "alternates" only with $ə_1$ and with $ə_2$ (and not with e or a). Hence allomorphs $pe{:}t \sim pə_1t$ and $pa{:}t \sim pə_2t$ parallel our earlier *pent* $\sim$ *pnt*. At this point we arbitrarily and provisionally rewrite $:$ as an allophone of $ə_1$ (rather than of $ə_2$). This will transform $pe{:}t \sim pə_1t$ into a simply alternating $peə_1t \sim pə_1t$ (compare *pent* $\sim$ *pnt*), while $pa{:}t \sim pə_2t$ becomes an automatically alternating $paə_1t \sim pə_2t$. By internal reconstruction we might conclude, however, that the alternation is a product of an earlier merger and that $paə_1t$ was at one time $paə_2t$.

Renewed examination of the etymologies reveals the fact that at the stage now reached $ə_1$ occurs never after a, and $ə_2$ never after e.[20] The two items $ə_1$ and $ə_2$ do contrast, however, between consonants. On the other hand, how generally do a and e themselves contrast with each other? The question is worth asking because of a notable restriction in the occurrence of a; the vowel a is found freely only before $ə_2$ and after ⚏ (i.e., initially). If it can be shown that initial $ə_2$ is lost, then a was at one time entirely conditioned by a neighboring (preceding or following) $ə_2$. Now, in the environment ⚏——e none of the sets $:/:/:$, $i/e/a$, $i/a/a$ exist. But there is evidence for an alternation between $ə_1$ and $ə_2$ (represented by their vowel length allophones), on the one hand, and initial $ø$ (which, of course, does "occur" between ⚏ and vowel), on the other: root morphemes of the type $ep{\sim}p$, $ap \sim p$ (on a par with *pent* $\sim$ *pnt* above) will appear, in a construction which calls for a prefix (or reduplication) ending in e and the lesser ("zero grade") allomorph of the root ($\ldots$ $e\text{-}pnt$), as follows: $..\ e\text{-}ə_1p\ ..\ a\text{-}ə_2p$ (i.e., $..\ e{:}p\ ..\ a{:}p$). From this it may be inferred that both $ə_1$ and $ə_2$ were lost initially before a vowel, that the contrast between e and a was a matter of secondary split, and that the one vowel in existence before the conditioned loss of $ə_1$ and $ə_2$ had an a-like allophone in the neighborhood of $ə_2$ and an e-like allophone elsewhere (including near $ə_1$). It may then be labeled e, with the explanation that $ə_1e > e$; $ə_2e > a$; $eə_1C > e{:}$; $eə_2C > a{:}$—in terms of the most recent stage of proto-Indo-European.

To return to the older stages, $ə_1$ and $ə_2$ are now seen to have once had a distribution very much like that of y and n (and other phonemes like them), in that all of them occur not only in V——C and in C——C but also in ⚏——e (words begin with $ye\ ..$, $ne\ ..$). There is a fourth type of environment which is of some interest: after vowel plus voiceless stop and before vowel (et——e). Here most consonants occur freely (*etye*, *etne*, etc.). In at least some cases where $ə_2$ comes to stand in the crucial environment, Indo-Iranian presents an otherwise unexplained correspondence. Thus if

---

[20] This is merely an explicit, digit-by-digit expression of the fact that $e{:}$ alternates with $ə_1$ and $a{:}$ alternates with $ə_2$.

Lat. *rota* (older *rotā*) 'wheel' continues an IE *roteə₂*, the Sanskrit word for '(wheeled) chariot', *ratha-* should represent *rotə₂-o-*, with a well-known adjective-forming suffix and the alternation $e \sim \emptyset$ noted above.

The discovery of the previously unknown Hittite brought partial confirmation of the hypothesis of which the foregoing is a small and schematic sample.[21] Roughly, it developed that, in about one-half the etymologies in which ə₂ would have to be reconstructed (and for which Hittite has a representative), the Hittite form shows a consonant ("laryngeal") phoneme (*ḫ* or *ḫḫ*), next to which the vowel *a* occurs, while *e* does not. In the remainder of the cases (again insofar as there is Hittite evidence at all), Hittite has $\emptyset$, but the same vocalic effect. Since the difference is in no way conditioned, it is necessary to recognize two "*a*-colored laryngeals": one which has survived as a Hittite consonant, and another which has the same history in Hittite as in the other languages and which therefore remains recoverable only in indirect fashion.

---

[21] See also 13.4. It goes without saying that this is not a full résumé of the laryngeal hypothesis; for such a résumé see, for instance, Polomé, *Revue belge* 30. It is important to realize, however, that the contribution of Hittite to the whole reconstruction is often exaggerated. See also Lehmann, *Proto-Indoeuropean Phonology*, 85–98.

13. CLASSIFICATION

13.1. Reconstruction from More than Two Related Languages

If the sister languages or putative sister languages are more than two in number, that is, if we are dealing with a LANGUAGE FAMILY, the theory of change, relationship, and reconstruction is in many respects merely an extension of those principles which hold for two sister languages. In a sense, any problem in the reconstruction of a proto-language for which there are more than only two later witnesses can be resolved into two-language problems. Three languages (A, B, C) which have been pronounced "related" may be subjected to reconstruction procedures by pairs: A/B, A/C, B/C.

In other ways, however, the extension from two to more than two languages presents special and historically very concrete problems. First, added evidence of a third or fourth daughter language may compensate for the uncertainties and ambiguities created, most of all, by duplicate merger (12.7.2.1, etc.). Second, pair-wise reconstructions from three related languages may pose the question of degrees of relationship within the language family. Since in either case the problem arises when the component pairwise reconstructions disagree with one another, the two contingencies are intimately connected. As in all historical and comparative work, it must also be remembered that sound change is not the only basis for reconstruction and that the phonemic shape of morphs is not the only feature to be reconstructed. In the treatment of what shall here be called the THREE-LANGUAGE problem, other processes and other features assume, in fact, particular prominence. Nevertheless, the phonological side remains exceptionally amenable to fuller statement. It is here taken up first.

13.2. Three-Language Phonology

13.2.1. Preliminary: Descent or Sister Relation

If we form all phonemic correspondence sets from two related languages, A and B (i.e., from the cognate morphs in the two languages, after elimination of non-inherited material [see chaps. 5 and 10]), the phonemes reconstructed for the proto-language *X according to chapter 12 may or may not be in a one-to-one relationship, morph by morph, with the phonemes of one of the two languages under comparison, say, with the phonemes of A. If they are, A is said to be the "same" as *X, and the reconstruction amounts to the simple discovery that A is an "earlier stage", or indistinguishable from an earlier stage, of B. It is to be expected that the chronology of the corpora, if available, bears this out and that the texts in language B are more recent than those in language A, except for the effects of artificial literary preservation. The alternative would be to assume that all phonemes (not only some, under 12.3–12.6) remained unchanged from *X to A—an assumption which becomes less likely the more time has elapsed between the two stages. If there is at least one instance in which *X is not the "same" as A—that is, at least one instance of merger or reassignment—A is not the ancestor of B.

In actual historical records the direct ancestor-descendant relationship is sometimes approximated. Modern Persian is very possibly the daughter language of Middle Persian, and Middle Persian, in turn, the daughter language of Old Persian. Ordinarily, however, there is a residue which represents the single telling instance referred to above whereby the older corpus is shown not to be the older stage or ancestor but the sister of the later stage. It is, in fact, an accident, not to be expected too frequently, that the same type of speech which happens to have been developed in a literary fashion and therefore to have been singled out for preservation should be precisely the one from which the later, equally unpredictably surviving dialects have come. It is well known that the relation between such languages as Latin and French, or Sanskrit and Bengali, is not strictly linear but collateral, although the distinction may for certain purposes be disregarded.

13.2.2. Subrelationships between Three Related Languages

a) With three language corpora (A, B, C) on record, it may be found that all phonemic correspondence sets taken from A/B, from A/C, and from B/C yield the same reconstruction and, further, that this reconstruction coincides with (is the "same" as) one of the extant languages, say, A. In that case, A is the ancestor, and B and C are daughter languages (Fig. 134).[1]

FIG. 134

---

[1] The relation between the so-called family-tree picture and the isogloss or wave picture is in effect dealt with later in this chapter. See also Pulgram, *Orbis* 1 Maas, *Textual Criticism*, contains striking parallels from a different field of scholarship, which nevertheless has influenced the development of historical linguistics considerably.

b) If, on the other hand, only A/B (*read:* the proto-language reconstructed from A and B) equals A, while A/C = B/C = *X, the table of descent is necessarily as shown in Figure 135. If, in turn, all sets from A/*X and from B/*X are formed, the reconstruction will in both cases coincide with *X itself.

c) If A/B = A/C = *X, while B/C yields a different reconstruction, *Y, it must be true that *X/*Y = *X (Fig. 136).

d) If A/B = A/C, and = A itself, with B/C reconstructing to a separate *Y, we shall also find that *Y/A = A itself (Fig. 137).

e) Lastly, A/B, A/C, and B/C may all yield one identical reconstruction *X which is not like any of the extant languages (Fig. 138).

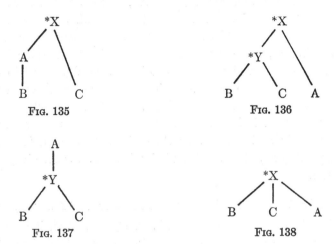

This exhausts the possible subrelationships for three related languages. In particular, it should be noted that A/B, A/C, and B/C (all combinations of A B C) cannot yield three different reconstructions. In (*b*), (*c*), and (*d*) two combinations (called A/C and B/C in [*b*]; A/B and A/C in [*c*] and [*d*]) are lined up against the remaining combination; in (*a*) and (*e*) all three combinations yield one and the same reconstruction.

13.2.3. Examples

In (*a*) A might be Vulgar Latin (thought of, in this example, as extant in informal inscriptions, authors like Petronius, etc.); B, French; and C, Spanish.

In (*b*) A might be Vulgar Latin; B, French; C, Oscan.

In (*c*) A might be Oscan; B, French; C, Spanish. Consider, for instance, the occurrence (greatly simplified, especially by the omission of secondary intervocalic *s* [10.2.1]) of the consonants "*r*" and "*s*" in these three languages. French (B) and Spanish (C) have two correspondence sets, r/r and s/s occurring in some contrast:

r/r occurs intervocalically and non-intervocalically ,
s/s occurs   non-intervocalically .

From this it is possible to reconstruct for *Y ("Vulgar Latin", this time conceived of as reconstructed proto-Romance):

*r occurring intervocalically and non-intervocalically ,
*s occurring   non-intervocalically .

Oscan (A) and French (B) yield the following:

r/r intervocalically and non-intervocalically
s/r intervocalically
s/s non-intervocalically .

Hence we might reconstruct for the common source of Oscan and French (12.5):

*r intervocalically and non-intervocalically, and
*s intervocalically and non-intervocalically ,

with a primary split, intervocalic *s > r, in French. Oscan (A) with Spanish (C) yields the same results, for the same morphs, as Oscan does with French: the common source (*X) of Oscan and French is also the common source of Oscan and Spanish; it will be called "proto-Italic". If we now form sets from the r's and s's as they occur in the reconstructed morphs of proto-Italic (*X) and of Vulgar Latin (*Y), in that order, we obtain once again:

*r/*r intervocalically and non-intervocalically ,
*s/*r intervocalically
*s/*s   non-intervocalically .

When reconstructed in turn, this yields:

**r intervocalically and non-intervocalically, and
**s intervocalically and non-intervocalically ,

with the same primary split, **s > *r, this time in Vulgar Latin. As the reconstruction from Vulgar Latin with proto-Italic thus turns out to be identical, morph by morph, with proto-Italic itself, the descendants of Vulgar Latin, viz., French and Spanish, form a SUBFAMILY within the family descended from proto-Italic. In particular, the sound change merging intervocalic s with r and thereby splitting the phoneme s is shown to have taken place between the proto-Italic (*X) and the Vulgar Latin (*Y) stage.

In (d), if A = (older) Classical Latin; B = French; C = Spanish; *Y = reconstructed Vulgar Latin (thought of as a linear descendant of Classical

Latin, ignoring 13.2.1 above), we find, among the sets formed from Latin (A) and French (B), these two in word-initial position before vowels: ϕ/ϕ and h/ϕ. We reconstruct, of course, $*\phi$ and $*h$ for the "common source". The same morphs, when reconstructed from Latin (A) and Spanish (C), yield the same contrast, $*\phi$ and $*h$. The common source for Latin-French, the common source for Latin-Spanish, and, third, Latin itself are the same; Latin is the common source. Reconstruction from French (B) and Spanish (C), however, leads to a different result: the morphs involved show ϕ/ϕ throughout, pointing to Vulgar Latin $*\phi$. Forming sets from the two reconstructions (or, what amounts to the same, from Classical Latin and reconstructed Vulgar Latin), we obtain:

$(*)\phi/*\phi$ initially before vowel ,
$(*)h/*\phi$ initially before vowel ;

that is, by further reconstruction (12.4):

$$**\phi ,$$

and

$$**h .$$

Since this is again identical with Classical Latin itself, we conclude that the common ancestor of French and Spanish is a descendant of Classical Latin and that the merger of ϕ and h took place between the Classical Latin and the Vulgar Latin stages.

13.2.4. Generalization for n Languages

The procedure for the discovery of subrelationships among any number of related languages may be stated as follows. If n related languages are known, there will be $n(n-1)/2$ pairs of languages from which to form phonemic correspondence sets (e.g., for 3 languages: 3 pairs; for 4 languages: 6 pairs; for 10 languages: 45 pairs). Examination of all phonemic correspondence sets for every language pair will show that the reconstructions from some pairs are the "same" (13.2.1). Each different reconstruction represents the proto-language of a subfamily. The component languages of those language pairs which yield identical reconstructions belong to one subfamily. If a language is found thus to belong to two subfamilies, that subfamily which is reconstructed from the smaller number of languages is, in turn, a subfamily within the subfamily reconstructed from the larger number of languages.

Thus four related languages (A, B, C, D) may exhibit these, and only these, subrelationships (the possibility that one of the four is at the same time a proto-language or sub-proto-language is now disregarded):

a) The six language pairs yield three different reconstructions:

A/B; proto-language *Z
A/C = B/C; proto-language *Y
A/D = B/D = C/D; proto-language *X

A and B are descendants of both *Z and *Y; *Z, being reconstructed from fewer languages, is therefore a descendant of *Y. A, B, and C are descendants of both *Y and *X; *Y, being reconstructed from fewer languages than *X, must be a descendant of *X. The diagram is therefore as shown in Figure 139.

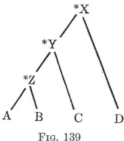

FIG. 139

b) Again, three different reconstructions:

A/B; proto-language *Z
C/D; proto-language *Y
A/C = A/D = B/C = B/D; proto-language *X

A and B are descendants of *Z and of *X; *Z is a descendant of *X. Likewise, C and D are descendants of *Y and of *X; *Y is a descendant of *X (Fig. 140).

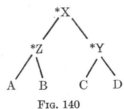

FIG. 140

c) Two different reconstructions:

A/B; proto-language *Y
A/C = A/D = B/C = B/D = C/D; proto-language *X

A and B are descended both from *Y and from *X; *Y, being reconstructed from one pair of two languages only, is a descendant of *X (Fig. 141).

d) Again, two different reconstructions:

A/B = A/C = B/C; proto-language *Y
A/D = B/D = C/D; proto-language *X

A, B, and C are descendants of both *Y and *X; *Y, involving fewer languages, is a descendant of *X. Diagrammatically, this is given in Figure 142.

e) One reconstruction from all six pairs, A/B = A/C = A/D = B/C = B/D = C/D = *X (Fig. 143).

A few corollaries are worth noting. Two or more related languages can belong to different subfamilies only if one subfamily is a subfamily within the other (i.e., only if the sub-proto-languages are in a descendant relationship) but not if they are in an ordinary sister relationship. French is both Romance and "Italic" (13.2.3 [c]), but it could not also be Celtic, since Celtic is neither a subfamily of Romance or of Italic nor vice versa. The proto-languages and sub-proto-languages (*X, *Y, *Z) identified and placed by means of the procedure outlined in this section may be themselves subjected to the comparative method as illustrated variously in 13.2.2. For instance, *Y/*X in Figures 139–42 reconstruct into *X itself. If all the possible pairs

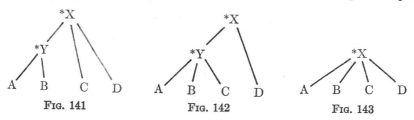

FIG. 141   FIG. 142   FIG. 143

among *n* related languages yield the same reconstruction, this is an indication that the common ancestor has split into *n* daughter languages simultaneously rather than successively (see 13.2.2 [e], Fig. 138; 13.2.4 [e], Fig. 143; and, for a sub-proto-language, 13.2.4 [d], Fig. 142). The same for 13.2.4 (c) at *X; if A and B are replaced by their common subancestor, *Y, *X may be reconstructed identically from *Y/C, *Y/D, and C/D.

13.3. Three-Language Morphemics

With the reservations occasioned by the lesser manageability of the processes of morph change, the operations outlined in the preceding sections also apply to morphological reconstructions. In two given Greek dialects, say, in Attic and in Laconian Doric, the dative morpheme has taken the place of an older pair of contrasting case morphemes, "dative" and "locative". It was shown (7.2) how that contrast might be reconstructed from a comparison between "Greek" (we now emend to "Attic") and Sanskrit (where the locative case is intact), or between Attic and Latin (where the locative also underwent merger, but not with the dative). Supposing it now to be our task to establish the relationships existing among Attic, Laconian, and Latin, we find that the pairs Attic/Latin and Laconian/

Latin yield the same reconstruction ("proto-Indo-European"; two case morphemes), while Attic/Laconian yields a different reconstruction ("proto-Greek"; one case morpheme). By analogy to 13.2.4, proto-Greek is a subancestor in proto-Indo-European. This may be confirmed by reconstructing from proto-Greek and proto-Indo-European: the result equals proto-Indo-European itself.

13.4. Subgrouping and Internal Reconstruction

The procedures of 13.2 and 13.3 are a technical and somewhat specialized illustration of the famous principle that subfamilies are established on the basis of "shared innovations". As it happens, sound changes and grammatical syncretisms are among the clearest instances of replacement and, therefore, of indisputable and reconstructable "innovation". Innovation, however, is probable in a great many cases of morphological change which are of particular importance for reasons set forth below. Quite often lexical and grammatical innovations may be spotted as such with the help of internal reconstruction—occasionally, in fact, internal reconstruction converging from more than one daughter language (chap. 7). Thus the naming of an animal by a self-descriptive term or paraphrase reminiscent of a taboo replacement (6.5) in one later stage, or in two daughter languages, with the simpler, unanalyzable term extant in another daughter languages, establishes a presumption of innovation. The highly irregular, unique paradigm of the Greek and Sanskrit demonstrative Gk. *ho, tón* 'he, him', Skt. *sa tam* may now be matched with a list of Hittite forms, *su, ta* connective particle, *-am* (as in *ta-an*) 'him', which seems to show that the Hittite state of affairs, representing, as it does, a productive construction of sentence-initial connectives with enclitic pronominals, is original and that Greek and Sanskrit contain an innovation.[2] The innovation may be regarded as working toward a new type of sentence syntax; the particle-and-enclitic device is given up. Greek and Sanskrit might have followed the typological trend by letting different particular examples of the old construction survive in isolation and thus develop into "pronouns"; but the significant fact is that exactly the same combinations survive in both languages (**so* and **tom*, to cite the forms in their sub-proto-language form; but not, e.g., †*to* and †*som*). If it is granted that this particular selection cannot well have taken place twice, we would have an argument in favor of thinking that Greek and Sanskrit (and most other Indo-European languages except Hittite) form one subfamily, and Hittite (only with its closest congeners) another within Indo-European.

---

[2] Sturtevant, *Lg.* 15.

13.4.1. Overlapping Innovations: Model and Examples

What makes problems of subgrouping difficult is the fact that, even in the field of sound change and of simple grammatical change, the clear-cut alignment constructed in 13.2 and 13.3 is likely to be obscured by other influences, the more so, the less time has elapsed between the proto-language and the sub-proto-language—in other words, the more closely the subrelationships resemble the original relationship. It may be said that the factors making for obscuration and uncertainty are more destructive to the relatively few phonemes of the language, with their typologically restricted avenues of further change, than they are to the more numerous and more variable morphs. The greater amenability of sound change to rigorous treatment is certainly in large part offset by this weakness.[3]

In dealing with sound change, the investigator, as soon as he begins to study "all" sets from language pairs, is typically confronted with a situation of the following sort. Three related languages, A, B, and C, correspond thus:

	A	B	C		A	B	C
(1)	a	b	c	(6)	j	m	n
(2)	d	e	c	(7)	o	p	q
(3)	f	g	h	(8)	r	p	s
(4)	f	g	i	(9)	t	u	v
(5)	j	k	l	(10)	t	w	v

Each numbered row is a (triple) set of correspondences. For the sake of simplicity it is assumed that the sets are in contrast with each other, so that occurrence of the same phoneme in more than one set in a given language represents simple unconditional merger (12.4) in one, or two, out of the three languages. The ultimate proto-language must be reconstructed as having all ten different phonemes, (1)–(10). In order to determine a subrelationship, if any, we note that not only are (1) and (2) merged in language C; (5) and (6) in language A; and (7) and (8) in language B—these mergers contributing nothing toward any subgrouping, since the three reconstructions from A/B, A/C, and B/C would still turn out identical. But we also note—ignoring sets (9) and (10) for the time being—that (3) and (4) are merged in both A and B. This (i.e., all the mergers and other innovations of which this would be true) would seem to establish a sub-proto-language (13.2.2 [c]), as shown in Figure 144.

If we consider (9) and (10), ignoring (3) and (4), the picture is, on the contrary, as illustrated in Figure 145. But (3)–(4) and (9)–(10) cannot both

---

[3] Greenberg, *Essays* 48; Dyen, *Lg.* 29, with references.

be considered "shared innovations" for the purpose of establishing a sub-relationship, since the subfamilies would overlap (13.2.2, end) rather than inclose and be inclosed.

Iranian is a simple example of a language group occupying the position A. It shares a great many innovations with Indic; for example, the sound change IE *e > *a; IE *o > *a (merger) with the attendant secondary split, *k^we > *ča; *k^wo > ka (9.2). On the other hand, Iranian shares inno-

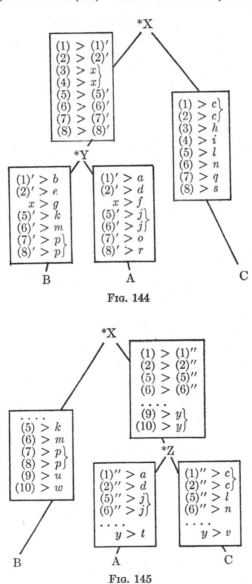

FIG. 144

FIG. 145

vations with Slavic, for example, the merger of IE *dh* and *d* (12.7.2.1). In Indic, *dh* and *d* are kept apart; in Slavic, *e* and *o* are kept apart.

If it is understood that phonemic merger stands here for any demonstrable replacement, such overlapping is indeed frequent, although apparently more so in some language families than in others. It is necessary to look for the principles available to help interpret the phenomenon.

13.4.2. Overlapping Innovations: Interpretation

First of all, while the effect of a replacement change suffered at the protostage or at a sub-proto-stage is "shared" by the daughter languages, the reverse does not hold: a replacement "shared" may owe its recurrence from sister language to sister language to the "accident" of independent identical change, for example, to duplicate phonemic merger (12.7.2.1). In the traditional view the vowel merger of IE *e* with *o* belonged to the Indo-Iranian subancestor, while the merger of *d* with *dh* was merely duplicate, that is, it took place separately in Iranian and in Slavic. Or the changes— (9) > *u*, (10) > *w* in language B; and (9), (10) > *t* in language A, > *v* in language C—may yet be reconciled with Figure 144 (and thereby with the merger of [3] and [4] between *X and *Y) by positing the merger of (9) and (10) as having taken place twice: once between *X and C and once between *Y and A.

13.4.2.1. Duplication

For this reason efforts at subgrouping frequently center around the task of estimating the chances for the same innovations to happen more than once: innovations shared by overlapping groups of languages within a language family are counted, analyzed, and weighed against one another. Since the force of the criteria depends in large part on generalizations concerning the predictability of change, these efforts tend to bog down in flat contradictions, depending on individual scholars' preconceptions (8.3, etc.).[4] We have seen that sound change has comparatively minor weight because the assimilative and otherwise physically plausible possibilities open to a given phonemic structure may be relatively few. The merging of *dh* and *d* or of any ordinary assimilatory merger may possibly be called phonetically trivial. If, however, the conditioning is very specific, or if a whole cluster of related changes, such as a secondary split dependent upon a merger, take place identically, as in the case of $*k^w e > *\check{c}a : *k^w o > ka$, the chances for duplicate (not to mention triplicate, etc.) occurrence appear to lessen. Morphological and lexical changes furnish better material; the particular

---

[4] The controversy between Senn, *KZ* 71, and Szemerényi, *Kratylos* 2, is a recent example.

strength of the case of the Indo-European demonstrative pronoun was pointed out above, though even this instance has been disputed. If one believes that inherent structural traits (gaps in the system, statistical instabilities) predetermine change, then the chances for independent identical developments from the same (ancestral) base are great in any event. Certainly, the ordinary analogic leveling of paradigms (6.3), which comes nearest to being predictable from formal premises, is always suspect.

13.4.2.2. Areal Interpretations

Often the data themselves intimate that the replacement changes which have occurred are neither entirely random (thus permitting a statistical computation of chance duplication) nor largely predetermined by structure (thus leading one to expect a great deal of duplicate change) but determined in part by specific outside factors (chap. 8, end). For instance, the overlapping subgroups, when plotted on a geographical map, are likely to occupy contiguous areas—a characteristic trait, in any synchronic picture, of isoglosses marking innovations (isoglosses marking mere retentions may, on the contrary, be of the discontinuous, "relic" type). The territory in which *dh and *d were merged covers, in historical times, an area which comprises Baltic, Slavic, Iranian, and apparently the imperfectly known Thracian and Macedonian. Indic, Greek, Italic, Germanic, and Armenian (where the two phonemes are not merged) form a disconnected, fragmentary rim. It is important that the innovating area, or part of it, is marked out by many other innovations, morphological and lexical, as well. This is not equally true of two outer languages, Hittite and Celtic, which nevertheless have also merged *dh and *d. But the Celtic process may indeed be looked upon as only superficially similar: if the merger of aspirates and voiced non-aspirates is followed through all the places of articulation, it develops that, while the solidly grouped innovator languages let *g^wh fall together with *g^w (into something like g and, with secondary split, $\check{j}$), Celtic achieves what, it must be admitted, is the same typological effect in a different way: *g^wh goes to g, but *g^w to b. Hittite remains to be judged; in view of its considerable isolation with regard to the remaining Indo-European languages, the loss of the aspiration in Hittite may be a truly accidental duplication (unless, of course, it is merely graphic).

It is an open question, however, whether small discrepancies in the scope of a replacement change (e.g., in the conditioning of a sound change) are necessarily a symptom of accidental duplication. Some of the eastern Indo-European languages agree in developing two allophones[5] (front and retract-

---

[5] Martinet, Économie 240.

ed) of *s into two phonemes. The conditioning is largely the same (e.g., retracted after i [see 12.7.3.1]), but not quite (the sequence isp becomes $i\check{s}p$ in Indo-Iranian but isp in Slavic). It is in perfect keeping with observations made in linguistic geography if we picture the change as possibly one single event insofar as the conditioning is the same or at least for part of the conditioning insofar as it is the same; if it is true that conditioned changes have a way of inducing further change which in effect widens the earlier conditioning (8.3), only the discrepant portion need represent duplication.

The geographical pattern of shared innovations allows different interpretations, or at least different emphases. It is possible (1) to regard all the intersecting innovation isoglosses (or at least all but one which is taken to represent a true subfamily) as the effect of the historical (often: the present-day) location of the speech communities. These isoglosses then amount to language areas such as may also be formed by unrelated languages (chap. 8); such language areas, it will be recalled, are characterized by developments toward typologically more similar structures. In the case of related languages,[6] the probability that the same areal trend is achieved through the same machinery is relatively great (e.g., if two related and at the same time neighboring languages have a three-tense $[A–B–C]$ verb paradigm, and an areal trend toward a two-tense paradigm is at work, the chances that both sister languages carry out the same change [drop C] are considerable). It is also possible, however, (2) to look upon the relative location of the daughter-language communities as essentially unchanged through time and to consider the intersecting isoglosses as typical dialect isoglosses surviving from the ancestor-language community. In this view, an area like the Indo-European speech territory has simply spread radially without great changes in the relative position of the former dialect areas on the map. Here a geographically discontinuous innovation (and one that is discontinuous not simply because a further innovation has arisen somewhere in the center of the area) might become crucial as an indication of a true disturbance in the relative position of the descendant languages. To say that the observable innovation isoglosses represent ancient dialect isoglosses is tantamount to saying that the dialects in question were still capable of undergoing certain changes in common at a time at which they were already different in some other respects.

---

[6] The uncertainty arises in practice only with related languages (see 8.4); and even here it is relieved by insights into relative chronology. If, e.g., sound change has affected part of the community and if the relationship between the neighboring but different phonemic systems is such that loanwords can be distinguished from commonly inherited words, the case is clear. Many examples of this sort are used by Porzig, *Gliederung*.

Obviously, the 'family-tree' patterns of 13.2 and 13.3, embodying as they do the principle that agreement on a replacement change is due either to subrelationship or accident, must fit a history of sudden, radical cleavage better than one of gradual differentiation without sharp dialect boundaries through extinction of intermediary zones. It is still remarkable, under these circumstances, that the Romance languages yield not only an over-all reconstruction which may be checked against literary Latin (a close sister language of proto-Romance, or "Vulgar Latin") but also reasonably well-defined subancestors.[7]

Sometimes the geographical argument is turned around: the pattern of location on the map is used for the purpose of discovering innovations and distinguishing them from retentions. Thus the fact that *caballa* 'mare' is common to a group of central Romance languages, as against *equa* on the periphery, tallies well with the fact that *equus* is (1) the inherited, Indo-European and also (2) the ordinary Classical Latin expression for 'horse': *caballus* is an innovation, certainly insofar as it is a replacement, in all areas, for *equus*. The phonemic correspondence sets which occur in the daughter forms of *caballa* (in the center) and of *equa* (at the periphery) are, to be sure, the same as those occurring in words of general Romance distribution: an indication, on the whole, that both words were part of the common Latin vocabulary (in different meanings—a fact which also happens to be recorded in the Latin texts) and that it is only their replacement relationship which is reflected on the map.

13.4.3. *Amorphous Change and Subgrouping*

Where no simple replacement pattern is involved, the presence of a form in one group of daughter languages and its absence in another usually permits two contradictory interpretations: (1) the ancestor language possessed the form, and it was lost through obsolescence in one group, and (2) the ancestor language did not possess the form; it emerged in a number of daughter languages through the usual processes: neologism or borrowing from a common source. If the form exhibits the standard phonemic correspondences (i.e., if it cannot be identified as a borrowing on phonemic grounds), its emergence must antedate the sound changes which set the languages in question up as separate daughter languages. Since, as a borrowing, it constitutes a "common innovation", it contributes to the understanding of subgrouping. In Indo-European, at least, the experience has been that the assumption of partial innovation (2) does not stand up well; it has been shown again and again by internal reconstruction in the lan-

---

[7] Hall, *Lg.* 26 (=*Readings in Linguistics* 303).

guages which lack the form in question that they are rather partial obsolescences (1). A common name for *Salmo salar* exists in Germanic (OE *leax*, etc.), Baltic, Slavic, and Iranian; in Tokharian B the word occurs, too, although in the wider meaning 'fish'. It had therefore been regarded as a regional innovation (with the Tokharian item borrowed from Germanic), old enough to show regular sound correspondences. But if the word can be internally reconstructed (chap. 7) in Sanskrit as *lakṣa* from such items as *lākṣā* 'red lac, lit. red (salmon-colored) substance' (with the "vṛddhi" lengthening regular in derived adjectives), the obsolescence of the animal name is a mere case of amorphous loss (3.6), natural after migration to a part of the world where the salmon is not found. As a retention, the name of the salmon, where it does occur, carries no weight in favor of any linguistic subgrouping.[8] Neither do neologisms which are amorphous; they are "innovations" of a sort but not replacements. Some Algonquian languages agree in having a compound 'fire-water, liquor', formed by a grammatical process which is productive in each one of them. Its common occurrence does not argue for a prehistoric subgrouping; it simply shows that the culture change which added new discourses in those corpora affected several languages similarly. The status of the components ('fire', 'water') in other constructions where they have "predictable" rather than "special" meanings is, of course, another matter; they are by and large general Central Algonquian morphs.[9]

13.5. Glottochronology and Subgrouping

It is conceivable that universal factors such as the necessity for intelligibility within speech communities put an upper limit to the rate of replacement change; it is, on the other hand, conceivable that there are other universal factors making for replacement change. If so, the rate of change would vary only within a relatively narrow band.[10] Even if this were not generally granted, it might still be true of conditions within a language family, at least so long as it does not straddle the boundary line between two widely different structural areas: the semantic or grammatical system through which the morphs are passed in the replacement process will then be comparatively stable, and whatever common structural heritage the

---

[8] This section may serve as an example of the extralinguistic (archeological) possibilities of linguistic reconstruction. It is not surprising that it is amorphous change which furnishes the more unmistakable cultural indications (3.6). The example is from Thieme, *Heimat*.

[9] Hockett, in *Lg.* 24.127 (=*Readings in Linguistics* 287).

[10] Gudschinsky, *Word* 12 with bibliography (especially M. Swadesh's writings).

daughter languages possess may also be supposed to produce a uniform pace. As the daughter languages become separated to the point where their specific replacement changes are no longer the same (although they continue to move within the same typological framework), the morphs occupying homologous structures, that is, primarily the words (or word stems, or the like, depending on the build of the language) with the same meanings, will become fewer and fewer the more time has gone by since the separation. If an absolute rate of replacement (say, 20 per cent per thousand years) is posited, this would make it possible to calculate the time depth for an ancestor language which is reconstructed from two or more languages, using the ratio between the same and different morphs in a given meaning. But, even if the idea of an absolute constant is given up, such a calculation would render valuable help in the task of determining subrelationships. This has been done, apparently with some success, although the difficulties are considerable. As in the case of the more conventional methods, lexicostatistics of this kind seems to work best where the splitting-up of the mother language approximates clear-cut disruption. Where, on the other hand, there is a long lapse of time between the first separate and the last common replacement change, the computation is likely to be vitiated by the large amount of commonly shared change with nevertheless postdates separation as that term would be applied, however vaguely, by the historian of the area. A particularly disturbing factor is literary borrowing from the language's own ancestor language (as between forms of modern Arabic, on the one hand, and classical Arabic, on the other); here a later stage may contain so much reintroduced material (which would otherwise have been lost) as to create a serious problem. It is true that this can to some extent be alleviated by applying the classical test of sound change: the "popular" words alone count, while the "learned" items are thrown out and counted as replacements. Unfortunately, this kind of knowledge is not available in a number of areas to which glottochronology has been applied.

It is one of the most remarkable features of this approach that it gives central importance to the distinction between replacement change and amorphous change; the latter is eliminated (by keeping to a "basic word list" with meanings presumably so general that cultural innovation or discontinuation—the very processes which are linked with amorphous change [3.6–3.7]—do not affect them greatly[11]). Sound change (which in our view is

---

[11] Difficult decisions in cases of large-scale borrowing (5.4, 8.4) are perhaps ultimately made on the assumption of a "basic" vocabulary which resists cultural borrowing. According to G. H. Fairbanks and H. H. Paper, there are few Iranian loanwords in the "basic" Armenian list.

a replacement change) is also disregarded, to be sure; if this were not done, the rate of common retention in sister languages would soon drop to zero. It is apparently possible to believe that the ratio of sound change to other replacement changes with a less sweeping effect also moves around a constant. The source of the replacement does not matter; in times of extensive foreign contact it is more likely to be borrowing, while in quieter periods it will consist more of semantic change.[12]

---

[12] Dyen, *Lg.* 32, systematizes the historical inferences which can be drawn from the location of the speech communities as such. On the Arabic problem above see Hymes, *IJAL* 25.267–69 (1959).

BIBLIOGRAPHY

[This is a list of books and articles referred to in the notes in some not readily identifiable form. Abbreviations for names of periodicals are also included.]

AA = American Anthropologist.

AGI = Archivio glottologico italiano.

AL = Acta linguistica.

ALLEN, W. SIDNEY. Relationship in comparative linguistics, TPS 1953.52–112.

AUSTIN, WILLIAM M. Criteria for phonetic similarity, Lg. 33.538–44 (1957).

BENNETT, EMMETT L., JR. Review of VENTRIS and CHADWICK, Documents in Mycenean Greek, Lg. 33.553–68 (1957).

BENVENISTE, ÉMILE. Problèmes sémantiques de la reconstruction, Word 10.251–64 (1954).

BERGSTRÄSSER, GOTTHELF. Einführung in die semitischen Sprachen. Munich, 1928.

BLOCH, BERNARD. Contrast, Lg. 29.59–61 (1953).

———. A set of postulates for phonemic analysis, Lg. 24.1–47 (1948).

BLOOMFIELD, LEONARD. Algonquian, Linguistic Structures, ed. H. HOIJER, 85–129.

———. Language. New York, 1933.

BONFANTE, GIULIANO. Additional notes on reconstruction, Word 2.155–56 (1946).

———. On reconstruction and linguistic method, Word 1.83–94, 132–61 (1945).

BURROW, THOMAS. The Sanskrit Language. London, 1955.

DEETERS, GERHARD. Armenisch und Südkaukasisch, Caucasica 3.37–82; 4.1–64 (1926/27).

DIRINGER, DAVID. The Alphabet. 2d ed. New York, 1953.

DYEN, ISIDORE. Language distribution and migration theory, Lg. 32.611–26 (1956).

———. Review of DAHL, Malgache et maanjan, Lg. 29.577–90 (1953).

Eighth Congress = Proceedings of the Eighth International Congress of Linguists. Oslo, 1957.

EMENEAU, MURRAY B. India as a linguistic area, Lg. 32.3–16 (1956).

———. Taboos on animal names, Lg. 24.56–63 (1948).

———. Review of KAKATI, Assamese, Its Formation and Development, Lg. 18.245–48 (1942).

Fourth Congress = Actes du IVᵉ congrès international de linguistes. Copenhagen, 1938.

FRIEDRICH, JOHANNES. Extinct Languages, trans. FRANK GAYNOR. New York, 1957.

GELB, IGNACE J. A Study of Writing. Chicago, 1952.

GILLIÉRON, JULES LOUIS. Pathologie et thérapeutique verbales. Paris, 1921.

GOETZE, ALBRECHT. Relative Chronologie von Lauterscheinungen im Italischen, IF 41.78–149 (1923).

———. Review of FRIEDRICH, Hethitisches Wörterbuch, Lg. 30.401–5 (1954).

GRAMMONT, MAURICE. *Traité de phonétique*. Paris, 1939.

GREENBERG, JOSEPH. *Essays in Linguistics*. Chicago, 1957.

GUDSCHINSKY, SARAH C. The ABC's of lexicostatistics (glottochronology), *Word* 12.175–210 (1956).

HALL, ROBERT A., JR. The genetic relationships of Haitian Creole, *Ricerche linguistiche* 1.194–203 (1950).

——. *Leave Your Language Alone!* Ithaca, N.Y., 1950.

——. The reconstruction of Proto-Romance, *Lg.* 26.6–27 (1950). (Reprinted in Joos [ed.], *Readings in Linguistics* 303–14.)

——. *A Theory of Graphemics*. Ithaca, N.Y., 1957. (Mimeographed.) (Definitive version to appear in *AL* 7.)

HALLE, M. (ed.). *For Roman Jakobson*. The Hague, 1956.

HAMP, ERIC P. Consonant allophones in proto-Celtic, *Lochlann* 1.209–17 (1959).

HARRIS, ZELLIG S. Componential analysis of a Hebrew paradigm, *Lg.* 24.87–91 (1948). (Reprinted in Joos [ed.], *Readings in Linguistics* 272–74.)

——. Co-occurrence and transformation in linguistic structure, *Lg.* 33.283–340 (1957).

——. *Development of the Canaanite Dialects*. New Haven, Conn., 1939.

——. Discourse analysis, *Lg.* 28.1–30 (1952).

——. *Methods in Structural Linguistics*. Chicago, 1947.

HAUDRICOURT, ANDRÉ G., and JUILLAND, ALPHONSE G. *Essai pour une histoire structurale du phonétisme français*. Paris, 1949.

HAUGEN, EINAR. Directions in modern linguistics, *Lg.* 27.211–22 (1951).

——. *The Norwegian Language in America*. Philadelphia, 1953.

——. Review of DEROY, *L'emprunt linguistique*, *Lg.* 33.587–89 (1957).

——. Review of WEINREICH, *Languages in Contact*, *Lg.* 30.380–89 (1954).

HAVERS, WILHELM. *Neuere Literatur zum Sprachtabu*. Vienna, 1946.

HENNING, W. B. Oktou, *TPS* 1948.68.

HILL, ARCHIBALD A. Juncture and syllable division in Latin, *Lg.* 30.439–47 (1954).

——. Phonetic and phonemic change, *Lg.* 12.15–22 (1936). (Reprinted in Joos [ed.], *Readings in Linguistics* 81–84.)

HOCKETT, CHARLES F. Central Algonquian /t/ and /c/, *IJAL* 22.202–7 (1956).

——. *A Course in Modern Linguistics*. New York, 1958.

——. Implications of Bloomfield's Algonquian studies, *Lg.* 24.117–31 (1948). (Reprinted in Joos [ed.], *Readings in Linguistics* 281–89.)

——. *A Manual of Phonology*. Baltimore, 1955.

HOENIGSWALD, HENRY M. Change, analogical and semantic, *Indian Linguistics* 16.233–36 (1955).

——. The phonology of dialect borrowing, *SinL* 10.1–5 (1952).

——. The principal step in comparative grammar, *Lg.* 26.357–64 (1950). (Reprinted in Joos [ed.], *Readings in Linguistics* 298–302.)

——. Some uses of nothing, *Lg.* 35.409–21 (1959).

——. Review of MARTINET, *Économie des changements phonétiques*, *Lg.* 33.575–83 (1957).

HOIJER, HARRY. Athapaskan kinship systems, *AA* 58.309–33 (1956).

——— (ed.). *Linguistic Structures of Native America.* New York, 1946.

HYMES, DELL. Positional analysis of categories, *Word* 11.10–23 (1955).

IF = *Indogermanische Forschungen.*

IJAL = *International Journal of American Linguistics.*

JAKOBSON, ROMAN. Prinzipien der historischen Phonologie, *TCLP* 4.247–67.

———, Sur la théorie des affinités phonologiques des langues, *Fourth Congress* 48–54.

———. Typological studies and their contribution to historical comparative linguistics, *Eighth Congress* 17–25.

JESPERSEN, OTTO. *A Modern English Grammar on Historical Principles.* Heidelberg, 1909–40.

JONES, DANIEL. *The Phoneme.* Cambridge, 1950.

JOOS, MARTIN. The medieval sibilants, *Lg.* 28.222–31 (1952). (Reprinted in Joos [ed.], *Readings in Linguistics* 372–78.)

——— (ed.). *Readings in Linguistics.* Washington, D.C., 1957.

KLUGE, FRIEDRICH. *Etymologisches Wörterbuch der deutschen Sprache.* 17th ed. by ALFRED SCHIRMER and WALTHER MITZKA. Berlin, 1957.

KROEBER, ALFRED L. *Anthropology.* Rev. ed. New York, 1948.

KRONASSER, HEINZ. *Handbuch der Semasiologie.* Heidelberg, 1952.

KURYŁOWICZ, JERZY. *L'accentuation des langues indo-européennes.* Cracow, 1952.

———. *L'apophonie en indo-européen.* 2d ed. Wrocław, 1958.

———. La nature des procès dits "analogiques," *AL* 5.15–37 (1945/49).

KZ = *Zeitschrift für vergleichende Sprachforschung auf dem Gebiete der indogermanischen Sprachen.*

LENORMAND, MAURICE H. The phonemes of Lifu, *Word* 8.252–57 (1952).

LEUMANN, MANU. *Lateinische Grammatik, Laut- und Formenlehre.* (5th ed. of Stolz-Schmalz, *Lateinische Grammatik.*) Munich, 1926.

———. Zum Mechanismus des Bedeutungswandels, *IF* 45.105–18 (1927).

Lg. = *Language.*

MAAS, PAUL. *Textual criticism.* Oxford, 1958.

MARCHAND, JAMES W. Internal reconstruction of phonemic split, *Lg.* 32.245–53 (1956).

MARTINET, ANDRÉ. *Économie des changements phonétiques.* Berne, 1955.

MEILLET, ANTOINE. *La méthode comparative en linguistique historique.* Oslo, 1925.

MEILLET, A., and VENDRYES, J. *Traité de la grammaire comparée des langues classiques.* 2d ed. Paris, 1948.

MENNER, ROBERT J. The conflict of homonyms in English, *Lg.* 12.229–44 (1936).

———. Multiple meaning and change of meaning in English, *Lg.* 21.59–76 (1945).

MOULTON, WILLIAM G. The stops and spirants of early Germanic, *Lg.* 30.1–42 (1954).

MURPHY, JOHN J. *The Book of Pidgin English.* 4th ed. Brisbane, 1954.

NAERT, P. Des mutations *ct, cs* > *pt, ps; gn* > *mn* et *mn* > *un* en roumain, *AL* 2.247–57 (1941).

OSGOOD, C., and SEBEOK, T. A. (eds.). *Psycholinguistics.* Baltimore, 1954.

PENZL, HERBERT. The evidence for phonemic changes, *Studies Presented to Joshua Whatmough on His Sixtieth Birthday* 193–208. The Hague, 1957.

PIKE, KENNETH L., *Axioms and Procedures for Reconstructions in Comparative Linguistics.* Rev. ed. Glendale, 1957.

POLOMÉ, EDGAR. Zum heutigen Stand der Laryngaltheorie, *Revue belge de philologie et d'histoire* 30.444–71, 1041–52 (1952).

PORZIG, WALTER. *Die Gliederung des indogermanischen Sprachgebiets.* Heidelberg, 1954.

PULGRAM, ERNST. Family tree, wave theory and dialectology, *Orbis* 2.67–72 (1953).

ROGGER, KASPAR. *Vom Wesen des Lautwandels.* Leipzig and Paris, 1934.

ROTHE, WOLFGANG. *Einführung in die historische Laut- und Formenlehre des Rumänischen.* Halle, 1957.

RUIPÉREZ, MARTIN S. Esquisse d'une histoire du vocalisme grec, *Word* 12.67–81 (1956).

SANDFELD, K. *Linguistique balkanique.* Paris, 1930.

SAPIR, EDWARD. *Language.* New York, 1921.

SCHWYZER, EDUARD. *Griechische Grammatik.* Munich, 1939–53.

SENN, ALFRED. Die Beziehungen des Baltischen zum Slavischen und Germanischen, *KZ* 71.162–88 (1953).

SinL = Studies in Linguistics.

Sitzungsberichte = Deutsche Akademie der Wissenschaften zu Berlin, Philosophisch-historische Klasse, Sitzungsberichte.

Sixth Congress = Proceedings of the Sixth International Congress of Linguists. Paris, 1949.

SMAL-STOCKI, ROMAN. Taboos on animal names in Ukrainian, *Lg.* 26.489–93 (1950).

STEINITZ, WOLFGANG. *Geschichte des wogulischen Vokalismus.* Berlin, 1955.

STERN, GUSTAF. *Meaning and Change of Meaning.* Göteborg, 1932.

STURTEVANT, EDGAR H. The pronoun **so *sā *tod* and the Indo-Hittite hypothesis, *Lg.* 15.11–19 (1939).

———. *The Pronunciation of Greek and Latin.* 2d ed. Philadelphia, 1940.

SZEMERÉNYI, OSWALD. The problem of Balto-Slav unity. *Kratylos* 2.97–123 (1957).

TCLP = Travaux du Cercle Linguistique de Prague.

THIEME, PAUL. *Die Heimat der indogermanischen Gemeinsprache.* Wiesbaden, 1954.

TPS = Transactions of the Philological Society.

TRUBETZKOY, NIKOLAI. Gedanken zum Indogermanenproblem, *AL* 1.81–89 (1939).

TWADDELL, W. FREEMAN. The prehistoric Germanic short syllabics, *Lg.* 24.139–51 (1948).

———. Pre-OHG */t/, For Roman Jakobson,* ed. M. HALLE, 559–66.

ULLMANN, STEPHEN. *The Principles of Semantics.* Glasgow, 1951.

VOGT, HANS. Language contacts, *Word* 10.365–74 (1954).

WACKERNAGEL, JAKOB. *Altindische Grammatik*. Göttingen, 1896——.

WARTBURG, WALTHER VON. *Einführung in die Problematik und Methodik der Sprachwissenschaft*. Halle, 1943.

WATKINS, CALVERT. Review of KURYŁOWICZ, *L'apophonie en indo-européen*, *Lg*. 34.381–98 (1958).

WEINREICH, URIEL. On the compatibility of genetic relationship and convergent development, *Word* 14.374–79 (1958).

——. On the description of phonic interference, *Word* 13.1–11 (1957).

——. Is a structural dialectology possible? *Lg*. 10.381–400 (1954).

——. *Languages in Contact*. New York, 1953.

WHITNEY, WILLIAM DWIGHT. *A Sanskrit Grammar*. 3d ed. Boston, 1896.

INDEX

Affinity (formal), 48, 52
Alliteration, 6
Allomorph, 17, 30, 47 ff.
Alternation, 48 ff., 56, 99 ff.
Amorphous change, 2, 14, 19, 38, 57, 157–58
Analogic change, 30, 46, 57, 60, 63, 155
Analogic creation (analogy), 11, 47, 59–60, 107 ff., 118
Ancestor language, 13, 119, 145 ff.
Animal cry, 12
Area, 82 ff., 155 ff.
Assimilation, 73–74
Automatic alternation, 101 ff.

Back formation, 24, 41 ff., 58, 60
Base (morphophonemic), 101 ff.
Basic vocabulary, 159
Bilingualism, 82
Borrowed phonemes, 96
Borrowing, 11, 22, 28–29, 58, 69, 111

Change, 2
Characteristic environment, 15, 28
Classification, 144 ff.
Comparative method, 69 ff., 119 ff.
Composite set, 126
Conditional statement, 3
Conditioned sound change, 73–74
Construction, 1, 24
Contamination, 47
Contrast, 16, 28, 87
Contrastive environment, 15, 28, 64
Convergence areas, 82 ff.
Correspondence, 13, 69 ff., 119 ff.

Daughter language, 145 ff.
Descent, 3, 13, 144 ff.
Diachrony, 2–3
Dialect borrowing, 50 ff., 66–67
Differentiation, 39, 57
Discourse, 1
Distinctive feature, 86, 89
Doublet, 39, 51, 57, 68, 109, 159
Duplicate change, 84, 154–55
Duplicate merger, 125–26, 130 ff.
Duplicate split, 129–30

Ease of articulation, 73–74
Economy (in reconstruction), 139
Ellipsis, 40
Emergence, 22
Empty morph, 35
Environment, 1, 15

Family tree, 145, 157
Folk etymology, 25, 47
Form, 22
Frequency, 99–100
Functional load, 79

Glottochronology, 158 ff.
Grammatical change, 46
Graph, 4 ff.
Grapheme, 4 ff.

Homonymy, 18, 26, 56, 58, 64, 69, 79
Hyperbole, 35
Hyperforms, 66, 74–75

Idiolect, 2
Increment, 40, 92–93
Indeterminacy, 101 ff.
Internal reconstruction, 68, 99 ff., 151, 158
Intonation, 1, 17
Invention, 22
Inverse spelling, 9–10
Irregular alternation, 103 ff.
Isogloss, 145, 155
Isolation, 61, 68

Juncture, 5, 49, 57

Language family, 144 ff.
Lexicostatistics, 159
Litotes, 35
Loan shift, loan translation, 22, 82
Logographic writing, 5
Loss, 40, 91

Meaning, 16, 19, 23, 29, 34–35, 45, 57, 69
Merger, 14, 33, 67, 77, 90, 99–100, 115 ff., 121–22, 124
Metaphor, 35, 45
Meter, 6
Metonymy, 35

167

Misunderstanding, 55, 63, 65
Morph boundaries, disappearing, 40
Morpheme, 16, 27 ff.
Morphophoneme, 48 ff., 68, 99 ff., 141

Narrowing (of meaning), 35, 45
Nil, 35, 40, 56, 58, 91–92, 134
Non-automatic alternation, 103 ff.

Obsolescence, 19, 58, 69

Paradigms, 46
Pejoration, 35
Phonemic substitution, 25, 80
Pitch, 57
Polysemy, 19
Primary split, 77, 91–92, 122
Productivity, 59 ff., 158
Proto-language, 119

Reassignment, 79, 88–89
Rectangular pattern, 115–16
Regular alternation, 105
Relative chronology, 112 ff.
Replacement, 2, 13, 57
Replacement pattern, 14, 27 ff., 75 ff., 86 ff.
Residue, 92, 95–96
Rhyme, 6

Secondary split, 38, 77, 93 ff., 123
Secondary transmission, 12
Semantic change, 29, 34, 45, 57, 69
Semantic field, 35, 45

Sentence, 1
Set of correspondences, 69–70, 119 ff.
Shift, 79, 86 ff.
Shortening, 40, 56
Sound change, 54, 58, 69, 72 ff., 151, 159
Sound substitution, 80
Split, 14, 37–38, 88 ff., 91 ff., 99 ff., 114 ff., 122–23
Stage, earlier and later, 3, 13, 144 ff.
Stress, 57
Style, 25, 66
Subrelationship, 144 ff.
Substratum, 55, 65
Suppletion, 48 ff., 57, 68, 70
Synchrony, 2–3
Syncretism, 36, 49, 70, 151
Synonymy, 16, 18, 47
Syntactic change, 46

Taboo, 65
Three-language problem, 144 ff., 150 ff.
Time, 1
Transformation, 1, 17, 20, 35, 61
Typology, 79, 83, 114, 118, 135–36, 155

Unconditional change, 3, 74

Widening (of meaning), 35, 45
Word order, 47
Writing, 4 ff.

Zero, 35